Learn 2D Game Development with C#

Jebediah Pavleas

Jack Keng-Wei Chang

Kelvin Sung

Robert Zhu

Apress·

Learn 2D Game Development with C#

ISBN-13 (pbk): 978-1-4302-6604-4

ISBN-13 (electronic): 978-1-4302-6605-1

President and Publisher: Paul Manning
Lead Editor: Gwenan Spearing
Technical Reviewer: Felipe Ramos
Editorial Board: Steve Anglin, Mark Beckner, Ewan Buckingham, Gary Cornell, Louise Corrigan, Jim DeWolf, Jonathan Gennick, Jonathan Hassell, Robert Hutchinson, Michelle Lowman, James Markham, Matthew Moodie, Jeff Olson, Jeffrey Pepper, Douglas Pundick, Ben Renow-Clarke, Dominic Shakeshaft, Gwenan Spearing, Matt Wade, Steve Weiss, Tom Welsh
Coordinating Editor: Mark Powers
Copy Editor: Brendan Frost
Compositor: SPi Global
Indexer: SPi Global
Artist: SPi Global
Cover Designer: Anna Ishchenko

Distributed to the book trade worldwide by Springer Science+Business Media New York, 233 Spring Street, 6th Floor, New York, NY 10013. Phone 1-800-SPRINGER, fax (201) 348-4505, e-mail orders-ny@springer-sbm.com, or visit www.springeronline.com. Apress Media, LLC is a California LLC and the sole member (owner) is Springer Science + Business Media Finance Inc (SSBM Finance Inc). SSBM Finance Inc is a Delaware corporation.

For information on translations, please e-mail rights@apress.com, or visit www.apress.com.

Apress and friends of ED books may be purchased in bulk for academic, corporate, or promotional use. eBook versions and licenses are also available for most titles. For more information, reference our Special Bulk Sales–eBook Licensing web page at www.apress.com/bulk-sales.

Any source code or other supplementary material referenced by the author in this text is available to readers at www.apress.com/9781430266044. For detailed information about how to locate your book's source code, go to www.apress.com/source-code/.

Contents at a Glance

Contents

About the Authors

Jebediah Pavleas is a graduate student in the Computer Science and Software Engineering program at the University of Washington Bothell (UWB). He received a Bachelor of Science in 2012 and was the recipient of the Chancellor's Medal for his class. During his time as an undergraduate he took a great interest in both computer graphics and games. His projects included an interactive math application that utilizes Microsoft's Kinect sensor to teach algebra, a 2D role-playing game designed to teach students introductory programming concepts, and a website where students can compete in various mini-games to control checkpoints around campus. Relating to these projects, he coauthored publications in *IEEE Computers and The Journal of Computing Sciences in Colleges* (CCSC). When not working towards his graduate degree, he enjoys designing, building, and playing games of all kinds as well as adapting technology for improved accessibility. A university student in computer science, he is interested in working as a game programmer, focusing on accessibility.

Jack Keng-Wei Chang is working on an MS in computer science and software engineering. He builds Kinect software for teaching math.

Kelvin Sung is a Professor with the Computing and Software Systems at University of Washington Bothell (UWB). He received his Ph.D. in Computer Science from the University of Illinois at Urbana-Champaign in 1992. His background is in computer graphics, hardware, and machine architecture. He came to UWB from Alias|Wavefront (now part of Autodesk) in Toronto, where he played a key role in designing and implementing the Maya Renderer, an Academy Award-winning image generation system. Before joining Alias|Wavefront, Kelvin was an Assistant Professor with the School of Computing, National University of Singapore. Kelvin's research interests are in studying the role of technology in supporting human communication. Funded by Microsoft Research and the National Science Foundation, Kelvin's recent work focused on the intersection of video game mechanics, real-world problems, and mobile technologies. Kelvin teaches both undergraduate and graduate classes in Computer Graphics, Game Development, and Mobile Computing.

Robert Zhu is a Principal Development Lead at Microsoft for Windows Operating System Group, is an expert in OS leading-edge development, research, design in computer engineering such as kernel, device driver, and board support packages. He leads the technical partnership with mobile carriers and OEM partners. Robert also gives training classes to OEMs on driver development and Windows OS research. Before working for Microsoft, he was with Digital Equipment Corporation (DEC), U.S.A. as senior software engineer on the 64-bit DEC Alpha platform for workstation server optimization and performance tuning for Windows, and a Software Lead with Motorola Wireless Division, Canada. He obtained Master of Computer Science at University of Washington; Master of Computing and Electrical Engineering, Simon Fraser University, Canada; B. Engineering, Tsinghua University; and was in the Ph.D. program with the SFU School of Engineering Science, Canada. Robert has published the book *Windows Phone 7 Programming for Android and iOS Developers*. He has also coauthored the book *Windows Phone Programming Essential*.

About the Technical Reviewer

Felipe Ramos was introduced to C++ at the age of 15 when a friend suggested they should make small video games. It is said that the act of creation is an addiction, and it was that addiction to software and video games that led him to enroll in the Game Design program at Keiser College back in early 2000. After becoming familiar with game development with DirectX and C++, managed languages started getting a foothold and he began promoting Frameworks like XNA and MonoGame by writing training materials covering different aspects of game development including best practices, AI, and UI development.

Professionally, Felipe has worked in different sectors of the industry encompassing a wide array of technologies and languages. Some of the industries include Health Care, ADP, Commerce, and Money Transfers.

Early in 2013, Felipe established a software company and is currently developing a game to be released for several devices in mid-2014.

Acknowledgments

The genesis of this book occurred as part of the XNA Based Game-Themed Programming Assignments for CS1/2 project, funded under the Computer Gaming Curriculum in Computer Science initiative from Microsoft External Research, and by Microsoft Research Connections. We would like to thank John Nordlinger for his recognition of our vision and Donald Brinkman and Lee Dirks for continual support, including their invaluable discussions and for allowing us incredible access. Throughout the project, Kent Foster has been our best advocate, connecting us with many end users who provided much-needed refinements to the examples. The final refinement of the materials and the book development efforts are part of the Game-Themed CS1/2: Empowering the Faculty project, funded by the Transforming Undergraduate Education in Science Technology Engineering and Mathematics (TUES) Program (National Science Foundation [NSF] award number DUE-1140410).

Students and the games they build from the course CSS385: Introduction to Game Development (see http://courses.washington.edu/css385) at the University of Washington Bothell have provided us with the ideal deployment vehicle and are a source of continuous inspiration. They have tested, retested, contributed to, and assisted in the formation and organization of the contents. The first two authors of this book are recent alumni of CSS385.

The University of Washington Bothell logo, which is used throughout this book, is a trademark owned by the University of Washington Bothell. The permission to use the logo is a courtesy of and does not represent endorsement from the institution. The Mind_Meld.mp3 audio clip used in the audio project from Chapter 7, "Sprites, Camera, Action!" was composed by Shane Krolikowski (http://skrolikowski.com/) using Apple's GarageBand samples.

We also want to thank Pei Zheng for introducing us to Russell Jones, who connected us to our editor Gwenan Spearing at Apress. A heartfelt thank-you to Gwenan for her appreciation of our vision and for her patience and expertise in guiding us through the book-writing process, and many thanks to Felipe Ramos, our technical reviewer. Finally, we would like to thank Mark Powers for his insightful technical feedback and writing guidance.

Introduction

Welcome to *Learn 2D Game Development with C#*. Because you have picked up this book, you are likely interested in creating your own games with the C# programming language. This book teaches you how to develop 2D games with C# and MonoGame by giving you background and conceptual information so you can play, examine, and develop 2D games.

This book identifies and presents relevant concepts from software engineering, computer graphics, mathematics, physics, and game development—all in the context of building 2D games. The projects you'll develop in this book are based on MonoGame, the open source implementation of of the popular XNA Framework discontinued by Microsoft. The presentations are tightly integrated with the analysis and development of source code; you'll spend much of the book building gamelike concept projects that demonstrate game principles and components. By building on concepts introduced early on, the book leads you on a journey through which you will master the basic concepts behind game development while simultaneously gaining hands-on experience developing simple but working 2D games.

By the end of the book, you will be familiar with the implementation details of 2D games, and you should feel competent in implementing commonly encountered 2D game behaviors using MonoGame.

Who should read this book

This book is targeted toward programmers who are familiar with basic object-oriented programming concepts and have a basic to intermediate knowledge of an object-oriented programming language like C# or Java. For example, if you are a student who has taken a few introductory programming courses, an experienced developer who is new to games and graphics programming, or a self-taught programming enthusiast, you will be able to follow the concepts and code presented in this book with little trouble. If you're new to programming in general, it is suggested that you first become comfortable with the C# programming language before tackling the content provided in this book.

Assumptions

You should be experienced with programming in an object-oriented programming language, such as C# or Java. The examples in this book were created with the assumption that readers understand data encapsulation and inheritance. In addition, you should also be familiar with basic data structures such as linked lists and dictionaries and be comfortable working with the fundamentals of algebra and geometry, particularly linear equations and coordinate systems.

Who should not read this book

This book is not designed to teach readers how to program, nor does it attempt to explain intricate details of C# or MonoGame. If you have no prior experience developing software with an object-oriented `programming language, you will probably find the examples in this book difficult to follow.

On the other hand, if you have an extensive background in game development for other platforms and with other programming languages, the content here will be too basic; this is a book intended for developers without 2D game development experience.

Organization of this book

This book divides the process of building 2D games into essential topic areas: tools, graphics, special effects, math and physics, and logic and behavior. These topics are organized into chapters. Each topic area (chapter) is then subdivided into essential concepts; for example, concepts related to computer graphics include coordinate spaces and camera abstraction. The book introduces each concept via a gamelike example organized as a section in a chapter. Each has an associated step-by-step project workflow. In this way, each section in the book corresponds to a single project or concept.

The first section begins with a simple project that you will build from scratch. Throughout the text, each subsequent section builds upon the sections that precede it. While this makes it a bit difficult to skip around in the book, it will give you practical experience and a solid understanding of how the different concepts relate to one another. In addition, rather than always working with new and minimalistic projects, you gain experience with building larger and more interesting projects.

The projects themselves start with simple concepts, such as creating objects and moving them across the screen, but quickly move to more complex concepts, such as implementing pixel-accurate collision detection and working with user-defined coordinate systems. In this way, while the concepts are presented in simple 2D gamelike examples, by the end of the book, your code base for the projects will include all the essential concepts covered.

That final code base, which you will have developed incrementally over the course of the entire book, serves as a great platform on which you can begin building your own 2D games. This is exactly what the very last chapter of the book does, leading you from conceptualization, to design, to implementation of a not-so-simple casual 2D game.

Finding your best starting point in this book

As a reader, there are several ways for you to follow along with this book. The first and most obvious is to enter the code into your project as you follow through each step in the book. From a learning perspective, this is probably the most effective way to absorb the information presented; however, we understand that it may not be the most realistic, due to the amount of code or debugging that approach may require. To help ameliorate this, each of the sections and projects in this book has two corresponding source code folders: the starter project in a 1.Starting folder, and the completed project in a 2.Completed folder. You can see an example of this structure in Figure 1. The starter projects allow you to follow along in the corresponding section by entering the code as you encounter it in the book, while the completed project lets you run and see the project in its completed state.

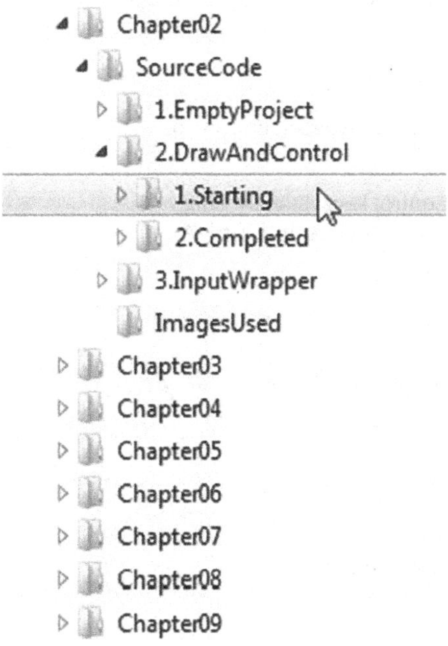

```
▲  Chapter02
   ▲  SourceCode
      ▷  1.EmptyProject
      ▲  2.DrawAndControl
         ▷  1.Starting
         ▷  2.Completed
      ▷  3.InputWrapper
         ImagesUsed
   ▷  Chapter03
   ▷  Chapter04
   ▷  Chapter05
   ▷  Chapter06
   ▷  Chapter07
   ▷  Chapter08
   ▷  Chapter09
```

Figure 1. *The folder structure for the book projects*

We recommend that you refer to the completed project when you begin a new section. Doing so lets you preview the current section's project, giving you a clear idea of the end goal, and letting you see what the project is trying to achieve. You may also find the completed project code useful when you have problems while building the code yourself, because you can compare your code with the completed project's code during difficult debugging situations.

■ **Note**   We have found the WinMerge program (`http://winmerge.org/`) to be an excellent tool for comparing source code files and folder.

Finally, after completing a project, we recommend that you compare the behavior of your implementation with the completed-project implementation provided. By doing so, you can observe whether your code is behaving as expected.

Conventions and features in this book

This book presents information using conventions designed to make the information readable and easy to follow:

- Each example is built on top of prior ones; however, complete source code is provided for each exercise, so you can use that to skip sections you don't need.

- A screen shot and an outlined overview of the steps involved precede each step-by-step procedure, so that you will know what to expect.

- When necessary, we provide relevant background information before beginning the analysis of how to implement the concept. For example, the book discusses differences between pixel and user-defined spaces before analyzing how to implement a user-defined coordinate system.

- Source code analysis is divided into distinct steps, where each step contributes to the eventual implementation of the concept.

- Items that you should type (excepting source code) appear in bold text.

- Programming-related items, such as class names, variable names, namespaces, and so on, appear in italics.

- When you need to press two keys at once, such as holding the Control key while pressing the A key, this book shows the two keys separated by a plus (+) sign—for example, Ctrl+A.

System requirements

You will need the following hardware and software in order to follow the examples in this book:

- Windows 7 or higher

- Microsoft Visual Studio 2010 or higher, any edition

- MonoGame V3.0 or higher

- A computer that has a 1.6 GHz or faster processor (2 GHz is recommended)

- More than 1 GB of RAM

- 1 GB of available hard disk space

- A Microsoft DirectX 9–capable video card that supports at least OpenGL 3 and can run at a resolution of 1,024×768 or higher

- An Internet connection, for downloading software or chapter examples

All of the projects in this book were built to use either your keyboard or a Microsoft Xbox 360 controller for Windows. You should be able to work with any wired Xbox 360 controller by plugging it into a USB port on your computer; however, wireless Xbox 360 controllers require an Xbox 360 wireless receiver for Windows to function on the PC. If you instead want to use a mouse with your Windows-based projects, you will need to make some code modifications. The types of changes you'll need to make are addressed near the end of the Draw and Control project in Chapter 2.

You can find details on how to download, install, and configure Visual Studio and MonoGame in Chapter 1, "Introducing 2D Game Development in C#."

Code samples

With the exception of the first chapter, all the chapters in this book include examples that let you interactively experiment with and learn the new materials. You can download all the code for all the projects, including the associated assets (images, audio clips, or fonts) in both their pre-example and completed states from the following page:

http://www.apress.com/9781430266044

Follow the instructions to download the source code file labeled 9781430266044.zip. To install the code samples, unzip the source code file. You should see the folder structure shown previously in Figure 1. As described previously, the starter project is in the 1.Starting folder, and the corresponding completed project is in the 2.Completed folder. With Visual Studio properly installed, you can double-click the corresponding solution (.sln) file to begin working with any of the provided projects.

CHAPTER 1

Introducing 2D Game Development in C#

C#, a modern object-oriented programming language from Microsoft, is one the easiest languages to develop applications with. When developing C# applications within the Microsoft Visual Studio Integrated Development Environment (IDE), programmers are especially empowered with near-transparent application programming interface (API) access, friendly editor-assisted code completion, and almost instantaneous compilations. For these reasons, C# is one the best programming languages for prototyping sophisticated ideas and for learning and experimenting with difficult concepts.

Developing games can be a challenging and lengthy process, partly due to the general programming knowledge and experience required to begin game development, and partly due to the steep learning curve associated with most graphics APIs, such as Microsoft Direct3D and OpenGL. The MonoGame Framework, an open source implementation of the popular XNA Framework discontinued by Microsoft, addresses these issues by creating a developer-friendly framework with a much shallower learning curve. This framework lets developers quickly learn the information needed to begin creating 2D games for many of the popular platforms, from machines running Microsoft (Windows 7 or 8), Apple (Mac OS X), or Linux operating systems to popular mobile devices (iOS, Android, or Windows Phone). The examples in this book are designed to run on Windows for easy demonstration, but the same core principles apply to 2D game development on any platform. So once you've mastered the basics, you'll have MonoGame's cross-platform support at your fingertips.

The MonoGame framework presents its interface in C#. Together with Microsoft Visual Studio or the MonoDevelop IDE, it becomes possible to focus on learning 2D game development concepts in C# and avoid being distracted by the peripheral requirements of computer graphics, input device interactions, or programming language nuances. For example, instead of working with separate graphical API and User Interface (UI) API for drawing and receiving input, MonoGame provides a straightforward way of drawing graphical objects to the application windows and a simple model for receiving player actions. These allow us to concentrate on the structures and logics for coordinating the drawing of gaming elements and interpreting the intentions of the players rather than being consumed by the details of converting information between the different APIs.

With the elegant C# programming language, we can take advantage of data abstraction and object inheritance in modeling game element behaviors while avoiding preoccupation with pointer manipulation or memory management. Best of all, with MonoGame being an open source project and C# being freely available for the general public, it is not only relatively straightforward, but also free to build games for multiple platforms. Since many vendors (e.g., Windows Marketplace, or Google play) encourage hobbyists to self-publish applications and games, it becomes possible to build, perfect, and eventually publish games in the marketplace!

This chapter first leads you through the steps of downloading, installing, and setting up the development environment: Visual Studio Express IDE, MonoGame framework, and XNB Builder. We then describe the coverage of 2D game development topics in the rest of this book, with brief discussions of related topics that are not covered and where interested readers can find additional information on them.

■ **Note** MonoDevelop is an IDE, while MonoGame framework, or MonoGame Library, is the library that we will be using throughout this book for building the games. We will be using Microsoft Visual Studio as the IDE for developing example projects.

If you wish to learn more about or brush up on the technologies discussed in this chapter, such as C#, MonoGame, XNA, DirectX, or OpenGL, see the "Technology References" section at the end of this chapter.

Downloading and Installing Development Tools

To use MonoGame and follow along with this book, you will need the Windows 7 or Windows 8 operating system and three additional pieces of software:

- An IDE: We will be working with the Microsoft Visual Studio IDE. This is the software with which you will edit, compile, and run your games.

- A game library software development kit (SDK) : We will be working with the MonoGame V3.0 (or higher) SDK. With proper installation, we will be able to access MonoGame functions from the Microsoft Visual Studio IDE and build our games.

■ **Note** If you are working on an Apple Mac machine, you can download the MonoDevelop IDE instead (URL is provided at the end of this chapter). Due to the similarities in the two IDEs, you should be able to follow the examples in this book using MonoDevelop.

- An asset builder: We will be using XNB Builder for converting formats of assets (images, audios, fonts) to those that are suitable for your games.

Download and install the IDE: Visual Studio Express

The first piece of software you need is the IDE. To develop in C# and MonoGame, you will need to use either a version of Visual Studio or MonoDevelop. The examples in this book use Visual Studio 2012 Express. Visual Studio Express is free to download, and you can find the latest versions, along with optional earlier versions such as Visual C# 2010 Express at the following link:

www.microsoft.com/visualstudio/downloads

All the examples in this book should work in any recent edition of Visual Studio Express, including the 2010 edition.

■ **Note** Through the Microsoft DreamSpark program, all full-time students have free access to the Professional version of the Visual Studio IDE. All that is required is a school e-mail account. Please refer to www.dreamspark.com/ for more details.

Figure 1-1 shows the page for initiating the installation of Microsoft Visual Studio 2010 Express.

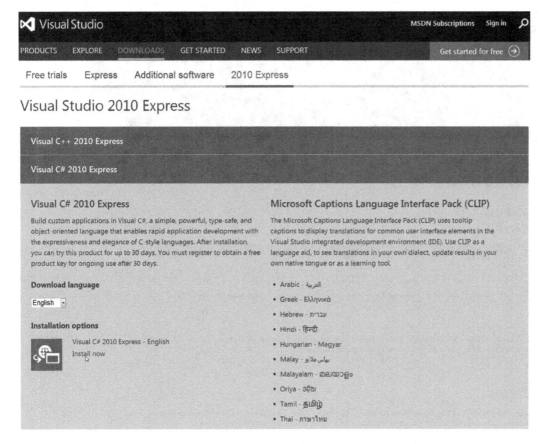

Figure 1-1. *Landing page for Visual Studio 2010 Express download*

Download and install the game SDK: MonoGame Framework

You will also need the MonoGame framework, which you can download from `www.monogame.net/downloads`. Figure 1-2 shows the download page at the time of writing. The version of MonoGame used in this book is V3.0.1 (released March 6, 2013), as indicated at the bottom of the screenshot.

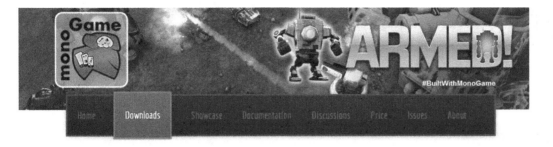

Downloads

Getting Started

There are a few pre-requisites that you should be aware of for the various platforms:

	Windows	Windows 8	iOS	Android	Mac OS X	Linux
Installer	Yes	Yes	No	Yes	No	No
Machine	PC	PC	Mac	Mac or PC	Mac	PC
IDE	Visual Studio	Visual Studio	Mono Develop	Visual Studio or Mono Develop	Mono Develop	Mono Develop
Examples	Yes	Yes	Yes	Yes	Yes	Yes

You can download MonoGame either as a binary installer or source code below. The installer will get you up and running quickly, but if you want to help adding features or contributing fixes you will need to get the source code.

Stable Releases

The Windows Installer supports for following platforms, Windows, Linux, Android. There is an Add In package for MonoDevelop which includes Windows, Linux, Android, Mac and iOS, although you will need a Mac to use the Mac and iOS project types.

MonoGame v3.0.1 (March 6th, 2013)

MonoGame v3.0 (January 21st, 2013)

Figure 1-2. Download page at www.monogame.net

Upon clicking the MonoGame 3.0.1 link, you will be brought to a page similar to the one shown in Figure 1-3. The recommended download is MonoGame 3.0.1 for Visual Studio 2010/2012. Although all examples in this book are built with Visual Studio 2012 Express, they will work with Visual Studio 2010 Express just fine.

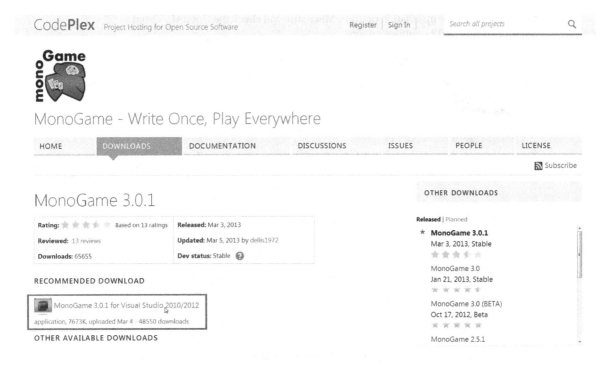

Figure 1-3. The MonoGame website provides a recommended download link for the latest SDK

To install the MonoGame SDK:

1. Double-click the downloaded installation file to see the following setup:

2.   Click Next to see the installation options. Make sure you check the OpenAL, Visual
     Studio 2010, and 2012 template options.

3.   Click Install. On successful completion you should see the following confirmation screen.

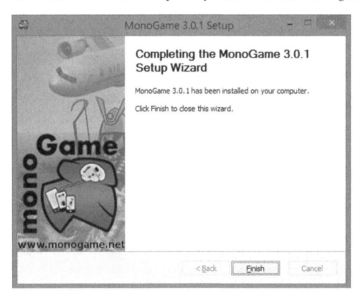

That's it! MonoGame is now installed on your computer. The final step is to download and install the asset builder, XNB Builder.

Download and install the asset builder: XNB Builder

In order for MonoGame to work with images, audio clips, and fonts (generally referred to as *assets* of your games), you need to download the XNB Builder. This can be found at the following site, shown in Figure 1-4:

```
http://sourceforge.net/projects/xnbbuilder/
```

***Figure 1-4.** Download page for XNB Builder*

The download takes the form of a zip file, XNAFormatter.zip. This file should be unzipped into the XNAFormatter folder that contains the XNAFormatter.exe program. Make sure you remember the location of the XNAFormatter program. You will need to use this program to build art assets for your game into formats that can be loaded by MonoGame.

■ **Note**   The XNAFormatter.exe program converts formats of images, audio files, and fonts into MonoGame's internal representation, the XNB format. This conversion is referred to as Content Pipeline processing for MonoGame. It is expected that in the future the XNAFormatter.exe will be integrated into the MonoGame SDK and this extra step of installing the asset importer will become unnecessary.

In the next chapter, we will begin by building our first empty template project. In the meantime, let's look at a brief overview of what we will cover in this book, and some recommendations on where to go to learn about other related topics in game development.

■ **Note**   Interested readers can refer to the excellent article by Dean Ellis overviewing MonoGame:
www.gamasutra.com/view/feature/192209/from_xna_to_monogame.php

---

What Is Covered in This Book?

Because this book is targeted toward individuals with some experience in software development, it jumps headlong into walking you through the technical details you need to know to create your own games from scratch. The overall goal is to guide you through this process as quickly and painlessly as possible while providing a solid foundation in the game development concepts used in the industry today.

Also note that *game development* is a catch-all term that actually includes many different disciplines. While some of these disciplines lie within the computer science and computer programming fields, there are several other areas of game development that are actually outside of the computer science and programming disciplines, including game design and asset creation (art). These areas are as crucial to the success of a game as the technical process. With that in mind, we'll detail the areas of development that are and are not covered in this book.

The following is an overview of the book and the topics we will cover:

Development tools (Chapter 1):

- Installation guide
- Conceptual framework behind MonoGame

Basic architecture of a 2D game engine using the MonoGame Framework (Chapter 2):

- Draw and update cycles
- Assets and resource-loading models
- Game object abstraction and encapsulation
- Game state implementation

Elementary math and physics (Chapters 3, 4, and 5):

- Drawing coordinate systems
- 2D camera abstraction
- Working with randomness
- Points, vectors, dot product, cross product, and their support for implementing speed, velocity, direction, collision responses

Game logic and behaviors (Chapters 5 and 6):

- Finite-state machines
- Game complexity and linear collections
- Pixel-accurate collisions
- Semiautonomous behaviors (controlled gradual turning, homing in, chasing, and following)

Graphics and effects (Chapters 7 and 8):

- 2D camera manipulation
- Sprite sheets and sprite animations

- Particle systems

- Fonts and audio effects

Building a complete game (Chapter 9):

- Design of a complete 2D game

- Enumerate functionality of all gaming elements

- Define C# classes implementing gaming element functionalities

- Synthesize all elements into a final fun game

This list represents fundamentals of technical knowledge required for developing videogames. By working through the activities in this book, you will gain a vital foundation in the technical building blocks that underlie all great games, from Pac-Man to Angry Birds! However, there are many other aspects to building successful video games. If you are serious about game development, you will also need to consider some of the topics discussed in the next section.

What Is *Not* Covered in This Book?

The following list describes some areas of development that *are not* covered in the book:

- *Game design:* This is the phase of brainstorming and creating the components and parts that comprise the game. In general, game design should be documented before the process of building the game begins; however, there are many different approaches to creating the game design document itself. Some people prefer to flesh out all the mechanics the game will have in a single large document, while others prefer to create a concise concept document of a few pages and then begin prototyping before completely fleshing out the mechanics.

- *Game development life cycle:* There are many approaches to the game development process. If you're starting out as a hobbyist, you won't need to worry too much about your development life cycle, and you can follow something like the simplified process shown in Chapter 9. Professional game development shops, on the other hand, need to manage not only their technical know-how, but also the team and their various talents, the schedule, testing etc. There are many life cycle processes in use today; one commonly used for software projects is agile development.

- *Game architecture planning:* This is about deciding how the game will be structured, including what objects the game will include, and how they will interact with one another. This phase relies heavily on knowledge of object-oriented programming. The game-building exercise in the last chapter, where we enumerate all the functionality of gaming elements and define how they should interact, gives a simplified peek into this area.

- *Asset creation:* This is the creation and preparation of assets (art, video, and audio) for the game. Asset creation includes everything from the process of creating sprite sheets to properly sizing images. In this book assets to all games are provided so that you do not have to be concerned with the creation of these while learning your way around game development.

If you're interested in some of these other areas of the game development process, or wish to dive more deeply into the technical aspects of creating 2D or 3D games, a plethora of resources exist. The authors have found the following books on game design and the development process to be very helpful and informative:

- *Game Design Workshop: A Playcentric Approach to Creating Innovative Games*, by Tracy Fullerton (CRC Press, 2008)

- *Fundamentals of Game Design (2nd Edition)*, by Ernest Adams (New Riders, 2009)

- *The Art of Game Design*, by Jesse Schell (CRC Press, 2008)

While the step–by–step tutorials from this book cover many of the foundational concepts in typical 2D game engines, the preceding areas can help you with the design and implementation of fun games. Together, these form a concrete foundation for building simple 2D games. In order to begin to understand and appreciate the intimate details of popular games like the Halo series, you need technical knowledge from standard computer science and computer engineering undergraduate curricula, including computer graphics, classical mechanics, artificial intelligence, networking, databases, human-computer interaction, software engineering, and so on. In addition, many of the advanced autonomous behaviors in games utilize concepts from linear algebra.

Very importantly, to be a successful game developer, you would need to know how to—and love to—work with people. Videogame creation is by nature a group effort. Artists, programmers, storytellers, managers, etc., must all work together in putting together a compelling and fun system. We should always remember that the modern blockbuster videogame titles, like the Halo series, are built by hundreds of full-time professionals. As aspiring indie developers, it is important to scope and design our projects accordingly. The technical concepts and knowledge you will learn from this book are important and great foundational first steps on your journey to becoming a successful game developer!

Technology References

The following list offers several links for obtaining additional information on topics related to this book.

- **C#** http://msdn.microsoft.com/library/vstudio/kx37x362.aspx

- **DirectX** http://msdn.microsoft.com/library/ms810424.aspx

- **OpenGL** www.opengl.org/

- **MonoGame** www.monogame.net

- **MonoDevelop** http://monodevelop.com

- **XNA Framework** http://msdn.microsoft.com/library/bb203940.aspx

- **Windows Marketplace** www.windowsmarketplace.com

- **Google play** http://play.google.com/store

- **Microsoft DreamSpark Program** www.dreamspark.com

- **Agile development** www.agilealliance.org/the-alliance/the-agile-manifesto

CHAPTER 2

Getting to Know the MonoGame Framework

After completing this chapter, you will be able to:

- Use the most important features of the Microsoft Visual Studio integrated development environment (IDE)

- Use the most appropriate MonoGame project development template

- Describe the functions of all the relevant files in a MonoGame project

- Work with the MonoGame project and application structure

- Use the functions and operations of the Draw/Update loop

Before diving headlong into game creation, it is a good idea to first become familiar with the development environment you will be using. The primary tools you will work with throughout this book are Visual Studio Express and MonoGame.

The fundamental concepts behind programming games are independent from any particular operating system or mobile device. For the purposes of this book and learning the universal building blocks of 2D game development, we will build examples using a Windows Desktop template, which is accessible to anyone using a Windows machine with Visual Studio and MonoGame.

MonoGame is designed to allow maximum code reuse and ease of porting between platforms, so once you're confident building 2D games, you will have the option to develop games for all popular operating systems including Windows, Mac OS, and Linux, and most popular mobile platforms including Windows Phone, iOS, and Android. MonoGame is even compatible with building games for Playstation Mobile and the OUYA console, and cross-platform support is improving all the time.

■ **Note**   MonoGame is free, but there may be other requirements and costs associated with some of the platforms you eventually want to target. For example, you will need a Mac to target Mac OS or iOS, and some mobile platforms require a paid developer license to sell or distribute your games. For more information on current requirements, see http://monogame.net/price.

The Visual Studio Development Environment

To follow along, you will need to download and install both Visual Studio and MonoGame. If you have yet to install either of these packages, you can refer to the download and installation instructions in the "Downloading and Installing Development Tools" section of Chapter 1 before proceeding.

After you have installed the required tools, you can start creating your first project. Luckily, Visual Studio Express with MonoGame lets you create new projects with minimal effort.

Creating a MonoGame project in Visual Studio

1. Open Visual Studio. Press Ctrl+Shift+N on your keyboard or select File ➤ New Project, as shown in the following image. A New Project window will appear.

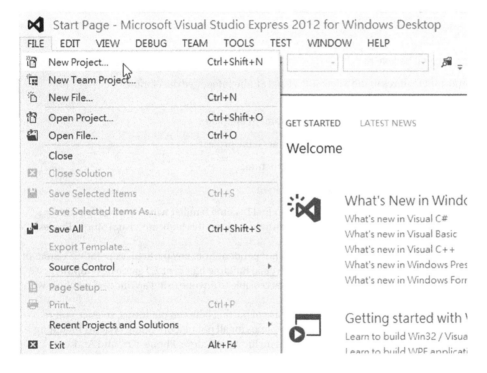

2. Under the Installed Templates section, expand the Visual C# section and then select MonoGame. A list of templates for both Windows and various mobile devices will appear. You can see an example of this in the following image:

3. Select MonoGame Windows OpenGL Project from the Installed Templates. A short description of the template will appear on the right.

4. Name the project SimpleMono.

■ **Note**   Optionally, you can also specify the solution name of the project. (By default, the solution name will be the same as the name of the project.)

---

5. If you like, you may specify a location for the project on your file system (the default location is in the Projects folder under `C:\YourUserName\Documents\Visual Studio 2012\Projects`).

6. Click the OK button.

Visual Studio generates a MonoGame project named SimpleMono for you. The project contains several default files that in turn contain a minimum skeleton of code required for the project to compile and run.

Go ahead and start the program now by selecting Debug ➤ Start Debugging or by pressing the F5 key on your keyboard. A new window will appear showing an empty game world in cornflower blue. Figure 2-1 shows an example of what the default project (which has no real content yet) looks like when you run it.

Figure 2-1. *Running the default game project*

■ **Note** Please refer to the following troubleshooting suggestions if you should run into any trouble compiling or running your SimpleMono game project.

To stop the program, either close the game world window or select Debug ➤ Stop Debugging in Visual Studio.

You have successfully run your first MonoGame project. Now that you have a working project, you'll use that to help you get oriented with the IDE.

If you should run into any trouble compiling or running your SimpleMono project, please refer to the following troubleshooting suggestions. You can skip the troubleshooting sections if you have not encountered any problems.

Troubleshooting: For Windows 8 machines only

If you are working on a machine that runs the Microsoft Windows 8 operating system, you may encounter the error where upon hitting compile and run the IDE complains that the SDL.dll file cannot be found, as indicated in Figure 2-2.

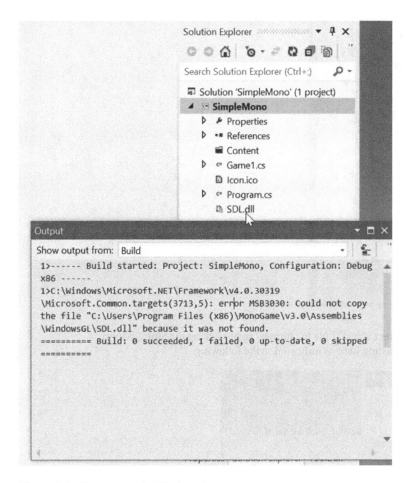

Figure 2-2. *Error screen in Windows 8*

Fortunately, this error can be easily remedied by removing and reestablishing the correct reference to the SDL.dll file. Here are the steps to accomplishing this task.

1. Remove the incorrect reference by right-clicking over the SDL.dll file and removing it as indicated in the following.

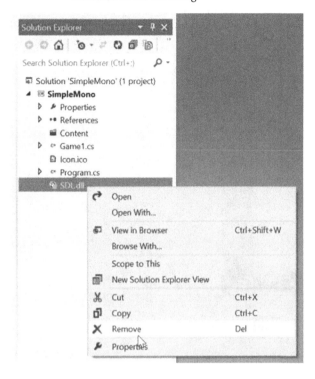

2. Add a new reference to the correct SDL.dll file location by right-clicking the SimpleMono project and selecting Add ➤ Existing Item as indicated in the following.

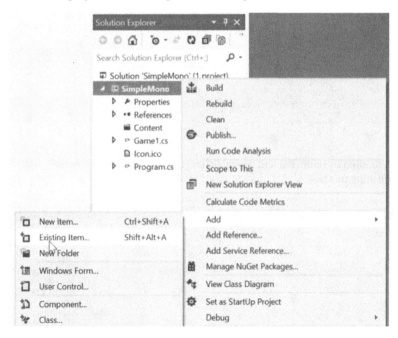

3. In the file dialog, make sure you set the filter to All Files (*.*) and navigate to:

   `C:\Program Files (x86)\MonoGame\v3.0\Assemblies\WindowsGL`

   select SDL.dll and click Add, as indicated in the following.

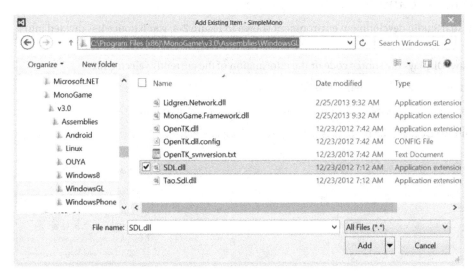

Now, your MonoGame project should compile and run.

Troubleshooting: OpenGL error

You might encounter the error shown in Figure 2-3 when trying to run your SimpleMono project.

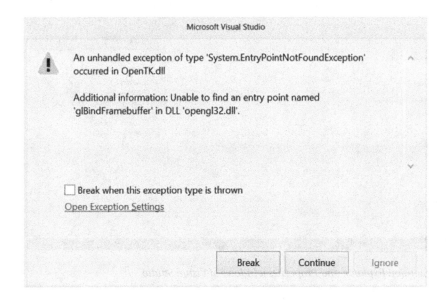

Figure 2-3. *Error screen in Visual Studio*

This means the device driver of your graphics card is not compatible with OpenGL 3. You need to update your graphics card driver, or you need to find a suitable graphics card in order to follow the rest of the examples in this book.

The Visual Studio layout and Solution Explorer

Upon first examining the Visual Studio development environment shown in Figure 2-4, you'll notice it is divided into four main sections:

- **Primary window:** Displays the source code or the information of the currently selected file
- **Error List window:** Displays the syntax errors in the code
- **Solution Explorer window:** Displays the projects and files for the current solution
- **Properties window:** Displays the properties of the currently selected object

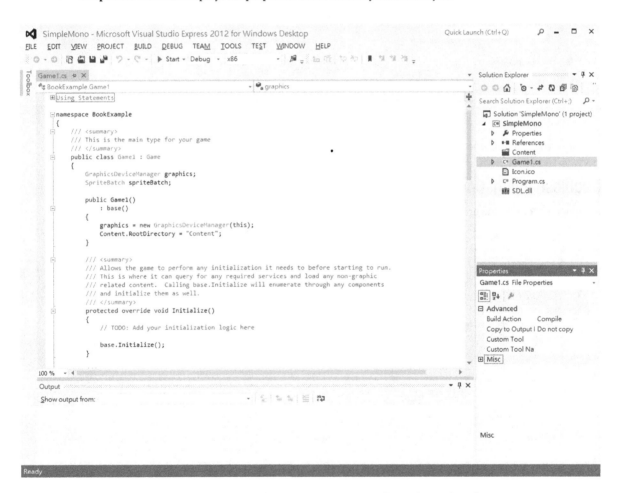

Figure 2-4. *The Primary, Error List, Solution Explorer, and Properties windows of Visual Studio*

■ **Note**   If you do not see the Error List, Solution Explorer, or Properties window in your IDE, click the View menu and then select the name of the missing window to display it in the IDE.

Because Solution Explorer is the least straightforward window in the bunch, it's worth exploring in more detail. In Figure 2-5, you can see that the SimpleMono solution contains a single project: SimpleMono. This project represents the game project itself. Within this project is the Content folder, which will contain the game's assets, such as art and sound. You can see the reference to the Content folder in Figure 2-5.

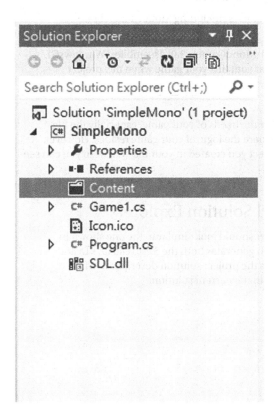

Figure 2-5. *The Solution Explorer window*

Table 2-1 describes the functions of the remaining files shown in Solution Explorer.

Table 2-1. *Purpose of Each File*

SimpleMono project: folder/file	Purpose
Icon.ico	Icon image in the top-left corner of the application window
Properties/AssemblyInfo.cs	Configuration and information of the game—for example, the window title and the Globally Unique Identifier (GUID), which gives the game a unique name. Further coverage of the content of this file will follow.
Program.cs	Container of the main() function. Content to this file will follow.
Game1.cs	Source code of the game. Content to this file will follow.
References	Reference to all required system libraries (including MonoGame libraries)
SDL.dll	This is the Simple DirectMedia Layer runtime library. This library should be installed in C:\Program Files (x86)\MonoGame\v3.0\Assemblies\WindowsGL and will be copied to the folder that contains your game when this project is compiled.

As you develop the game, you'll modify most of these files to suit the needs of your game, especially the file Game1.cs. Along with the source code files you create, Game1.cs is where the logic of your game resides. However, before tackling the source code in more detail, take a look at the project you created in your file system so you can see its relation to Solution Explorer.

The relationship between the file system and Solution Explorer

Open the SimpleMono project location on your file system. The folder should look similar to the one shown in Figure 2-6. Let's examine these files a little more closely. Visual Studio generates both the SimpleNono.sln and SimpleMono.suo files when you create the project. SimpleMono.sln is the project solution description, while SimpleMono.suo records various Visual Studio settings associated with the current solution.

Name	Date modified	Type	Size
SimpleMono	10/27/2013 9:41 ...	File folder	
SimpleMono.sln	10/27/2013 9:38 ...	Microsoft Visual S...	2 KB

Figure 2-6. *Contents of the SimpleMono project folder*

By opening the SimpleMono\SimpleMono subfolder (Figure 2-7), you will see that it contains the files and folders you saw in Visual Studio's Solution Explorer—along with a few additions. The bin and obj folders are hidden by default in Solution Explorer. They contain the project's executable and compiled files, respectively. The SimpleMono.csproj file contains the project description and is also hidden by Solution Explorer. The last additional file is OpenTK.dll, the Open Toolkit runtime library. By default OpenTK.dll is also installed in C:\Program Files (x86)\MonoGame\v3.0\Assemblies\WindowsGL. Together with SDL.dll, these runtime libraries allow your MonoGame projects access to low-level graphics and media functionalities. The remaining files all appear within Solution Explorer and were described in Table 2-1.

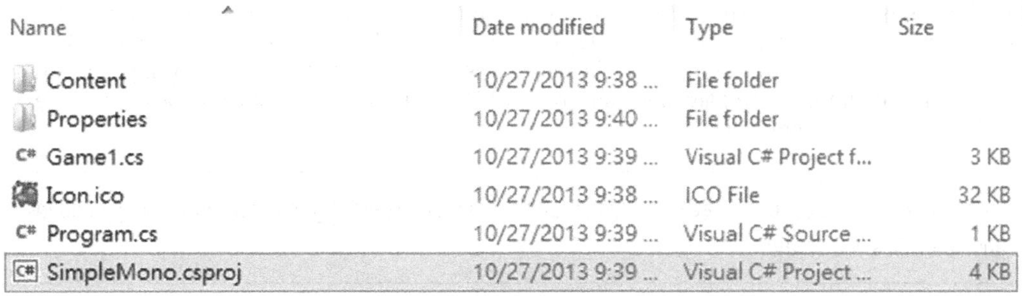

Name	Date modified	Type	Size
Content	10/27/2013 9:38 ...	File folder	
Properties	10/27/2013 9:40 ...	File folder	
C# Game1.cs	10/27/2013 9:39 ...	Visual C# Project f...	3 KB
Icon.ico	10/27/2013 9:38 ...	ICO File	32 KB
C# Program.cs	10/27/2013 9:39 ...	Visual C# Source ...	1 KB
C# SimpleMono.csproj	10/27/2013 9:39 ...	Visual C# Project ...	4 KB

Figure 2-7. *Contents of the SimpleMono\SimpleMono project folder*

■ **Note**   To display the hidden files within Solution Explorer, toggle the Show/Hide button in the top-left corner of the Solution Explorer window.

Understanding the MonoGame Framework

The first file you should know about is AssemblyInfo.cs. You can find that file in the Properties folder in Solution Explorer. Overall, AssemblyInfo.cs is not the most interesting source file. However, there are a few important aspects that we can touch upon, the first being the title of the game window. The following code shows the contents of the file. The first line reads [assembly: AssemblyTitle("SimpleMono")]. This code, which was generated automatically, sets the game window's title to SimpleMono when the project executes. Following this line are many other descriptors for the project, including company and trademark. Also, note the line of code that reads [assembly: Guid("64ac7fb4-d5bf-45ed-b760-92ca9bfc3905")], which represents the unique ID generated for this project.

```
// General Information about an assembly is controlled through the following
// set of attributes. Change these attribute values to modify the information
// associated with an assembly.
[assembly: AssemblyTitle("SimpleMono")]
[assembly: AssemblyProduct("SimpleMono")]
[assembly: AssemblyDescription("")]
[assembly: AssemblyCompany("")]
[assembly: AssemblyCopyright("Copyright © 2013")]
[assembly: AssemblyTrademark("")]
[assembly: AssemblyCulture("")]

// Setting ComVisible to false makes the types in this assembly not visible
// to COM components. If you need to access a type in this assembly from
// COM, set the ComVisible attribute to true on that type.
[assembly: ComVisible(false)]

// The following GUID is for the ID of the typelib if this project is exposed to COM
[assembly: Guid("64ac7fb4-d5bf-45ed-b760-92ca9bfc3905")]
```

The next file of interest is Program.cs. This is the source file that runs your game. Another way to look at it is that this file contains the main() function, or entry point for code execution. First, at the top of the following code is the using System; statement. For those with experience in other languages, the keyword using in this line is similar to the keywords include (of C++) and import (of Java). As you look inside main(), you will see that the code instantiates a Game1 object and invokes its Run() command.

■ **Note** When starting out, it is a good idea to avoid making modifications to this file. Try to keep all the game code in the Game1 object and other files you create.

```
#region Using Statements
using System;
using System.Collections.Generic;
using System.Linq;
#endregion

namespace BookExample
{
#if WINDOWS || LINUX
    /// <summary>
    /// The main class.
    /// </summary>
    public static class Program
    {
        /// <summary>
        /// The main entry point for the application.
        /// </summary>
        [STAThread]
        static void Main()
        {
            using (var game = new Game1())
                game.Run();
        }
    }
#endif
}
```

The last project-generated source code file you should look at is Game1.cs. A shortened example of Game1.cs is shown in the following. First, note that the file inherits from (is a subclass of) the MonoGame's Game class. This provides the Game1 class with access to code designed to assist in common game tasks, such as initialization, rendering, loading, and updating. You can see this reflected in the override functions that were generated for you (shown following). These functions are invoked by the MonoGame's Game library in a fixed sequence to support proper initialization and runtime functionality. Because you will be using these Game functions often, you'll explore them in more depth in upcoming sections.

```
namespace BookExample
{
    public class Game1 : Game
    {
        GraphicsDeviceManager graphics;
        SpriteBatch spriteBatch;
```

```csharp
        public Game1()
        {
            ...
        }

        protected override void Initialize()
        {
            ...
        }

        protected override void LoadContent()
        {
            ...
        }

        protected override void UnloadContent()
        {
            ...
        }

        protected override void Update(GameTime gameTime)
        {
            ...
        }

        protected override void Draw(GameTime gameTime)
        {
            ...
        }
    }
}
```

■ **Note** The full name of the Game class that we inherited from is actually Microsoft.Xna.Framework.Game. For this reason, you may sometimes see the Game1 class defined as follows:

```csharp
public class Game1 : Micrrosoft.Xna.Framework.Game { ... }
```

with the full name of the Game class spelled out. The results are the same in either case; with or without full name for the Game class, we are defining a subclass of Microsoft.Xna.Framework.Game. In the following discussion, we choose to use the full name to avoid causing confusion between Game and Game1 classes.

The *Microsoft.Xna.Framework.Game* Class

Like most classes, a Microsoft.Xna.Framework.Game subclass starts with a constructor. The constructor is responsible for allocating and initializing the internal memory of the game. It also handles the internal initialization of MonoGame by creating and initializing the graphics hardware. You can see this reflected in the following code, which shows the constructor of the Game1 class with the line graphics = new GraphicsDeviceManager(this). This line causes MonoGame to obtain and prepare the graphics device on your machine so you can use it for your game.

```
namespace Book_Example
{
    /// <summary>
    /// This is the main type for your game
    /// </summary>
    public class Game1 : Game
    {
        GraphicsDeviceManager graphics;
        SpriteBatch spriteBatch;

        public Game1()
        {
            graphics = new GraphicsDeviceManager(this);
            Content.RootDirectory = "Content";
        }


        ...

    }
}
```

The Initialize() function gets called next. This function initializes the game's graphics requirements, such as the window size. However, by default, the only call within the initialize function is its superclass function call, base.Initialize(), as shown in the following example. As you will see in many of the examples in the rest of this book, you will typically add custom non-default initialization code in this function.

```
protected override void Initialize()
{
    // TODO: Add your initialization logic here

    base.Initialize();
}
```

After the initialize function, MonoGame calls the LoadContent() function shown next. This function is fairly self-explanatory; it loads all the content or assets of your project, such as the game art and audio. It is important to note that this function is called only once per execution. Similarly, UnloadContent() is also called once per execution. However, as you may have guessed, UnloadContent() is called at the end of the game. It should unload all the content loaded by LoadContent().

```
/// <summary>
/// LoadContent will be called once per game and is the place to load
/// all of your content.
/// </summary>
protected override void LoadContent()
{
    // Create a new SpriteBatch, which can be used to draw textures.
    spriteBatch = new SpriteBatch(GraphicsDevice);

    // TODO: use this.Content to load your game content here
}
```

```
/// <summary>
/// UnloadContent will be called once per game and is the place to unload
/// all content.
/// </summary>
protected override void UnloadContent()
{
    // TODO: Unload any non-ContentManager content here
}
```

The next two functions, Update() and Draw(), behave fundamentally differently from LoadContent() and UnloadContent() in that they are both called many times per second throughout game execution. For example, it's not unusual for Draw() to be called 60 times per second and Update() to be called at an even higher rate.

The Update() function handles any change to the game state and is also responsible for polling the input devices. This means that whenever the position of a game object within the game world is modified, or an input device (such as a controller) needs its state checked, that change gets passed through the Update() function. The following code shows the Update() function polling the state of a gamepad to see if it should exit the game.

```
protected override void Update(GameTime gameTime)
{
    // Allows the game to exit
    if (GamePad.GetState(PlayerIndex.One).Buttons.Back == ButtonState.Pressed)
        this.Exit();

    // TODO: Add your update logic here
    base.Update(gameTime);
}
```

The Draw() function draws the game world to the screen each time it is called, which is often around 60 times per second. Draw() clears the screen every cycle and redraws all the rendered game objects. In the example code for this game, the screen is cleared with cornflower blue at every draw cycle.

■ **Note** It is true that in general the Draw() function is called at a rate that is similar to the refresh frequency of your display monitor. However, these two rates are completely independent from each other. For example, changing your monitor's refresh rate has no effect on how often the Draw() function is called.

```
protected override void Draw(GameTime gameTime)
{
    GraphicsDevice.Clear(Color.CornflowerBlue);

    // TODO: Add your drawing code here

    base.Draw(gameTime);
}
```

It is important to note that the purposes and operations of Update() and Draw() are well defined and distinct. The Update() function should update the state of the game (typically by changing instance variables) and should never draw anything, while the Draw() function should only display the game state (typically by rendering the relevant instance variables) and never change the game state. Mixing these two functions will cause many problems.

Adding, Drawing, and Controlling Content

Now that you have a basic understanding of some of the functionality provided by MonoGame's Game class, let's go through the process of drawing and controlling something on the screen.

■ **Note** You can develop and test MonoGame projects using a game controller or computer keyboard. For each project in the book we have listed both options. We used an Xbox 360 controller while writing the projects for this book. You can use an Xbox 360 compatible controller or you can simply use the keyboard on your computer. The Input Wrapper project later in this chapter shows you how to simplify input options so you won't have to worry about which input type you are using.

The Draw and Control project

This project demonstrates how to load images into a MonoGame project. Draw these image files as textures and manipulate their positions. Figure 2-8 shows an example of what the project looks like when running.

Figure 2-8. *The Draw and Control project when it is running*

The project's controls are as follows:

- **Back button (on the controller) or F1 key on the keyboard:** Exits the program
- **Left thumbstick or the WSAD keys on the keyboard:** Moves the image with the white background
- **Right thumbstick or the arrow keys on the keyboard:** Moves the image with the transparent background

The goals of the project are as follows:

- To understand and experience working with the Content folder and external images
- To understand the differences between .jpg and .png images (the transparency)
- To work with simple game states (position of images)
- To experience the basic drawing coordinate system and the Update/Draw loop

Creating the Draw and Control project

1. Start by creating a new project and naming it DrawAndControl. Recall that in this book we work with the MonoGame Windows OpenGL Project template; however, if you need to, you can refer back to the "Visual Studio Development Environment" section for a more detailed procedure.

2. Next, add the images to the content project in your game. Add a .jpg and a .png file to the project. This project uses UWB.jpg and UWB.png, which you can find in the sample code, in the Chapter02\ImagesUsed folder.

   To add an image, right-click the Content folder and select Add ➤ Existing Item, as shown in the following image. Images you add to the project will be copied to the bin folder when the project is built. It is essential that these images exist in the bin folder such that they can be deployed as a part of the game.

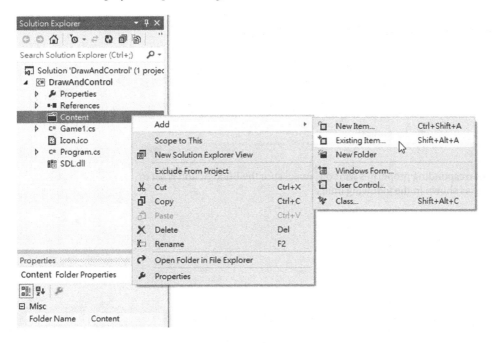

■ **Note**   The .png format supports transparency, or alpha, while the .jpg format does not. Transparency support for an image format means that areas of the image can be clear or partially clear. When an image has transparent parts, it uses the background to fill in those areas. When running the Draw and Control project, as shown in Figure 2-7, the difference between having and not having transparency support is easily recognizable.

An alternative way of adding images to the Content folder is by dragging images from your file system and dropping them directly into the Content folder. However, with this approach, you must manually set the content build properties of the images added. The following steps show you the procedure.

a.   Right-click over the image you just dragged into the Content folder and select Properties, as shown in the following image.

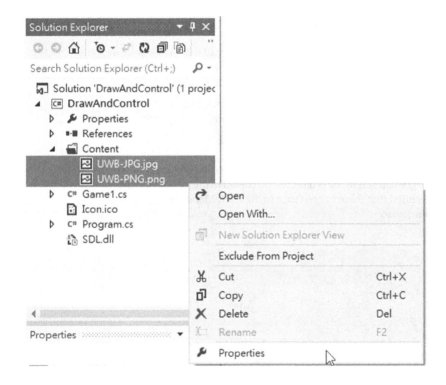

b.   In the corresponding properties window, make sure the Build Action is set to Content, as shown in the following image.

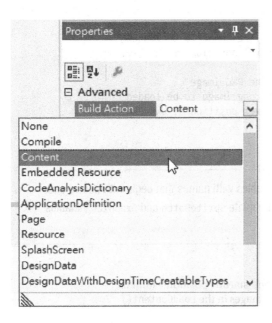

c. In addition, still in the Properties window, ensure the Copy to Output Directory option is set to Copy if newer, as shown in the following image.

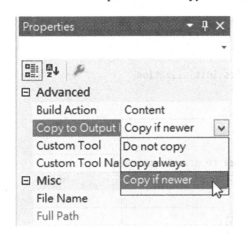

3. With the images in your project, you can now define the game state. Do this by inserting the following lines of code into your Game1 class.

a. Declare the following instance variables: Texture2D mJPGImage, Vector2 mJPGPosition, Texture2D mPNGImage, and Vector2 mPNGPosition, as shown in the following code:

```
public class Game1 : Game
{
    GraphicsDeviceManager mGraphics;
    SpriteBatch mSpriteBatch;
```

```
        // Support for loading and drawing the JPG image
        Texture2D mJPGImage;      // The UWB-JPG.jpg image to be loaded
        Vector2 mJPGPosition;     // Top-Left pixel position of UWB-JPG.jpg

        // Support for loading and drawing of the PNG image
        Texture2D mPNGImage;      // The UWB-PNG.png image to be loaded
        Vector2 mPNGPosition;     // Top-Left pixel position of UWB-PNG.png
        ...
    }
```

▮ **Note** This book follows the convention of naming all instance variables with names that begin with a lowercase "m." Notice that in the preceding code listing we have renamed the template SpriteBatch and Graphics variables accordingly.

---

d. Next, initialize the game state by setting your images' starting position within the Initialize() function and loading your external images in the LoadContent() function:

```
protected override void Initialize()
{
    // Initialize the initial image positions.
    mJPGPosition = new Vector2(10f, 10f);
    mPNGPosition = new Vector2(100f, 100f);

    // Important to let the base class perform its initialization
    base.Initialize();
}

protected override void LoadContent()
{
    // Create a new SpriteBatch, which can be used to draw textures.
    mSpriteBatch = new SpriteBatch(GraphicsDevice);

    // Load the images.
    mJPGImage = Content.Load<Texture2D>("UWB-JPG");
    mPNGImage = Content.Load<Texture2D>("UWB-PNG");
}
```

4. With the images loaded and ready, you can now draw them to your game world. You do this with the provided SpriteBatch object. As shown in the following code, the SpriteBatch.Begin() call initializes the drawing process, and the two SpriteBatch.Draw() calls add images to the batch to be rendered. When all desired drawing is done, you flush and display the drawn images with a call to the SpriteBatch.End() function. Notice that in the SpriteBatch.End() function, you simply draw the state of the game by rendering the images at the corresponding positions. You should avoid changing the game state information in the Draw() function.

■ **Important** Changes to the game state belong in the Update() function, with a few exceptions. Mixing the two functions will cause trouble because their calling frequencies are independent from each other.

```
protected override void Draw(GameTime gameTime)
{
    // Clear to background color
    GraphicsDevice.Clear(Color.CornflowerBlue);

    mSpriteBatch.Begin(); // Initialize drawing support

    // Draw the JPGImage
    mSpriteBatch.Draw(mJPGImage, mJPGPosition, Color.White);

    // Draw the PNGImage
    mSpriteBatch.Draw(mPNGImage, mPNGPosition, Color.White);

    mSpriteBatch.End(); // Inform graphics system we are done drawing

    base.Draw(gameTime);
}
```

5. The last step is to update the position of the images based on the input from the user. As you can see in the following code, at every update you add to the images' current position by the gamepad's thumbstick displacement values. In this case, notice that the Update() function updates the game state only by changing the various instance variables. You should avoid drawing any of the game objects in the Update() function. Additionally, if you prefer to use the mouse and keyboard, code for this is also provided. Both the keyboard and mouse are handled by polling the current state for the key or button of interest and modifying the appropriate values. From this point on, projects will use only the game controller for input. If you wish to use the keyboard and mouse, you will need to add the code to your project.

```
protected override void Update(GameTime gameTime)
{
    #region Game Controller
    // Allows the game to exit
    if (GamePad.GetState(PlayerIndex.One).Buttons.Back == ButtonState.Pressed)
        this.Exit();

    // Update the image positions with left/right thumbsticks
    mJPGPosition += GamePad.GetState(PlayerIndex.One).ThumbSticks.Left;
    mPNGPosition += GamePad.GetState(PlayerIndex.One).ThumbSticks.Right;
    #endregion

    #region Keyboard
    // Allows the game to exit
    if (Keyboard.GetState().IsKeyDown(Keys.Escape))
        this.Exit();
```

```
                // Update the image positions with Arrow keys
                if (Keyboard.GetState().IsKeyDown(Keys.Left))
                    mJPGPosition.X--;
                if (Keyboard.GetState().IsKeyDown(Keys.Right))
                    mJPGPosition.X++;
                if (Keyboard.GetState().IsKeyDown(Keys.Up))
                    mJPGPosition.Y--;
                if (Keyboard.GetState().IsKeyDown(Keys.Down))
                    mJPGPosition.Y++;

                // Update the image positions with AWSD
                if (Keyboard.GetState().IsKeyDown(Keys.A))
                    mPNGPosition.X--;
                if (Keyboard.GetState().IsKeyDown(Keys.D))
                    mPNGPosition.X++;
                if (Keyboard.GetState().IsKeyDown(Keys.W))
                    mPNGPosition.Y--;
                if (Keyboard.GetState().IsKeyDown(Keys.S))
                    mPNGPosition.Y++;
                #endregion

                #region Mouse
                // Poll mouse state
                MouseState mMouseState = Mouse.GetState();

                // If left mouse button is pressed
                if (mMouseState.LeftButton == ButtonState.Pressed)
                    mJPGPosition = new Vector2(mMouseState.X, mMouseState.Y);

                // If right mouse button is pressed
                if (mMouseState.RightButton == ButtonState.Pressed)
                    mPNGPosition = new Vector2(mMouseState.X, mMouseState.Y);
                #endregion

                base.Update(gameTime);
            }
```

The project is now ready. Build the project to see if any errors occur. If not, run the project and explore the program by moving the images around.

■ **Note** If you're using a game controller, remember to have it connected before executing the program.

Wrapping Game Controller with the Keyboard

As illustrated in the previous example, MonoGame supports the game controller, keyboard, and mouse. However, to maintain the support for all three types of input devices can involve a large amount of code and can complicate the explaining and learning of new concepts. In this example, we introduce the InputWrapper class to wrap game controller functionality with the keyboard. In this way, you can continue reading and experimenting with the examples in this book by using a game controller or the keyboard. However, you will not have to be concerned with the details of either one.

The Input Wrapper project

This project demonstrates how to unify the interaction with game controller and keyboard input devices. Figure 2-9 shows an example of what the project looks like when running. Note that this project appears identical to the previous one with the only difference being the code that handles user's input.

Figure 2-9. *The Input Wrapper project when it is running*

The project's controls are as follows:

- **Back button (on the controller) or F1 key on the keyboard:** Exits the program

- **Left thumbstick or the WSAD keys on the keyboard:** Moves the image with the white background

- **Right thumbstick or the arrow keys on the keyboard:** Moves the image with the transparent background

The goal of the project is as follows:

- To understand how to design a wrapper class to unify the game controller and keyboard input

Creating the Input Wrapper project

1. Start by creating a new project and naming it InputWrapper.

2. Add a new source file into your project by right-clicking over the project name and selecting Add ➤ New Item, as shown in the following image.

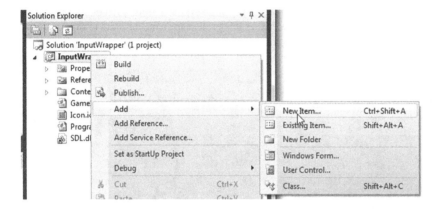

3. Select a new C# class, and name the file InputWrapper.cs, as show in the following image.

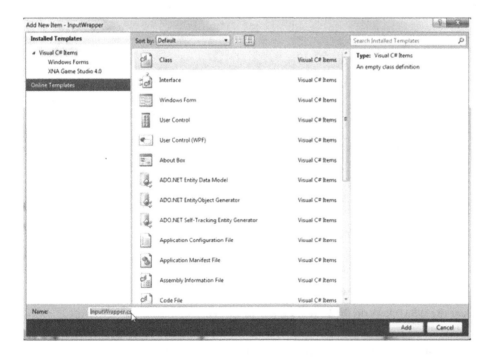

4. Double-click the newly created InputWrapper.cs file to open it for editing.

   a. Include all the references to necessary libraries for working with the keyboard with the following using statements.

```
using Microsoft.Xna.Framework;
using Microsoft.Xna.Framework.Input;
using Microsoft.Xna.Framework.Graphics;
```

   b. Define AllInputButtons outside of the InputWrapper class, an internal structure that captures button functionality of the game controller. The internal keyword ensures that the AllInputButtons structure is accessible only from within this library.

```
internal struct AllInputButtons
{
            ...
}
```

   c. Within the AllInputButtons structure, define the keys for all the buttons that we will work with. In the following, we define the K key for the game controller A button, L key for the B button, and so on.

```
private const Keys kA_ButtonKey = Keys.K;
private const Keys kB_ButtonKey = Keys.L;
private const Keys kX_ButtonKey = Keys.J;
private const Keys kY_ButtonKey = Keys.I;
private const Keys kBack_ButtonKey = Keys.F1;
private const Keys kStart_ButtonKey = Keys.F2;
```

■ **Note**   Variables that begin with the letter k represent a constant.

---

   d. Continue to work in AllInputButtons structure, define a GetState() function to poll the state of the corresponding keyboard key or the game controller button if one is connected. Notice the order upon which the states are polled: keyboard followed by game controller. This order means that when a game controller and the keyboard are both present, if a player types on the keyboard and presses the corresponding game controller button at the same time, we will process the keyboard input.

```
private ButtonState GetState(ButtonState gamePadButtonState, Keys key)
{
        if (Keyboard.GetState().IsKeyDown(key))
            return ButtonState.Pressed;

        if ((GamePad.GetState(PlayerIndex.One).IsConnected))
            return gamePadButtonState;

        return ButtonState.Released;
}
```

e. Final task in `AllInputButtons` structure is to define assessors with corresponding button names that will call the `GetState()` function. The following shows the assessors for the A, B, Back, Start, X, and Y buttons.

```
public ButtonState A {
        get { return GetState(GamePad.GetState(PlayerIndex.One).Buttons.A,
                                kA_ButtonKey); } }
public ButtonState B {
        get { return GetState(GamePad.GetState(PlayerIndex.One).Buttons.B,
                                kB_ButtonKey);  } }
public ButtonState Back {
        get { return GetState(GamePad.GetState(PlayerIndex.One).Buttons.Back,
                                kBack_ButtonKey); } }
public ButtonState Start {
        get { return GetState(GamePad.GetState(PlayerIndex.One).Buttons.Start,
                                kStart_ButtonKey); } }
public ButtonState X {
        get { return GetState(GamePad.GetState(PlayerIndex.One).Buttons.X,
                                kX_ButtonKey); } }
public ButtonState Y {
        get { return GetState(GamePad.GetState(PlayerIndex.One).Buttons.Y,
                                kY_ButtonKey); } }
```

f. We must repeat the preceding steps b to e to define internal structures `AllInputTriggers` and `AllThumbSticks` for wrapping game controller triggers and thumbsticks.

g. For `AllInputTriggers`, the left and right triggers are defined to be the N and M keys, and a keyboard trigger will return a floating point value of 0.75. The `GetTriggerState()` function implements the similar priority of checking the keyboard before the game controller.

```
internal struct AllInputTriggers
{
        private const Keys kLeftTrigger = Keys.N;
        private const Keys kRightTrigger = Keys.M;
        const float kKeyTriggerValue = 0.75f;

        private float GetTriggerState(float gamePadTrigger, Keys key)
        {
            if (Keyboard.GetState().IsKeyDown(key))
                return kKeyTriggerValue;

            if ((GamePad.GetState(PlayerIndex.One).IsConnected))
                return gamePadTrigger;

            return 0f;
        }
```

```
        public float Left
        {
                get { return GetTriggerState(
                                GamePad.GetState(PlayerIndex.One).Triggers.Left,
                                kLeftTrigger); }
        }

        public float Right
        {
                get { return GetTriggerState(
                                GamePad.GetState(PlayerIndex.One).Triggers.Right,
                                kRightTrigger); }
        }
}
```

h. For AllThumbSticks, the left thumbstick's positive and negative X movements are
    mapped to A and D keys, the corresponding Y movements are mapped to W and
    S keys. The right thumbstick's movements are mapped to the corresponding arrow
    keys. The defined ThumbStickState() function polls both the game controller
    and keyboard to accumulate the returned movement values.

```
internal struct AllThumbSticks
{
        const Keys kLeftThumbStickUp = Keys.W;
        const Keys kLeftThumbStickDown = Keys.S;
        const Keys kLeftThumbStickLeft = Keys.A;
        const Keys kLeftThumbStickRight = Keys.D;

        const Keys kRightThumbStickUp = Keys.Up;
        const Keys kRightThumbStickDown = Keys.Down;
        const Keys kRightThumbStickLeft = Keys.Left;
        const Keys kRightThumbStickRight = Keys.Right;

        const float kKeyDownValue = 0.75f;

        private Vector2 ThumbStickState(Vector2 thumbStickValue,
                                Keys up, Keys down, Keys left, Keys right)
        {
            Vector2 r = new Vector2(0f, 0f);
            if ((GamePad.GetState(PlayerIndex.One).IsConnected))
            {
                r = thumbStickValue;
            }
            if (Keyboard.GetState().IsKeyDown(up))
                r.Y += kKeyDownValue;
            if (Keyboard.GetState().IsKeyDown(down))
                r.Y -= kKeyDownValue;
            if (Keyboard.GetState().IsKeyDown(left))
                r.X -= kKeyDownValue;
```

```
                     if (Keyboard.GetState().IsKeyDown(right))
                         r.X += kKeyDownValue;

                     return r;
                 }

                 public Vector2 Left
                 {
                     get {
                         return ThumbStickState(GamePad.GetState(PlayerIndex.One).ThumbSticks.Left,
                                       kLeftThumbStickUp, kLeftThumbStickDown,
                                       kLeftThumbStickLeft, kLeftThumbStickRight); }
                 }

                 public Vector2 Right {
                         return ThumbStickState(GamePad.GetState(PlayerIndex.One).ThumbSticks.Right,
                                       kRightThumbStickUp, kRightThumbStickDown,
                                       kRightThumbStickLeft, kRightThumbStickRight); }
                     }
             }
```

i. With all the supporting structures, the InputWrapper class can simply define instances of corresponding structures with names identical to those from the GamePad class.

```
static class InputWrapper
{
        static public AllInputButtons Buttons = new AllInputButtons();
        static public AllThumbSticks ThumbSticks = new AllThumbSticks();
        static public AllInputTriggers Triggers = new AllInputTriggers();
}
```

5. Finally, we can poll input status by calling the newly defined InputWrapper facilities instead of checking the system GamePad and Keyboard classes. This is achieved by replacing the corresponding functions in the Update() function of the Game1 class (in Game1.cs).

```
protected override void Update(GameTime gameTime)
{
        // Allows the game to exit
        if (InputWrapper.Buttons.Back == ButtonState.Pressed)
            this.Exit();

        // Update the image positions with left/right thumbsticks
            mJPGPosition += InputWrapper.ThumbSticks.Left;
        mPNGPosition += InputWrapper.ThumbSticks.Right;
}
```

For the rest of examples in this book, we will always poll input devices using the InputWrapper class. In this way, all examples will function correctly with or without a compatible game controller.

Summary

This chapter has shown you how to create and explore a default generated MonoGame project. You saw ways to customize that MonoGame project by working with the `Initialize()`, `Load()`, `Draw()`, and `Update()` functions provided by the framework. Using those four functions, you created a simple project that allows you to interact with your own graphical objects.

In general, the `Initialize()`, `Load()`, `Draw()`, and `Update()` functions provide you with the core functionality you need to build most games. These four functions afford you the ability to create games of limitless variety and complexity while also allowing you to work within the provided framework.

Lastly, you should pay special attention to the `Draw/Update` loop concept, because that concept spans nearly every technology and programming language as a practical and reliable way to build games. As you will see in the next chapter, you will increasingly use these functions in various ways as the projects become more complex.

Quick Reference

To	Do this
Create a new Mono project	In Visual Studio, select File ➤ New Project and choose MonoGame Windows OpenGL Project. Remember to name the project before you click OK.
Open the Solution Explorer tab	In Visual Studio, select View ➤ Solution Explorer.
Change the game window title	In Solution Explorer, open the Properties tab, and in `AssemblyInfo.cs`, modify `[assembly: AssemblyTitle("YourTitle")]`.
Change the unique name of the project	In Solution Explorer, open the Properties tab, and in `AssemblyInfo.cs`, modify `[assembly: Guid("Your new GUID")]`.
Add source code to your game	Modify the `Game1.cs` source code file.
Include an image in your project	In Solution Explorer, right-click over the Content folder, select Add ➤ Existing Item and browse to locate your image.
Include an image by dragging and dropping the image directly into the Content folder	Make sure you remember to update the properties of the image: Build Action to Content, and Copy to Output Directory should be set to Copy if newer.

Load an image into your game	In the `Game1.cs` source code file, define an instance variable for referencing to the image, like so:
	
	 `Texture2D mTheImage;`
	
	 Load the image into the variable in `LoadContent()` function, as follows:
	
	 `mTheImage = Content.Load<Texture2D>("TheImageFileName");`
	
	 In the `Game1.cs` source code file, define a variable to hold the image position, like so:
	
	 `Vector2 mTheImagePosition;`

(continued)

To	Do this
Draw the loaded image at a specific position	Draw the image in the Draw() function, as follows: `mSpriteBatch.Draw(mTheImage, mTheImagePosition, Color.White);`

Move the image in your game	Update the image position with the gamepad's thumbstick movement in the Update() function, like so:
	
	`mTheImagePosition += GamePad.GetState(PlayerIndex.One).ThumbSticks.Left;`
	
	Draw the image Draw() function, as previously:
	`mSpriteBatch.Draw(mTheImage, mTheImagePosition, Color.White);`

■ **Note**   Do not attempt to draw in `Update()`, and do not attempt to change any instance variables in `Draw()`.

CHAPTER 3

■ ■ ■

2D Graphics, Coordinates, and Game State

After completing this chapter, you will be able to:

- Control the game window size

- Create and use a custom C# class to support the drawing and simple behaviors of textures

- Differentiate between pixel and user-defined coordinate systems

- Design and create your own coordinate system that best supports your game

- Create simple game objects

- Create a simple game state

Introduction

Most games these days use graphics in some form or another to represent or communicate their state, and 2D games are no different. Whether they use a texture used to represent a hero character or particles to show an explosion, 2D games also rely on graphics and effects to bring their game world to life. This chapter will cover some of the basic building blocks needed to achieve the desired graphics and effects for your game.

As in general for this book, you can follow along with the sections using the example projects contained in the Chapter03\SourceCode folder. An even better approach is to create your own project and follow along by inserting the required code as you step through the procedures. Building the projects yourself will give you both hands-on development experience and better insight into the concepts covered. It is also important to note that most of the projects build upon one another and therefore often reuse code from prior sections.

The Game Window

The first aspect to address is the game window. A game window is commonly displayed in one of two modes: windowed mode or full-screen mode. In *windowed* mode, you can specify the desired resolution of your game window, and it will be contained in the operating system's (Windows) default window. *Full-screen* mode will fit your game to the entire screen—even if the window size does not match, which can cause the game to look stretched or pixelated unless you plan for and handle the full-screen situation carefully.

The Game Window Size project

This project demonstrates how to toggle between full-screen mode and windowed mode. Figure 3-1 shows an example of the project running in windowed mode.

Figure 3-1. *Running the Game Window Size project in windowed mode*

The project's controls are as follows:

- **Back button (F1-key)** Exits the program
- **A button (K-key)** Toggles to full-screen mode
- **B button (L-key)** Toggles to windowed mode

The goals of the project are as follows:

- To understand how to control the application game window size using code
- To be able to toggle between full-screen and windowed mode
- To identify the need for graphical objects

Modifying the game window

1. Create a new project named *GameWindowSize* or follow along with the example project in the Chapter03\SourceCode\1.GameWindowSize folder. If you need a reminder on how to create a new project with Visual Studio and MonoGame, refer back to the example in Chapter 2, "Getting to know the MonoGame Framework."

2. In the Game1 class, declare the variables kWindowWidth and kWindowHeight to hold your desired window size, as shown in the following code:

```
public class Game1 : Game
{
    GraphicsDeviceManager mGraphics;
    SpriteBatch mSpriteBatch;

    // Prefer window size
    const int kWindowWidth = 1000;
    const int kWindowHeight = 700;
    ...
}
```

3. Next, as illustrated in the following code, set your window size by creating a graphics device manager and setting its PreferredBackBufferWidth and PreferredBackBufferHeight in the constructor. This is all it takes to specify your initial window size!

```
public Game1()
{
    mGraphics = new GraphicsDeviceManager(this);
    Content.RootDirectory = "Content";

    // Set preferred window size
    mGraphics.PreferredBackBufferWidth = kWindowWidth;
    mGraphics.PreferredBackBufferHeight = kWindowHeight;

    ...
}
```

4. Now add support for toggling to and from full-screen mode by inserting the code shown following into your Update() function. This code adds an if statement that allows the game to exit, and two more if statements that support toggling to and from full-screen mode. The first of the latter two if statements is responsible for toggling into full-screen mode. The code checks the A button's state (whether the button has been pressed) during every update cycle. If the button has been pressed, the code checks whether the game is already in full-screen mode. If not, the code uses the graphics device manager to set IsFullScreen to true, and then calls ApplyChanges() to apply the change immediately, because you are modifying the window state at run time. The second if statement is similar, but checks whether the B button has been pressed. If so, it checks to see whether the game is currently in full-screen mode, and if it is, toggles out of full-screen mode and then applies the change immediately.

```
    protected override void Update(GameTime gameTime)
    {
        // Allows the game to exit
        if (InputWrapper.Buttons.Back == ButtonState.Pressed)
            this.Exit();

        // "A" to toggle to full-screen mode
        if (InputWrapper.Buttons.A == ButtonState.Pressed)
        {
            if (!mGraphics.IsFullScreen)
            {
                mGraphics.IsFullScreen = true;
                mGraphics.ApplyChanges();
            }
        }

        // "B" toggles back to windowed mode
        if (InputWrapper.Buttons.B == ButtonState.Pressed)
        {
            if (mGraphics.IsFullScreen)
            {
                mGraphics.IsFullScreen = false;
                mGraphics.ApplyChanges();
            }
        }
    }
```

While modifying the window size and state is useful, it is not very interesting without any graphical objects in the game to show the changes. Next, you'll see what it takes to add some graphical objects to the game.

Textured Primitives

Most games use images, or textures, to represent characters or objects. With proper support, images or textures provide a straightforward way of getting assets or art into the game. In general, you can use textures for a wide variety of purposes within the game, including background representation and UI layout. This section guides you through the process of implementing a project designed to support textures.

The Textured Primitive project

This project demonstrates how to import textures and manipulate their position and size. It also demonstrates how to select the textures you want to control. Figure 3-2 shows the project running.

***Figure 3-2.** Running the Textured Primitive project*

The project's controls are as follows:

- **Back button (F1-key)** Exits the program
- **A button (K-key)** Toggles to full-screen mode
- **B button (L-key)** Toggles to windowed mode
- **Left thumbstick (WSAD-keys)** Moves the currently selected texture
- **Right thumbstick (arrow-keys)** Changes the size of the currently selected texture
- **X button (J-key)** Switches the currently selected texture

The goals of the project are as follows:

- To understand the abstraction of graphical primitives (TexturedPrimitive)
- To understand how to create and use a TexturedPrimitive
- To observe the limitations of working with the default pixel space

The steps for creating the project are as follows:

1. Create a new C# class for the project.

2. Define the behavior for the class.

3. Use the new class.

Abstracting TexturedPrimitive into a class enables you to easily reuse, modify, and build upon the object in the future, which is the purpose of object-oriented programming.

Creating the *TexturedPrimitive* class

1. To continue, you should use the previous project or follow along with the example project in the Chapter03\SourceCode\2.TexturedPrimitive folder.

2. Modify the Game1 class to support static variables for SpriteBatch, ContentManager, and GraphicsDeviceManager, as shown in the following code. Making these variables static allows you to access them globally and allows convenient drawing and loading of textures and fonts.

```
public class Game1 : Game
{
    static public SpriteBatch sSpriteBatch;       // Drawing support
    static public ContentManager sContent;        // Loading textures
    static public GraphicsDeviceManager sGraphics; // Current display size


    ...
}
```

■ **Note** Variables that begin with the letter s (for example, sStaticVariable) indicate that they are static.

---

3. The next step is to create a new C# class to display textures. As you probably know, making a class designed for texture support lets you reuse the same code without having to write it again. For example, when your game requires multiple textures, you can simply instantiate multiple instances of the object.

    a. Before creating the class itself, however, you should first create a folder to keep your project organized. To create a folder, right-click the project name in Solution Explorer, and then select Add ➤ New Folder, as shown in the image that follows. Name the folder GraphicsSupport.

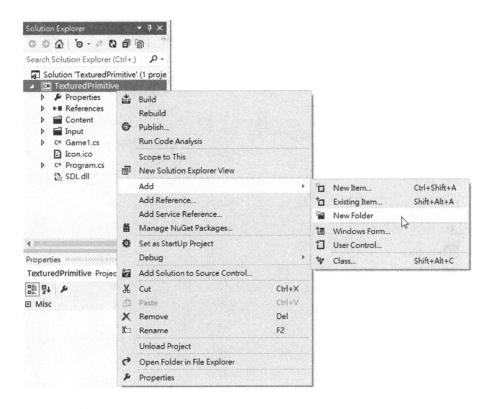

b. Now that you have created the GraphicsSupport folder for organizing the class, you can create the new class. To create a new C# class, right-click the GraphicsSupport folder and select Add ➤ New Item, as shown following. A new template window will appear.

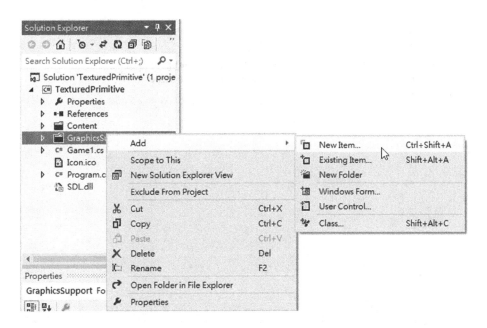

    c.   Select the Class template as shown following and name it TexturedPrimitive. Click the Add button, and the new class will appear within Visual Studio under your GraphicsSupport folder.

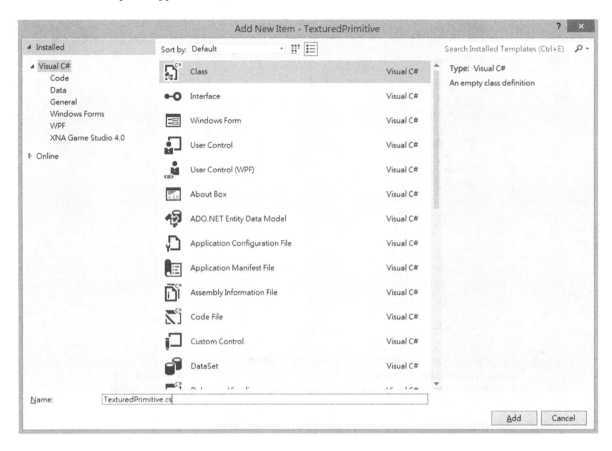

    d.   The image that follows shows the new class file inside the GraphicsSupport folder. This file is accessible from your current project as long as it shares the same namespace with the rest of the source code files.

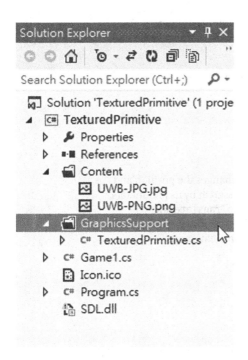

You have successfully created a new C# class file within the project. Next, you'll define functionality and behavior for this new class.

Adding custom functionally and behavior to TexturedPrimitive enables it to handle its own draw and update cycles, which keeps the object self-contained and simpler to manage.

Adding *TexturedPrimitive* functionality and behavior

1. You can now add the code needed to support textures in the TexturedPrimitive.cs source file. Start by declaring three instance variables: a Texture2D variable to hold the image and two Vector2 variables for the position and size of the image or texture.

```
protected Texture2D mImage;      // The UWB-JPG.jpg image to be loaded
protected Vector2 mPosition;     // Center position of image
protected Vector2 mSize;         // Size of the image to be drawn
```

■ **Note**   Variables that begin with the letter m are instance variables. These variables are accessible within the scope of the class.

---

2. Next, initialize these variables in the constructor with corresponding parameters. You can see an example of this in the code shown following. Notice how you access the static sContent variable of Game1 in order to load the texture.

```
public TexturedPrimitive(String imageName, Vector2 position, Vector2 size)
{
    mImage = Game1.sContent.Load<Texture2D>(imageName);
    mPosition = position;
    mSize = size;
}
```

3. The next step is to create an Update() function. This function changes the position and size of the texture when it is called by applying the amounts passed in by its parameters. You can see this represented in the following code, where deltaTranslate and deltaScale are added to the current position and size. If deltaTranslate and deltaScale have not changed, then the texture will remain the same size and stationary.

```
public void Update(Vector2 deltaTranslate, Vector2 deltaScale)
{
    mPosition += deltaTranslate;
    mSize += deltaScale;
}
```

4. The last function you need is the Draw() function. This function is responsible for drawing the texture to the screen. You can do this by creating a rectangle object for the size and position of the texture and using the Game1.sSpriteBatch.Draw call, which accepts a texture object, a primitive (rectangle) object, and a color.

```
public void Draw()
{
    // Defines where and size of the texture to show
    Rectangle destRect = new Rectangle((int)mPosition.X, (int)mPosition.Y,
                                       (int)mSize.X, (int)mSize.Y);
    Game1.sSpriteBatch.Draw(mImage, destRect, Color.White);
}
```

Now that you have completed the TexturedPrimitive class, it can be used within the Game1 class.

Using the *TexturedPrimitive* class

1. Open the Game1 class (by double-clicking the Game1.cs file in Solution Explorer) and declare the variables kNumObjects, mGraphicsObjects, and mCurrentIndex, as shown following. The integer kNumObjects represents the number of objects you will be working with, the TexturedPrimitive array mGraphicsObjects holds the texture objects, and the integer mCurrentIndex holds the index of the currently selected texture. The following code shows the changes in the Game1.cs file:

```
public class Game1 : Game
{
    static public SpriteBatch sSpriteBatch;          // Drawing support
    static public ContentManager sContent;           // Loading textures
    static public GraphicsDeviceManager sGraphics;   // Current display size
```

```
    // Preferred window size
    const int kWindowWidth = 1000;
    const int kWindowHeight = 700;

    const int kNumObjects = 4;
    // Work with the TexturedPrimitive class
    TexturedPrimitive[] mGraphicsObjects; // An array of objects
    int mCurrentIndex = 0;


    ...
}
```

2. The next step is to load the textures within LoadContent(). Add the following lines of code to the LoadContent() function of Game1 to create the texture array and set its starting image, position, and size. Remember from Chapter 2 that content such as images should be loaded into the content project (in this case, TexturedPrimitiveContent) before being used. Do this by right-clicking the content project and selecting Add ➤ Existing Item. Add both UWB-JPG.jpg and UWB-PNG.png to TexturedPrimitiveContent. They can be found in this chapter's Book_Img folder.

```
protected override void LoadContent()
{
    // Create a new SpriteBatch, which can be used to draw textures.
    Game1.sSpriteBatch = new SpriteBatch(GraphicsDevice);

    // Create the primitives.
    mGraphicsObjects = new TexturedPrimitive[kNumObjects];
    mGraphicsObjects[0] = new TexturedPrimitive("UWB-JPG",              // Image file name
                                        new Vector2(10, 10),     // Position to draw
                                        new Vector2(30, 30));    // Size to draw
    mGraphicsObjects[1] = new TexturedPrimitive("UWB-JPG",
                                        new Vector2(200, 200), new Vector2(100, 100));
    mGraphicsObjects[2] =  new TexturedPrimitive("UWB-PNG",
                                        new Vector2(50, 10), new Vector2(30, 30));
    mGraphicsObjects[3] = new TexturedPrimitive("UWB-PNG",
                                        new Vector2(50, 200), new Vector2(100, 100));
}
```

3. Now that you have properly prepared the LoadContent() function, the next step is to draw the textures to the screen. As you probably have guessed, this is done within Draw() function of Game1. Add the code shown following, which loops through each TexturedPrimitive and calls its Draw() function:

```
protected override void Draw(GameTime gameTime)
{
    // Clear to background color
    GraphicsDevice.Clear(Color.CornflowerBlue);

    Game1.sSpriteBatch.Begin(); // Initialize drawing support
```

```
    // Loop over and draw each primitive
    foreach (TexturedPrimitive p in mGraphicsObjects)
    {
        p.Draw();
    }

    Game1.sSpriteBatch.End(); // Inform graphics system we are done drawing

    base.Draw(gameTime);
}
```

4. The final portion of code needed lies within the Update() function. First, to support changing between the selected textures, use the gamepad's X button to modify the current index variable (mCurrentIndex). Next, use the Update() function of TexturedPrimitive in combination with the gamepad's left and right thumbstick to update the currently selected texture's size and position. You can see this reflected in the following code:

```
protected override void Update(GameTime gameTime)
{
    // Allows the game to exit
    ...
    // "A" to toggle to full screen
    ...
    // "B" toggles back to window
    ...

    // Button X to select the next object to work with
    if (InputWrapper.Buttons.X == ButtonState.Pressed)
        mCurrentIndex = (mCurrentIndex + 1) % kNumObjects;

    // Update currently working object with thumb sticks.
    mGraphicsObjects[mCurrentIndex].Update(
        InputWrapper.ThumbSticks.Left,
        InputWrapper.ThumbSticks.Right);

    base.Update(gameTime);
}
```

Observations

With all the necessary components of the TexturedPrimitive project completed, it is time to build and run the project while making some observations. Run the project and experiment with its functionality. Observe the behavior of the images when moving each thumbstick separately, as well as when toggling to and from full-screen mode. In particular, you should make the following observations:

- Notice the inversion of the y-axis. When moving the gamepad's left thumbstick upward, the selected image moves downward. This behavior is not intuitive for most users.

- When moving the right thumbstick, the images do not scale with respect to their centers; rather, the scaling is with respect to the top-left corner. You can identify this behavior by recognizing that the top-left corner retains its position during the scaling operation.

- Pay attention to the relative size of the images in windowed mode versus full-screen mode. As you'll notice, the image size does not change between windowed mode and full-screen mode. This is troublesome for you as a developer because you do not know the relative size of an object in relation to the game window size. We will touch upon this concept more in the next section.

In the upcoming projects, you will learn the necessary concepts to address and correct each of these behaviors to support a more intuitive experience for the user, as well as a more straightforward game world for you to develop in.

Coordinate System and Camera

As you saw at the end of the previous section, the TexturedPrimitive project was successful in adding multiple images to the game world and supporting straightforward interaction with the images. However, it also shed light on several issues that arise when using the default pixel space. These and many other issues that will arise by using default pixel space can be addressed by creating your own user-defined coordinate system.

For the purposes of this discussion, *pixel space* describes the area that the game window occupies in units of pixels. Each pixel in the game window represents a point in a discrete coordinate system where the origin lies in the top-left corner of the window, the x-axis points toward the right, and the y-axis points downward. A *user-defined coordinate system* is a Cartesian coordinate system created by you to suit your needs for the project. The user-defined coordinate system is different from the pixel space in two unique ways: first, the unit of the user-defined system is independent of pixels; second, the y-axis of the user-defined system points upward. The user-defined coordinate system acts as a layer between the default pixel space and you, the developer, in order to standardize the game world across different window sizes and views.

■ **Note** The terms *user-defined coordinate system* and *user-defined coordinate space* will be used interchangeably from here on.

Creating a user-defined coordinate system makes your job as a developer easier from a technical standpoint as well as a design standpoint. For example, imagine you are creating a game that uses human-sized characters. Under a user-defined coordinate system, you could use a meter as your basic unit and design you characters to be two units tall. However, under a pixel-space system, a character becomes an arbitrary amount of pixels tall. The problem becomes even worse when considering effects like camera zooming, since the character's pixel height has already been specified. A user-defined coordinate system allows the flexibility of adding new functionality while maintain the core functionality needed to standardize the game's look.

The User-Defined Coordinate System project

This project builds infrastructure support for a user-defined coordinate system and allows you to move away from pixel space. This infrastructure support includes defining a new Camera class and building new functionality in the TexturedPrimitive class. The functionality of the project is the same as the Textured Primitive project. However, as a developer you will be able to specify the position and size of an object independent from pixel resolution. Figure 3-3 shows the project running.

Figure 3-3. *Running the User-Defined Coordinate System project*

The project's controls are as follows:

- **Back button (F1-key)** Exits the program
- **A button (K-key)** Toggles to full-screen mode
- **B button (L-key)** Toggles to windowed mode
- **Left thumbstick (WSAD-keys)** Moves the currently selected texture
- **Right thumbstick (arrow-keys)** Changes the size of the currently selected texture
- **X button (J-key)** Switches the currently selected texture

The goals of the project are as follows:

- To understand the details and requirements of a coordinate system
- To understand how to create a coordinate system
- To define and work with a camera window within a user-defined coordinate system

The steps for creating the project are as follows:

1. Create a user-defined coordinate system. This is accomplished by creating a new Camera class and modifying the TexturedPrimitive class.

2. Use the Camera class. This allows navigation in the user-defined coordinate system.

Understanding pixel space and user-defined space

Before we go into the details of creating a user-defined coordinate system, we'll first discuss the default pixel space, which is shown in Figure 3-4. Upon inspection, you'll notice that the origin lies in the top-left corner of the game window rather than the bottom-left corner. Additionally, the y-axis increases in value in the downward direction rather than upward, as would generally be expected. It is also important to note that we use W_p to represent the width of the game window and H_p to represent the height of the game window.

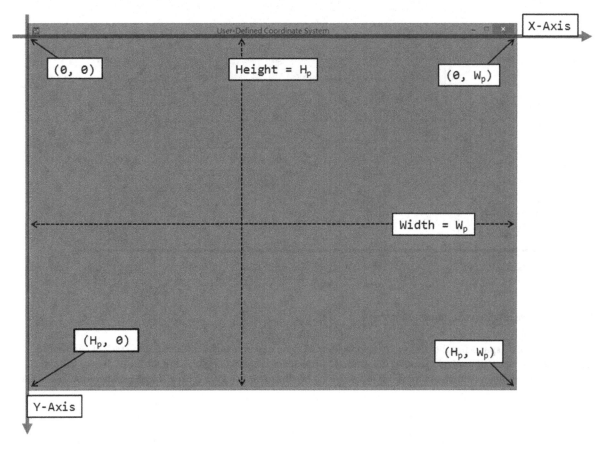

Figure 3-4. *Default pixel space*

Now that you know the layout of the default pixel space, you can begin to design the user-defined coordinate system to reflect a more intuitive layout. To start, it is a good idea to first specify the desired user-defined space. Usually this is done by creating a camera region that views a specified section of the game world. In Figure 3-5 you can see an example of a user-defined space where the light-blue rectangle represents the camera region (or camera window) that should be displayed in the game window. You can see outside the camera window that the desired user-defined space has its origin located in the bottom-left corner and a y-axis that increases in the upward direction. The camera window itself is defined by its bottom-left corner (X_c and Y_c), its width (W_c), and its height (H_c).

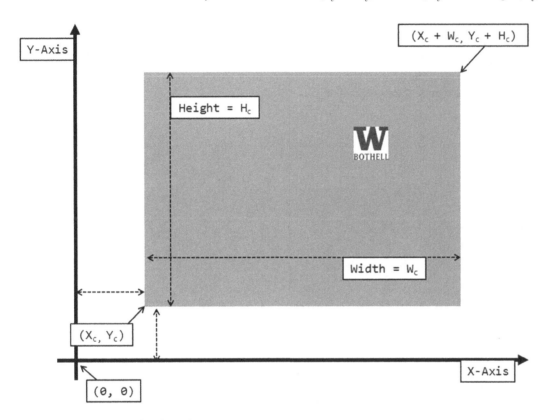

Figure 3-5. *The user-defined coordinate system*

With the pixel space and the desired user space defined, you can now begin addressing the task of converting from the user space to that pixel space. To transition to pixel space, you first need to shift, or translate, the camera window to the origin, as shown in Figure 3-6. This is done by subtracting X_c and Y_c from the camera window's position.

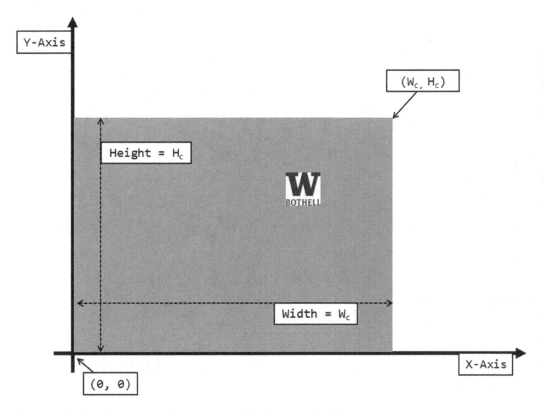

Figure 3-6. *User-defined coordinate system with a translated origin*

Next, the user-defined space needs to be resized (or scaled) to match the width and height of the pixel space. This can be achieved by multiplying the width W_c by W_p/W_c and the height H_c by H_p/H_c, which a leaves you with W_p, H_p for your width and height. You can see this in Figure 3-7.

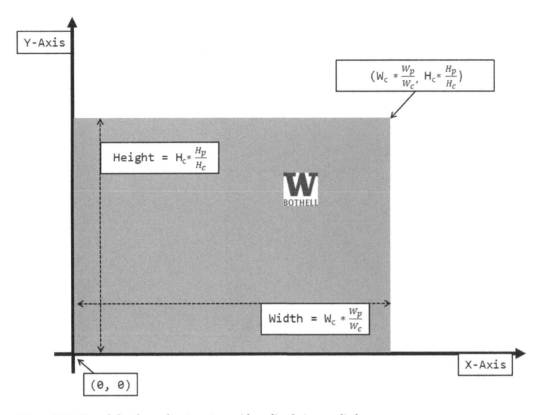

Figure 3-7. User-defined coordinate system with scaling being applied

The last step for converting to pixel space is to flip the y-axis so that the origin lies in the top-left corner. This can be done by taking the height of the pixel space and subtracting the y value from it. This leaves you with an origin in the top-left corner of the window, as shown in Figure 3-8.

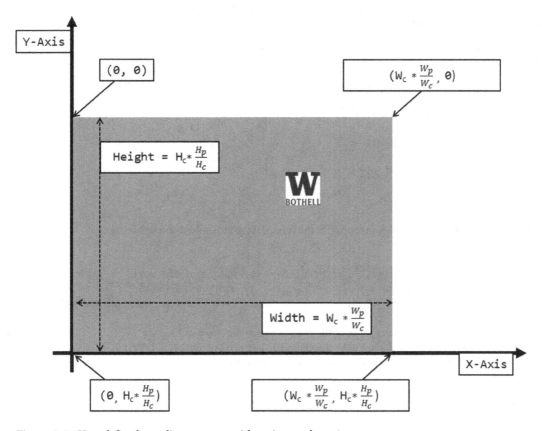

Figure 3-8. *User-defined coordinate system with an inverted y-axis*

Now that you know the process of converting to pixel space, take a look at the following formulas, where camera positions are represented with (C_x, C_y) in the user-defined space and the corresponding pixel space positions are presented as (P_x, P_y):

$$P_x = (C_x - X_c) * \left(\frac{W_p}{W_c} \right)$$

$$P_y = H_p - (C_y - Y_c) * \left(\frac{H_p}{H_c} \right)$$

If you follow the equation for the y values, you can see each step in the process of conversion happen in order. First, you translate to the origin by subtracting Y_c from C_y. Next, you scale to match the pixel space's size by multiplying by (H_p/H_c). Finally, the y-axis is flipped with subtraction by H_p. The formula is similar for the x-axis values, except there's no need to flip the horizontal axis.

Now that you have an understanding of the process and mathematics involved in converting from user-defined space to pixel space, you'll take a look at how a Camera class can be created to support this conversion. To proceed, continue using the Textured Primitive project from earlier in the chapter as camera support is added, or follow along with the 3.UserDefinedCoordinateSystem example provided in the Chapter03\SourceCode folder.

Creating a user-defined coordinate system

1. Start by creating a new class in the GraphicsSupport folder in your project. Name the class Camera.

2. Make the class static, since you want to avoid multiple instantiations of the Camera class.

```
namespace Book_Example
{
    static public class Camera
    {
        ...
    }
}
```

3. Next, add the following variables to represent the origin, the width, and the ratio between the camera and pixel window:

```
static private Vector2 sOrigin = Vector2.Zero;    // Origin of the world
static private float sWidth = 100f;               // Width of the world
static private float sRatio = -1f;                // Ratio between camera window and pixel
```

4. Now create a private function that returns the ratio between the two windows, as shown in the following code. If you follow the code, you can see that Game1.sGraphics. PreferredBackBufferWidth / sWidth represents (W_p/W_c) from the formula derived earlier.

```
static private float cameraWindowToPixelRatio()
{
    if (sRatio < 0f)
        sRatio = (float) Game1.sGraphics.PreferredBackBufferWidth / sWidth;
    return sRatio;
}
```

5. Now you need a function to set the camera window's position and size. This is easily done by creating a set function like the one shown following:

```
static public void SetCameraWindow(Vector2 origin, float width)
{
    sOrigin = origin;
    sWidth = width;
}
```

▪ **Note**   Notice that only the width of camera window can be specified. This is because once the width is defined, the height of the camera window depends on the actual height of the game window. Allowing only the width to be modified guarantees that the camera can draw to the entire game window with the proper aspect ratio.

---

6. Next, you need to implement the conversion of a position from user-defined space to pixel space for drawing. This can be accomplished by implementing the P_x and P_y equations shown earlier in this section. Notice again that only the y-axis is flipped.

```
static public void ComputePixelPosition(Vector2 cameraPosition, out int x, out int y)
{
    float ratio = cameraWindowToPixelRatio();

    // Convert the position to pixel space
    x = (int)(((cameraPosition.X - sOrigin.X) * ratio) + 0.5f);
    y = (int)(((cameraPosition.Y - sOrigin.Y) * ratio) + 0.5f);

    y = Game1.sGraphics.PreferredBackBufferHeight - y;
}
```

7. The last function for the Camera class needs to convert a rectangular area from user-defined coordinate space to pixel space. This is accomplished by converting the camera window's position and size to the corresponding pixel space. You can see this reflected in the following code:

```
static public Rectangle ComputePixelRectangle(Vector2 position, Vector2 size)
{
    float ratio = cameraWindowToPixelRatio();

    // Convert size from camera window space to pixel space.
    int width = (int)((size.X * ratio) + 0.5f);
    int height = (int)((size.Y * ratio) + 0.5f);

    // Convert the position to pixel space
    int x, y;
    ComputePixelPosition(position, out x, out y);

    // Reference position is the center
    y -= height / 2;
    x -= width / 2;

    return new Rectangle(x, y, width, height);
}
```

Using the *Camera* class

1. Use the Camera class by defining a camera window with the SetCameraWindow() function inside the LoadContent() function of Game1. Set its origin to (10, 20) and width to 100. Notice how the width is independent from how many pixels are covered by the game window in pixel space.

```
protected override void LoadContent()
{
    // Create a new SpriteBatch, which can be used to draw textures.
    Game1.sSpriteBatch = new SpriteBatch(GraphicsDevice);

    // Define camera window bounds
    Camera.SetCameraWindow(new Vector2(10f, 20f), 100f);

    // Create the primitives
    mGraphicsObjects = new TexturedPrimitive[kNumObjects];
    mGraphicsObjects[0] = new TexturedPrimitive("UWB-JPG",
                              new Vector2(15f, 25f), new Vector2(10f, 10f));
    mGraphicsObjects[1] = new TexturedPrimitive("UWB-JPG",
                              new Vector2(35f, 60f), new Vector2(50f, 50f));
    mGraphicsObjects[2] = new TexturedPrimitive("UWB-PNG",
                              new Vector2(105f, 25f), new Vector2(10f, 10f));
    mGraphicsObjects[3] = new TexturedPrimitive("UWB-PNG",
                              new Vector2(90f, 60f), new Vector2(35f, 35f));
    // NOTE: Since the creation of TexturedPrimitive involves loading of textures,
    // the creation should occur in or after LoadContent()
}
```

2.   Finally, it is important to convert all positions and sizes from user-defined coordinate to pixel space before each drawing. As shown in the following code of the Draw() function from the TexturedPrimitive.cs file, Camera.ComputePixelRectangle() is called to perform the proper transformation:

```
public void Draw()
{
    // Defines where and size of the texture to show
    Rectangle destRect = Camera.ComputePixelRectangle(Position, Size);
    Game1.sSpriteBatch.Draw(mImage, destRect, Color.White);
}
```

Build and run the project. The results should be the same as those shown previously in Figure 3-3, in pixel space. Now let's take a look at user-defined space. Figure 3-9 shows the game world in the user-defined space.

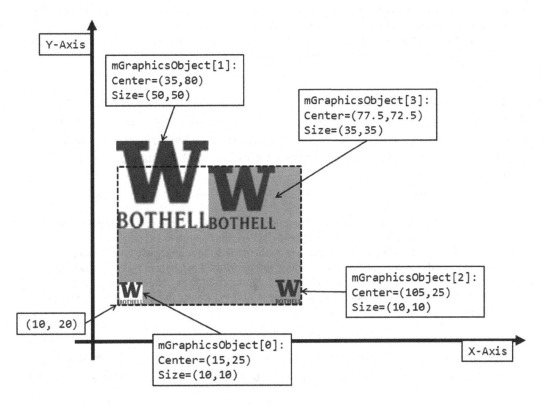

Figure 3-9. *User-defined coordinate system within the pixel space*

Now try toggling buttons A and B to switch between windowed and full-screen modes. Notice how the relative sizes of the objects remain constant—an object that occupies half of the game window will continue to occupy the half in full-screen mode. As a game developer, you can now focus on designing the relative sizes and positions of your game objects without concerning yourself with the eventual pixel resolution of the game window.

It is important to recognize the difference in the camera's width and position between coordinate spaces. The camera only covers 100 units in width in the user-defined coordinate space, while in pixel space it covers 1,000 pixels. Similarly, the camera's origin is located in the bottom-left corner, at (10, 20), while the game window's origin is located in the top-left corner, at (0, 0). This indicates that you have successfully decoupled the user-defined coordinate system from the game window's pixel space.

Font Output

A valuable tool that many games use for a variety of tasks is text output. This is because text provides an efficient way to communicate information to the user as well as you, the developer. For example, it can be used to communicate the game's story, the player's score, or the debugging information during development. However, unlike in console programming, the game window that MonoGame provides does not include direct text output support. Fortunately, this can be easily remedied by using the SpriteFont class to create a custom class to produce output of text to the game window.

The `SpriteFont` class takes your desired font and converts the characters into a texture during build time. To use the `SpriteFont` class, a font file, such as `Arial.spritefont`, must be created, this file must then be conveted into the xnb format, and finally added to the project. Similar to images, fonts should be added to the content folder before they are used. This is because, like images, the font file is an external resource.

■ **Note**   SpriteFonts are XML files that can be generated from existing fonts on your PC. In order to create or customize your own SpriteFont, refer to `http://msdn.microsoft.com/library/bb447673.aspx`. For more information on the `SpriteFont` class and its properties, refer to `http://msdn.microsoft.com/library/bb447759.aspx`. It is also important to note that while you can create SpriteFonts from fonts that exist on your PC, you may need permission to use those fonts in your game.

Before you create a class to support fonts, you should first find the `Arial.spritefont` font description resource file in the `Chapter03\SourceCode\ImagesAndFontUsed` folder and convert this file into `Arial.xnb`. This conversion can be accomplished by invoking the XNAFormatter program from the XNB Builder utility you have downloaded and unzipped as part of the "Downloads and Installations" operations you performed in Chapter 1. Once converted, you can then include the `Arial.xnb` file into the MonoGame project in a similar fashion as image files we have worked with: either by right-clicking over the Content folder and navigating to Add ➤ Existing Item, or by dragging and dropping the file into the Content folder.

■ **Note**   As with images, if you choose to drag and drop the `Arial.xnb` file into the Content folder, you must remember to bring up the Properties window and change the Build Action field to Content, and Copy to Output Directory to Copy if Newer.

The Font Output project

This project demonstrates how to draw text to the game screen by using a `FontSprite` asset. Two types of print function are supported. One prints to the top-left corner of the screen, and the other prints the message to any specified location in user-defined coordinate space. Printing to a location is useful when it is necessary to print text on an object; notice that the currently selected texture in Figure 3-10 is identified.

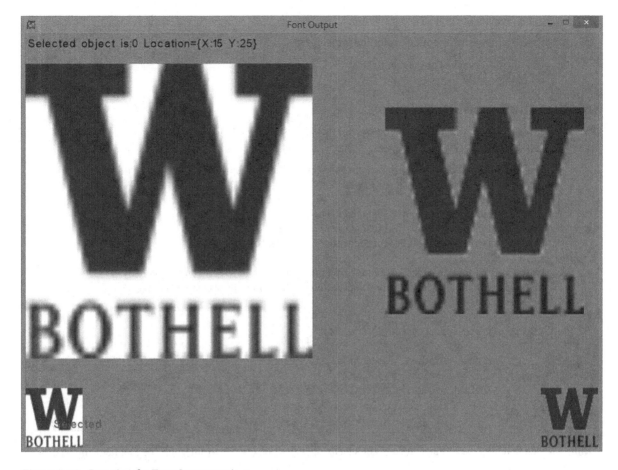

Figure 3-10. Running the Font Output project

The project's controls are as follows:

- **Back button (F1-key)** Exits the program
- **A button (K-key)** Toggles to full-screen mode
- **B button (L-key)** Toggles to windowed mode
- **Left thumbstick (WSAD-keys)** Moves the currently selected texture
- **Right thumbstick (arrow-keys)** Changes the size of the currently selected texture
- **X button (J-key)** Switches the currently selected texture

The goals of the project are as follows:

- To understand how text can be output to the screen
- To understand how to use a FontSprite asset
- To create and use a FontSupport class

The steps for creating the project are as follows:

1. Create a new FontSupport class for the project.

2. Use and observe the FontSupport class.

Creating the *FontSupport* class

1. Create a class named FontSupport in your GraphicsSupport folder and make the class static.

2. Declare three static variables in the FontSupport.cs file—the sprite font, the color, and the location—as shown in the following code:

```
static private SpriteFont sTheFont = null;
static private Color sDefaultDrawColor = Color.Black;
static private Vector2 sStatusLocation = new Vector2(5, 5);
```

3. Now create a function called LoadFont(), which initializes the SpirteFont variable by loading it with the font resource that was added to the content project (in this case, Arial.spritefont).

```
static private void LoadFont()
{
    // For demo purposes, loads Arial.spritefont
    if (null == sTheFont)
        sTheFont = Game1.sContent.Load<SpriteFont>("Arial");
}
```

■ **Note** Notice that the Load() function does not specify the extension (.spritefont), only the font name (Arial).

---

4. Next, add a simple function called ColorToUse(), which allows the color to be changed from the default (black) to any specified color. In the following code, you can see that if the incoming color is null, the default color is returned; otherwise, the specified color is returned.

```
static private Color ColorToUse(Nullable<Color> c)
{
    return (null == c) ? sDefaultDrawColor : (Color)c;
}
```

5. To complete the class, add two functions to support printing to the game window.

   a. Name the first function PrintStatus and give it two parameters: one for the message that will be printed, and the other for the font color. This function will place the message in the top-left corner of the game window. You can see how this is achieved in the following code. Notice again that the static SpriteBatch variable is used to draw to the screen.

```
static public void PrintStatus(String msg, Nullable<Color> drawColor)
{
    LoadFont();
    Color useColor = ColorToUse(drawColor);

    // Compute top-left corner as the reference for output status
    Game1.sSpriteBatch.DrawString(sTheFont, msg, sStatusLocation, useColor);
}
```

        b.   Name the second function PrintStatusAt. This function is similar to the
             PrintStatus function; however, it supports printing to a specified location by
             accepting a position parameter and converting that position into user-defined
             coordinate space by using the ComputePixelPosition() function of the Camera class.
             You can see this reflected in the following code:

```
static public void PrintStatusAt(Vector2 pos, String msg, Nullable<Color> drawColor)
{
    LoadFont();

    Color useColor = ColorToUse(drawColor);

    int pixelX, pixelY;
    Camera.ComputePixelPosition(pos, out pixelX, out pixelY);
    Game1.sSpriteBatch.DrawString(sTheFont, msg,
                                  new Vector2(pixelX, pixelY), useColor);
}
```

A full listing of the FontSupport class is shown in Listing 3-1.

Listing 3-1. The complete *FontSupport* class

```
static public class FontSupport
{
    static private SpriteFont sTheFont = null;
    static private Color sDefaultDrawColor = Color.Black;
    static private Vector2 sStatusLocation = new Vector2(5, 5);

    static private void LoadFont()
    {
        // for demo purposes, loads Arial.spritefont
        if (null == sTheFont)
            sTheFont = Game1.sContent.Load<SpriteFont>("Arial");
    }

    static private Color ColorToUse(Nullable<Color> c)
    {
        return (null == c) ? sDefaultDrawColor : (Color)c;
    }

    static public void PrintStatusAt(Vector2 pos, String msg, Nullable<Color> drawColor)
    {
        LoadFont();
```

```
        Color useColor = ColorToUse(drawColor);

        int pixelX, pixelY;
        Camera.ComputePixelPosition(pos, out pixelX, out pixelY);
        Game1.sSpriteBatch.DrawString(sTheFont, msg,
                                        new Vector2(pixelX, pixelY), useColor);
    }

    static public void PrintStatus(String msg, Nullable<Color> drawColor)
    {
        LoadFont();
        Color useColor = ColorToUse(drawColor);

        // compute top-left corner as the reference for output status
        Game1.sSpriteBatch.DrawString(sTheFont, msg, sStatusLocation, useColor);
    }

}
```

Using and observing the *FontSupport* class

To use the FontSupport class, all you need to do is call the PrintStatus and PrintStatusAt functions inside the Draw() function of Game1. PrintStatus will print the message to the top-left corner of the game window, and PrintStatusAt will print the message at your specified location. It's that simple.

```
protected override void Draw(GameTime gameTime)
{
    // Clear to background color
    ...
    // Loop over and draw each primitive
    ...
    // Print out text message to echo status
    FontSupport.PrintStatus("Selected object is:" + mCurrentIndex +
                    " Location=" + mGraphicsObjects[mCurrentIndex].Position, null);

    FontSupport.PrintStatusAt(mGraphicsObjects[mCurrentIndex].Position, "Selected", Color.Red);
    ...
}
```

If you build and run the program, you can see it behave as expected (as shown previously in Figure 3-10). It is important to understand that the PrintStatus() function never converts the position of its message into the user-defined coordinate space. This means that it will remain at the top-left corner of the game window, even when the camera is repositioned.

A Simple Game Object

Now that you have an understanding of how the user-defined coordinate system functions via the Camera class and can now output text to the game window, it is time to create your first game object. Let's start simple and create a ball with some basic functionality, such as multiple instantiation, movement control, and bounds-collision detection.

The Simple Game Object project

This project demonstrates how to create soccer balls that collide with the edge of the screen. Figure 3-11 shows the project running.

Figure 3-11. *Running the Simple Game Object project*

The project's controls are as follows:

- **Back button (F1-key)** Exits the program
- **A button (K-key)** Spawns a new soccer ball
- **Right thumbstick (arrow-keys)** Moves the newly spawned soccer ball

The goals of the project are as follows:

- To understand how to create objects with simple behaviors and the reasons for doing so
- To work with the interaction of objects and the bounds of the camera window
- To experience working with an object's bounds

The steps for creating the project are as follows:

1. Modify existing classes to include bounds support.

2. Add support for collision detection.

3. Create a ball class called SoccerBall.

4. Use the SoccerBall class.

Before you can implement bounds support, you need an understanding of what the bounds of an object entail. Take a look at Figure 3-12. It shows the bounds of a texture represented as MinBound and MaxBound. MinBound is in the bottom-left corner and MaxBound is in the top-right corner of the texture. This is a fairly common way to represent the bounds of a rectangular object, as it uses only two points. With the bounds of an object defined, you can add behavior such as collision.

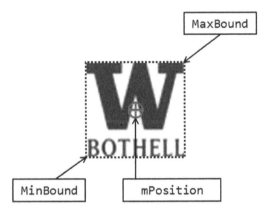

Figure 3-12. *The bounds and center position of the texture*

You can calculate the values of these bounds by using the position and size of the texture, which are already known. Let's try it.

Modifying the classes to include bounds support

1. Add a MinBound and MaxBound variable to your TexturedPrimitive class. You can see this done in the following code. Using both the position and size of the texture allows the bounds to be calculated and returned. Notice that neither bound can be set. This is because the bounds of the texture only change if the position or size of the texture changes. Using both position and size in your calculation ensures that the bounds will be accurate.

```
public Vector2 MinBound { get { return mPosition - (0.5f * mSize); } }
public Vector2 MaxBound { get { return mPosition + (0.5f * mSize); } }
```

2. Now add similar bounds to the camera. Do this by using its position (sOrigin) and size (sWidth, sHeight). However, remember that sOrigin is located in the bottom-left corner of the camera, and thus is the MinBound of the camera. You can easily calculate the MaxBound by adding the sWidth and sHeight to the sOrigin. You can see this reflected in the following code:

```
/// Accessors to the camera window bounds
static public Vector2 CameraWindowLowerLeftPosition
    { get { return sOrigin; } }
static public Vector2 CameraWindowUpperRightPosition
    { get { return sOrigin + new Vector2(sWidth, sHeight); } }
```

Adding collision detection support

1. Start by creating an enum (enumerated date type) in the Camera class called CameraWindowCollisionStatus to represent the five simple states that an object can have in colliding with the camera window: Top, Bottom, Left, Right, and Inside.

■ **Note**   For more information on enums, please refer to http://msdn.microsoft.com/library/sbbt4032.aspx.

```
// Support collision with the camera bounds
public enum CameraWindowCollisionStatus {
    CollideTop = 0,
    CollideBottom = 1,
    CollideLeft = 2,
    CollideRight = 3,
    InsideWindow = 4
};
```

2. Next, you need to add a collision detection function for the camera. The following code shows the CollidedWithCameraWindow() function, which accepts a TexturedPrimitive object, tests its collision with the camera bounds, and returns the collision status:

```
static public CameraWindowCollisionStatus CollidedWithCameraWindow(TexturedPrimitive prim)
{
    Vector2 min = CameraWindowLowerLeftPosition;
    Vector2 max = CameraWindowUpperRightPosition;

    if (prim.MaxBound.Y > max.Y)
        return CameraWindowCollisionStatus.CollideTop;
    if (prim.MinBound.X < min.X)
        return CameraWindowCollisionStatus.CollideLeft;
    if (prim.MaxBound.X > max.X)
        return CameraWindowCollisionStatus.CollideRight;
    if (prim.MinBound.Y < min.Y)
        return CameraWindowCollisionStatus.CollideBottom;

    return CameraWindowCollisionStatus.InsideWindow;
}
```

3. Lastly, add a simple random number generator to the Game1 class by creating a Random type variable and initializing that within the constructor:

```
static public Random sRan; // For generating random numbers

public Game1()
{
    ...
    Game1.sRan = new Random();
}
```

Since all the necessary supporting code is now complete, it is time to create the SoccerBall class.

Creating the *SoccerBall* class

1. Start by adding the image Soccer.png into your content project. The image can be found in the Chapter03\SourceCode\ImagesAndFontUsed folder.

2. Create a new class, name it SoccerBall, and have it inherit from TexturedPrimitive. This will allow you to take advantage of all the TexturedPrimitive functionality within the SoccerBall class, as well as define specialized behaviors.

```
public class SoccerBall : TexturedPrimitive
{
    ...
}
```

3. Add a variable called mDeltaPosition to represent the change in the object's position. This will be used to move the ball during updates.

```
private Vector2 mDeltaPosition; // Change current position by this amount
```

4. Create the constructor according to the following code. Start by initializing the position and size of the SoccerBall and passing those values to the base class (TexturedPrimitive). Then define the amount of change for mDeltaPosition by using the random number support from the Game1 class.

```
public SoccerBall(Vector2 position, float diameter) :
        base("Soccer", position, new Vector2(diameter, diameter))
{
    mDeltaPosition.X = (float) (Game1.sRan.NextDouble()) * 2f - 1f;
    mDeltaPosition.Y = (float) (Game1.sRan.NextDouble()) * 2f - 1f;
}
```

5. Add a variable for modifying and retrieving the radius of the ball. Remember that the SoccerBall class is a rectangle; therefore, changing its radius means changing the size of the rectangle's width and height. You can see an example of this in the following image:

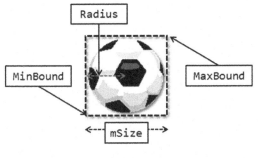

```
public float Radius {
    get { return mSize.X * 0.5f; }
    set { mSize.X = 2f * value; mSize.Y = mSize.X;}
}
```

6. Next, define the behavior of the soccer ball upon a collision. You can do this in the Update() function of the SoccerBall class. Add the Update() function, as shown in the following code. Notice how the x or y direction of mDeltaPosition reverses based on where the ball collides with a camera bounds. The last line in the Update() function changes the ball's position by the value of mDeltaPosition. Now the ball should bounce off the bounds of the camera. The following image shows an example of collision cases:

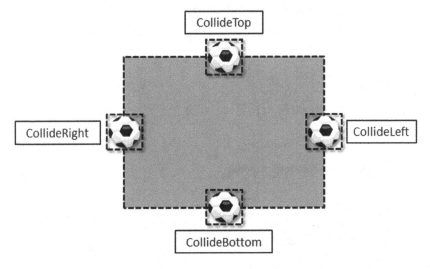

```
public void Update()
{
    Camera.CameraWindowCollisionStatus status = Camera.CollidedWithCameraWindow(this);
    switch (status) {
        case Camera.CameraWindowCollisionStatus.CollideBottom:
        case Camera.CameraWindowCollisionStatus.CollideTop:
            mDeltaPosition.Y *= -1;
        break;
```

73

```
            case Camera.CameraWindowCollisionStatus.CollideLeft:
            case Camera.CameraWindowCollisionStatus.CollideRight:
                mDeltaPosition.X *= -1;
            break;
        }
        Position += mDeltaPosition;
}
```

That is all that is currently needed for the SoccerBall class. It is now ready to be used. A full code listing of SoccerBall.cs is shown in Listing 3-2.

Listing 3-2. The complete *SoccerBall* class

```
public class SoccerBall : TexturedPrimitive
{
    private Vector2 mDeltaPosition; // Change current position by this amount

    /// <summary>
    /// Constructor of SoccerBall
    /// </summary>
    /// <param name="position">center position of the ball</param>
    /// <param name="diameter">diameter of the ball</param>
    public SoccerBall(Vector2 position, float diameter) :
            base("Soccer", position, new Vector2(diameter, diameter))
    {
        mDeltaPosition.X = (float) (Game1.sRan.NextDouble()) * 2f - 1f;
        mDeltaPosition.Y = (float) (Game1.sRan.NextDouble()) * 2f - 1f;
    }

    // Accessors
    public float Radius
        {
            get { return mSize.X * 0.5f; }
            set { mSize.X = 2f * value; mSize.Y = mSize.X;}
        }

    /// <summary>
    /// Compute the soccer ball's movement in the camera window
    /// </summary>
    public void Update()
    {
        Camera.CameraWindowCollisionStatus status =
                        Camera.CollidedWithCameraWindow(this);
        switch (status) {
            case Camera.CameraWindowCollisionStatus.CollideBottom:
            case Camera.CameraWindowCollisionStatus.CollideTop:
                mDeltaPosition.Y *= -1;
                break;
```

```
            case Camera.CameraWindowCollisionStatus.CollideLeft:
            case Camera.CameraWindowCollisionStatus.CollideRight:
                mDeltaPosition.X *= -1;
                break;
        }
        Position += mDeltaPosition;
    }
}
```

All that's left is to use the SoccerBall in your game. You can do this in the Game1 class.

Using the *SoccerBall* class

1. First, declare a SoccerBall variable named mBall and a TexturedPrimitive variable named mUWBLogo in the Game1 class:

```
TexturedPrimitive mUWBLogo;
SoccerBall mBall;
Vector2 mSoccerPosition = new Vector2(50, 50);
float mSoccerBallRadius = 3f;
```

2. Next, load the ball into the game by instantiating mBall and mUWBLogo within the LoadContent() function, as shown following:

```
protected override void LoadContent()
{
    ...
    // Create the primitives
    mUWBLogo = new TexturedPrimitive("UWB-PNG", new Vector2(30, 30), new Vector2(20, 20));
    mBall = new SoccerBall(mSoccerPosition, mSoccerBallRadius*2f);
}
```

3. Now update the ball in the Update() function by calling the ball's Update() function; remember to pass in the controls (right thumbstick) as a parameter. In addition, add support for instantiating a new ball when the gamepad's A button is pressed.

```
protected override void Update(GameTime gameTime)
{
    ...
    mUWBLogo.Update(InputWrapper.ThumbSticks.Left, Vector2.Zero);
    mBall.Update();
    mBall.Update(Vector2.Zero, InputWrapper.ThumbSticks.Right);

    if (InputWrapper.Buttons.A == ButtonState.Pressed)
        mBall = new SoccerBall(mSoccerPosition, mSoccerBallRadius*2f);
    ...
}
```

4. Lastly, remember to draw the ball by calling its Draw() function within the Draw() function of Game1.

```
protected override void Draw(GameTime gameTime)
{
    // Clear to background color
    ...
    mUWBLogo.Draw();
    mBall.Draw();

    // Print out text message to echo status
    FontSupport.PrintStatus("Ball Position:" + mBall.Position, null);
    FontSupport.PrintStatusAt(mUWBLogo.Position,
            mUWBLogo.Position.ToString(), Color.White);
    FontSupport.PrintStatusAt(mBall.Position, "Radius" + mBall.Radius, Color.Red);
    ...
}
```

Build and run the program. The output should look similar to Figure 3-11. Although the program should run, upon using it you'll notice many unintended quirks. For example, if the size of the ball is changed when near the window's boundary, the ball will get stuck on the boundary. Additionally, sometimes the ball will travel outside the window's bounds and essentially disappear. You can circumvent this by creating a new ball when the A button is pressed; however, this is not ideal. To understand and solve these problems, you need to delve into some mathematics and physics (which we will discuss in the next chapter).

Simple Game State

Now that you have successfully added simple behaviors to the TexturedPrimitive class, it is time to explore how to support simple game-like interactions, or a *game state*. However, before digging into the details of creating a project with a game state, we'll first help organize your thoughts.

Thus far, you have been modifying Game1.cs to handle the initializing, loading, updating, and drawing of your project. Ideally, it is a good practice to avoid using Game1.cs directly to prevent complexity in functions like initialization or draw functions, which can cause wasted debugging time further down the road. Additionally, a new class is needed to assist in the management of the game state.

You can isolate your interaction with Game1.cs and handle the management of the game state by creating a separate class that acts as an interface between you and Game1.cs. We will refer to this class as MyGame. The MyGame game state class will contain the Update() and Draw() functions that that will handle the updating and drawing of every object in your game. These two functions provide you with the functionality needed from Game1.cs for your game. Another aspect worth noting from the previous project (Simple Game Object) is the practice of subclassing. In that project, you subclassed the SoccerBall class from TexturedPrimitive to take advantage of the predefined behavior. Doing this afforded you the functionality of the TexturedPrimitive class and the ability to add new or specialized behaviors to SoccerBall. The subclassing not only avoided unnecessary code, but also reduced the potential of future bugs and the need to refactor your code. It is important to grasp this concept, because you will encounter it many times throughout the remainder of your time as a developer, as well as throughout the remainder of this book.

The Simple Game State project

This project demonstrates how to move a character or hero around the screen to collect (or net) basketballs. The basketballs will be generated randomly and continuously increase in size over time. Once the basketballs have reached a certain size, they will explode. Netting enough basketballs before they explode will give you the win, and allowing too many basketballs explode will make you lose. Figure 3-13 shows the project running.

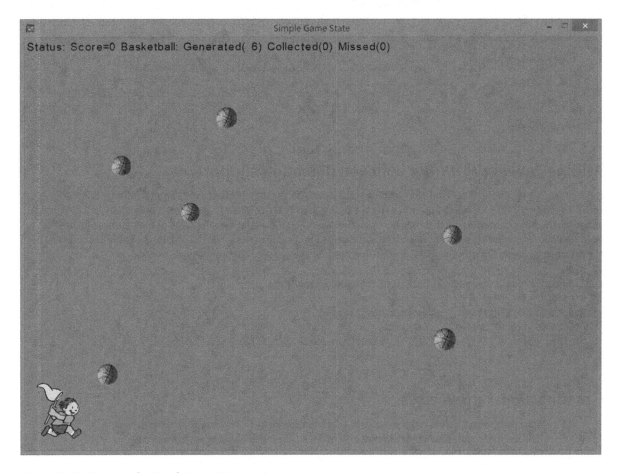

Figure 3-13. *Running the Simple Game State project*

The project's controls are as follows:

- **Back button (F1-key)** Exits the program
- **A button (K-key)** Starts a new game
- **Right thumbstick (arrow-keys)** Controls the movement of the hero

The goals of the project are as follows:

- To understand the needs for game state organization
- To implement the GameState class to house the game logic and control

The steps for creating the project are as follows:

1. Add TexturedPrimitive collision detection support.

2. Create a BasketBall class.

3. Create the GameState class.

4. Modify Game1.cs to support the game state.

Add the following resources, which can be found in the Chapter03\SourceCode\ImagesAndFontsUsed folder, into your content project before you begin:

-   BasketBall.png

-   Loser.jpg

-   Winner.jpg

-   Me.png

Adding *TexturedPrimitive* collision detection support

Before creating new objects and defining a game state, open the TexturedPrimitive class and add the following code. The PrimitivesTouches() function detects whether two TexturedPrimitive objects overlap in space. This is accomplished by comparing the distance between the two objects' positions against half of the combined width of both objects. A straightforward way of understanding this function is to notice that it is using a simple comparison of the distance between the objects, while accounting for their size, to see if the two objects overlap.

```
public bool PrimitivesTouches(TexturedPrimitive otherPrim)
{
    Vector2 v = mPosition - otherPrim.Position;
    float dist = v.Length();
    return (dist < ((mSize.X / 2f) + (otherPrim.mSize.X / 2f)));
}
```

Creating a *BasketBall* class

1. Start by creating a class named BasketBall that inherits from TexturedPrimitive. Next, add the three variables kIncreaseRate, kInitSize, and kFinalSize, as shown in the following code.

-   kIncreaseRate is the rate at which the basketball increases in size.

-   kInitSize is the initial size of the basketball.

-   kFinalSize is the size at which the basketball will explode.

```
private const float kIncreaseRate = 1.001f;
private Vector2 kInitSize = new Vector2(5, 5);
Private const float kFinalSize = 15f;
```

2. Now give the class a constructor that initializes the basketball's position to a random spot and sets its initial size. Remember to use the base function provided by TexturedPrimitive.

```
public BasketBall() : base("BasketBall")
{
    mPosition = Camera.RandomPosition();
    mSize = kInitSize;
}
```

3. The last function needed for the BasketBall class provides the object with some specialized behavior. Create an UpdateAndExplode() function that will increase the ball size and check whether the ball should explode or expire if the final size is reached.

```
public bool UpdateAndExplode()
{
    mSize *= kIncreaseRate;
    return mSize.X > kFinalSize;
}
```

That is all that is needed for the BasketBall class. Listing 3-3 shows a full code listing of the BasketBall class.

Listing 3-3. The complete *BasketBall* class

```
public class BasketBall : TexturedPrimitive
{
    // Change current position by this amount
    private const float kIncreaseRate = 1.001f;
    private Vector2 kInitSize = new Vector2(5, 5);
    private const float kFinalSize = 15f;

    public BasketBall() : base("BasketBall")
    {
        mPosition = Camera.RandomPosition();
        mSize = kInitSize;
    }

    public bool UpdateAndExplode()
    {
        mSize *= kIncreaseRate;
        return mSize.X > kFinalSize;
    }
}
```

Creating the game state object

1. Start by creating a new class named `MyGame`.

2. Next, you need to declare the variables the game will need. This includes the variables required for the hero, the basketballs, and the game state.

    a. For the hero, declare a `TexturedPrimitive`, and declare two `Vector2`s—one for the hero size and one for the position:

    ```
    // Hero stuff ...
    TexturedPrimitive mHero;
    Vector2 kHeroSize = new Vector2(15, 15);
    Vector2 kHeroPosition = Vector2.Zero;
    ```

    b. For the basketballs, you'll need a list of `BasketBall` objects, because you will be creating many new basketballs throughout the course of the game. Additionally, you'll need a timespan and integer for keeping track of when to spawn the next `BasketBall` object and add it to the list. Lastly, you'll use another integer to store the total number of balls created.

    ```
    // Basketballs ...
    List<BasketBall> mBBallList;
    TimeSpan mCreationTimeStamp;
    int mTotalBBallCreated = 0;
    // this is 0.5 seconds
    const int kBballMSecInterval = 500;
    ```

    c. The last variables you need to declare are relevant for the game state. The following code shows the variables needed to keep track of the game score, as well as the `TexturedPrimitive` object to display when a player wins or loses.

    ```
    // Game state
    int mScore = 0;
    int mBBallMissed=0, mBBallHit=0;
    const int kBballTouchScore = 1;
    const int kBballMissedScore = -2;
    const int kWinScore = 10;
    const int kLossScore = -10;
    TexturedPrimitive mFinal = null;
    ```

Now it's time to add the constructor, update, and draw functions.

3. Begin by initializing your hero object with the specified texture, position, and size. Also initialize the basketball list and the `mCreationTimeStamp`:

    ```
    public MyGame()
    {
        // Hero ...
        mHero = new TexturedPrimitive("Me", kHeroPosition, kHeroSize);

        // Basketballs
        mCreationTimeStamp = new TimeSpan(0);
        mBBallList = new List<BasketBall>();
    }
    ```

4. Next, you need to create the update function. This is slightly more complicated; here are the steps:

   a. *Check whether an update is necessary.* The first thing you need to check here are the win-or-loss conditions. This is achieved by checking whether mFinal is equal to null. If mFinal is not equal to null, then a win-or-loss condition has been met, and the game no longer needs to be updated.

```
public void UpdateGame(GameTime gameTime)
{
    #region Step a.
    if (null != mFinal) // Done!!
    return;
    #endregion Step a.
    ...
}
```

   b. *Update all objects.* Next, you update every game object by calling its update function. In the hero's update function, the gamepad's right thumbstick is passed in to allow control. In the list of BasketBall objects, the UpdateAndExplode() function is called, and if the return value is true (meaning the ball did explode), then the corresponding object is removed from the list and the score is updated.

```
public void UpdateGame(GameTime gameTime)
{
    ...
    #region Step b.
    // Hero movement: right thumb stick
    mHero.Update(InputWrapper.ThumbSticks.Right);

    // Basketball ...
    for (int b = mBBallList.Count-1; b >= 0; b--)
    {
        if (mBBallList[b].UpdateAndExplode())
        {
            mBBallList.RemoveAt(b);
            mBBallMissed++;
            mScore += kBballMissedScore;
        }
    }
    #endregion Step b.
        ...
}
```

   c. *Handle interactions among all objects.* Now you need to handle any interaction between the game objects. Specifically, you want to loop through the list of basketballs to check whether the hero has collided with them using the PrimitivesTouches() function. If an object has collided, you remove that BasketBall object from the list and update the score.

```
            public void UpdateGame(GameTime gameTime)
            {
                ...
                #region Step c.
                for (int b = mBBallList.Count - 1; b >= 0; b--)
                {
                    if (mHero.PrimitivesTouches(mBBallList[b]))
                    {
                        mBBallList.RemoveAt(b);
                        mBBallHit++;
                        mScore += kBballTouchScore;
                    }
                }
                #endregion Step c.
                    ...
            }
```

d. *Spawn new enemies*. Next, you want to check to see whether a new BasketBall object needs to be created. You do this by recording the current time and the last time a ball was created, and then checking to determine whether the difference between those two times is greater than the time creation interval (kBballMSecInterval). If so, you create a new BasketBall object, add it to the list, and increment the ball total.

```
            public void UpdateGame(GameTime gameTime)
            {
                ...
                #region Step d.
                // Check for new basketball condition
                TimeSpan timePassed = gameTime.TotalGameTime;
                timePassed = timePassed.Subtract(mCreationTimeStamp);
                if (timePassed.TotalMilliseconds > kBballMSecInterval)
                {
                    mCreationTimeStamp = gameTime.TotalGameTime;
                    BasketBall b = new BasketBall();
                    mTotalBBallCreated++;
                    mBBallList.Add(b);
                }
                #endregion Step d.
                ...
            }
```

e. *Check for a win-or-loss condition*. The last thing you need to check in the update function is whether the win-or-loss condition has been met. For this game, you can do this easily by determining whether the current score (mScore) is greater than the winning score or less than the losing score. If either of those conditions has been met, you can assign the appropriate corresponding texture to the mFinal TexturedPrimitive object.

2D GRAPHICS, COORDINATES, AND GAME STATE

```
public void UpdateGame(GameTime gameTime)
{
    ...
    #region Step e.
    // Check for winning condition ...
    if (mScore > kWinScore)
        mFinal = new TexturedPrimitive("Winner",
                                        new Vector2(75, 50), new Vector2(30, 20));
    else if (mScore < kLossScore)
        mFinal = new TexturedPrimitive("Looser",
                                        new Vector2(75, 50), new Vector2(30, 20));
    #endregion Step e.
}
```

Although it's not trivial, you can usually divide the update function of the game state into distinct logical steps according to game rules. The five steps just described are (1) check whether an update is necessary, (2) update all game objects, (3) handle interactions among all game objects, (4) spawn new enemies, and (5) check for a win-or-loss condition. These steps can serve as a template for many simple games.

5. The last function required is the draw function. This function draws the hero, the basketball objects, and the win-or-loss picture by calling their corresponding draw function. Additionally, the status is printed out to show the score and stats of the game.

```
public void DrawGame()
{
    mHero.Draw();

    foreach (BasketBall b in mBBallList)
        b.Draw();

    if (null != mFinal)
        mFinal.Draw();

    // Drawn last to always show up on top
    FontSupport.PrintStatus("Status: " +
                            "Score=" + mScore +
                            " Basketball: Generated( " + mTotalBBallCreated +
                            ") Collected(" + mBBallHit + ") Missed(" + mBBallMissed + ")",
null);
}
```

Modifying *Game1* to support the game state

The last task you need to accomplish is to initialize and connect the game state (MyGame) in Game1.cs. As shown in the following code, you can easily achieve this by declaring a new MyGame object, initializing it in the LoadContent function, updating it in the update function of Game1, and drawing it in the draw function. In addition, notice that we added the ability to start a new game by instantiating a new MyGame object if the A button is pressed.

```
public class Game1 : Game
{
    ...
    MyGame mTheGame;
```

```
    public Game1()
    {
        ...
    }

    protected override void LoadContent()
    {
        ...
        mTheGame = new MyGame();
    }

    protected override void Update(GameTime gameTime)
    {
        ...
        mTheGame.UpdateGame(gameTime);

        if (InputWrapper.Buttons.A == ButtonState.Pressed)
            mTheGame = new MyGame();
        ...
    }

    protected override void Draw(GameTime gameTime)
    {
        ...
        mTheGame.DrawGame();
        ...
    }
}
```

Your game state project is now complete. Try building and running the program. It should look similar to Figure 3-13, shown previously. Remember to test the program by winning, losing, and starting a new game to verify the behaviors of the game.

Summary

In this chapter, you have learned many of the basic graphics and effects principles needed to create your own customized game. This includes modifying the game window, creating textured primitives, and outputting text to the game window.

Another important concept that was touched on was the user-defined coordinate system. The user-defined coordinate system provides the flexibility and functionality needed to properly control what the user sees of the game world. It also provides the customization needed for a wide variety of games.

Lastly, you have seen what is required to provide an object with simple behavior and your game with a simple game state. Game state and object behavior are critical pieces needed to create a game from both technical and design standpoints. The way an object behaves in the game world and how it interacts with the user and game state is often referred to as gameplay. You will see how to create more advanced object behavior and game states in the upcoming chapters.

Quick Reference

To	Do this
Change the game window size	Modify `mGraphics.PreferredBackBufferWidth` and `mGraphics.PreferredBackBufferHeight`. Remember to call the `mGraphics.ApplyChanges()` function to activate the window size change.
Change the window to a full-screen display	Set `mGraphics.IsFullScreen` to either `true` or `false`. Once again, remember to call the `mGraphics.ApplyChanges()` function to activate the change.
Draw and interact with multiple copies of the same graphical object	Define a class to abstract the desired behaviors—for example, the `TexturedPrimitive` class. Remember that it is convenient to define both `Update()` and `Draw()` functions for your class. These functions can be called from the `Update()` and `Draw()` functions for updating and drawing of your objects.
Work with your own game object class	1. Define instance variables to represent your game objects. 2. Instantiate and initialize the game objects in `LoadContent()`. 3. Poll the user and change the game objects in `Update()`. 4. Draw the game objects in `Draw()`.
Work with the user-defined coordinate system	Allow the user to define the desired coordinate space by specifying the position for the lower-left corner and the width that the game window represents. Define functions to transform the user-defined coordinate space to pixel coordinate space by translating, scaling, and flipping the y-axis. In the case of this chapter, this functionality is defined in the `Camera` class. The `SetCameraWindow()` function allows the user to define the coordinate system. The `ComputePixelPosition()` and `ComputePixelRectangle()` functions implement the transform of positions and rectangles from user-defined to pixel coordinate space.
Draw in the user-defined coordinate system	1. Define a coordinate space by calling the `Camera.SetCameraWindow()` function. 2. Define all game objects in the defined coordinate space. 3. Before drawing a game object, remember to call the `Camera.ComputePixelRectangle()` function to transform from user-defined to pixel coordinate space.
Load a font into the project	Follow the same steps as loading an image: right-click over the ContentProject and locate the font file. In general, these are the same steps to follow to load any external files or resources into your project.
Draw fonts in your game	You can work with the `FontSupport` class and call the `PrintStatus()` function to output text to the top-left corner of the game window, or call the `PrintStatusAt()` function to print text to a user-defined coordinate system position.
Define specific behavior for a game object	One convenient approach is to define a subclass from the `TexturedPrimitive` class: 1. Add a new file into the project. 2. Implement the behavior (for instance, by changing the `Update()` function). 3. Reuse the `Draw()` function if possible. 4. Work with your new class.

(continued)

To	Do this
Avoid complex code in the Game1.cs file	Create a separate *GameState* object to create, maintain, and control your own game state.
Implement the Update() function of your GameState object	Follow these simple steps: 1. Check for the need to update (for example, for pausing or ending the game). 2. Call the Update() function for all game objects. 3. Handle interactions among all relevant game objects. 4. Spawn new enemies if necessary. 5. Check for a win-or-loss condition.

CHAPTER 4

■ ■ ■

Getting Things Moving

After completing this chapter, you will be able to:

- Program with rotated texture objects effectively
- Understand the concept of rotation reference position
- Implement autonomous controlled gradual turning and target-locked chasing behaviors

As you saw at the end of Chapter 3, "2D Graphics, Coordinates and Game State," the behavior of your game objects has become more complex. You may have noticed this in the Simple Game Object and Simple Game State projects, in which you created soccer ball and basketball game objects. The behavior given to those objects allows them to move around the game window, detecting and responding to collisions with the window's edges.

This chapter covers the basic math you need to implement some common behaviors and concepts used across many games, including concepts for projectiles, velocity, and more advanced collision-based behaviors.

Rotating textures

Understanding how a texture rotates is a good place to start, because texture rotation can be useful for a variety of tasks, including orienting your objects in the game world, adding rolling support to an object, modifying the direction an object faces, and creating more natural collision reactions. However, before you can implement behaviors like this, it's worth exploring the basics of rotation, which you'll do in this next project.

The Rotate Textured Primitive project

This project demonstrates how to move an object around the game window and rotate it—either clockwise or counterclockwise. It also demonstrates how to select the Ball object (an instance of TexturedPrimitive) or Logo object (another instance of TexturedPrimitive) and scale it. You can see an example of this project running in Figure 4-1.

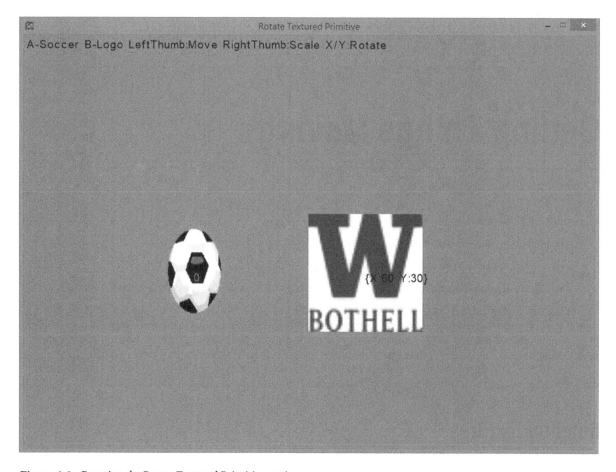

Figure 4-1. *Running the Rotate Textured Primitive project*

The project's controls are as follows:

- **Left thumbstick (WSAD-keys)** Moves the selected image
- **Right thumbstick (arrow-keys)** Scales the selected image
- **Button A (K-key)** Selects the ball
- **Button B (L-key)** Selects the logo
- **Button Y (I-key)** Rotates the selected image clockwise
- **Button X (J-key)** Rotates the selected image counterclockwise

The goals of the project are as follows:

- To understand how to rotate a texture
- To understand the rotation reference position

The steps for creating the project are as follows:

1. Modify the TexturedPrimitive class to support rotation.

2. Modify the GameState class to rotate the textures.

3. Observe and test the results.

Modifying the *TexturedPrimitive* class

1. Modify the TexturedPrimitive class by adding the variable mRotateAngle. This variable holds the clockwise rotation angle of the texture in *radians*. Radians are an alternative unit for describing angles; for example, a circle circumscribes 360 degrees, or 2π radians. MonoGame and other games and graphics APIs use radians because of their relation to trigonometric functions. Because such functions are used throughout the APIs in many areas, they have naturally become the industry standard for describing angles.

■ **Note**   If you need to review or refresh the concept of radians, refer to http://reference.wolfram.com/legacy/teachersedition/Teacher/AlgebraTrigMathematica24.Radiansanddegrees.html. If the cognitive leap from degrees to radians is cumbersome, the library provides convenient helper methods called MathHelper.ToRadians() and MathHelper.ToDegrees().

```
public class TexturedPrimitive
{
    ...

    protected float mRotateAngle; // In radians, clockwise rotation

    ...
}
```

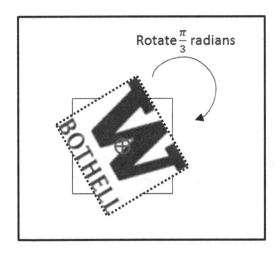

2. Now that you have declared the rotation angle variable, it is important to remember to initialize it within the constructor. The TexturedPrimitive class contains two constructors; therefore, the rotation angle is initialized within both. Both constructors initialize the variable to zero, meaning the TexturedPrimitive object has no angle of rotation upon creation.

```
public TexturedPrimitive(String imageName, Vector2 position, Vector2 size)
{
    ...

    mRotateAngle = 0f;
}

public TexturedPrimitive(String imageName)
{
    ...

    mRotateAngle = 0f;
}
```

3. Next, because you're going to want to modify the rotation angle, you should provide an accessor. The accessor simply needs to let you get or set the rotation variable, as shown here:

```
public float RotateAngleInRadian
{
    get { return mRotateAngle; }
    set { mRotateAngle = value; }
}
```

4. You also need to modify the update function of TexturedPrimitive to provide support for updating the rotation angle—something you can do easily by adding another parameter to specify the angle of rotation. In the following code, the change in angle gets added to the current angle of rotation:

```
public void Update(Vector2 deltaTranslate, Vector2 deltaScale, float deltaAngleInRadian)
{
    mPosition += deltaTranslate;
    mSize += deltaScale;
    mRotateAngle += deltaAngleInRadian;
}
```

■ **Note**   As you may already know, the term delta is used as a synonym for change in mathematics. Therefore, when a parameter is named deltaAngleInRadian, you can think of it as the angle of change, in radians.

5.   The last function that you need to modify is the Draw() function of TexturedPrimitive. This function includes three main steps: converting the position and size of TexturedPrimitive into pixel space for drawing; calculating the rotation origin or pivot; and drawing the texture to the screen using the SpriteBatch.

   a.   To convert from user-defined coordinate space to pixel space, you can use the ComputePixelRectangle() function you created in the Camera class in Chapter 3. Simply pass in the texture's position and size, and store the results in a local Rectangle variable called destRect, which you'll use for drawing.

   b.   Next, you can calculate the rotation origin, or org, by dividing both the image's width and height by two. It's handy to think of the rotation origin as the pivot point around which the texture rotates.

Center of image : $(\dfrac{\texttt{mImage.Width}}{2}, \dfrac{\texttt{mImage.Height}}{2})$

   c.   Lastly, the SpriteBatch.Draw() function is where you use the converted pixel-space rectangle (destRect), the rotation angle (mRotationAngle), and the rotation origin or image reference position (org).

```
virtual public void Draw()
{
    // Define location and size of the texture
    Rectangle destRect = Camera.ComputePixelRectangle(Position, Size);

    // Define the rotation origin
    Vector2 org = new Vector2(mImage.Width / 2, mImage.Height / 2);

    // Draw the texture
    Game1.sSpriteBatch.Draw(
            mImage,
            destRect,              // Area to be drawn in pixel space
            null,
            Color.White,
            mRotateAngle,          // Angle to rotate (clockwise)
            org,                   // Image reference position
            SpriteEffects.None, 0f);
}
```

Modifying the *GameState* class

1. Now that the TexturedPrimitive class supports rotation, you can use it within the GameState class to demonstrate that it is functioning correctly. Start by adding the following TexturedPrimitive variables and initializing them within the constructor:

```
// Work with TexturedPrimitive
TexturedPrimitive mBall, mUWBLogo;
TexturedPrimitive mWorkPrim;

public GameState()
{
    // Create the primitives
    mBall = new TexturedPrimitive("Soccer",
                        new Vector2(30, 30), new Vector2(10, 15));
    mUWBLogo = new TexturedPrimitive("UWB-JPG",
                        new Vector2(60, 30), new Vector2(20, 20));
    mWorkPrim = mBall;
}
```

2. Next, change the update function to support the selection of the current primitive and also the rotation of that primitive if either the X or the Y button is pressed:

```
public void UpdateGame()
{
    #region Select which primitive to work on
    if (InputWrapper.Buttons.A == ButtonState.Pressed)
        mWorkPrim = mBall;
    else if (InputWrapper.Buttons.B == ButtonState.Pressed)
        mWorkPrim = mUWBLogo;
    #endregion

    #region Update the work primitive
    float rotation = 0;
    if (InputWrapper.Buttons.X == ButtonState.Pressed)
        rotation = MathHelper.ToRadians(1f);        // 1 degree pre-press
    else if (InputWrapper.Buttons.Y == ButtonState.Pressed)
        rotation = MathHelper.ToRadians(-1f);       // 1 degree pre-press
    mWorkPrim.Update(
        InputWrapper.ThumbSticks.Left,
        InputWrapper.ThumbSticks.Right,
        rotation);
    #endregion
}
```

3. Lastly, modify the DrawGame() function to draw both of the TexturedPrimitive objects and output their angles of rotation via the FontSupport class:

```
public void DrawGame()
{
    mBall.Draw();
```

```
FontSupport.PrintStatusAt(
    mBall.Position,
    mBall.RoateAngleInRadian.ToString(),
    Color.Red);

mUWBLogo.Draw();
FontSupport.PrintStatusAt(
    mUWBLogo.Position,
    mUWBLogo.Position.ToString(),
    Color.Black);

FontSupport.PrintStatus(
    "A-Soccer B-Logo LeftThumb:Move RightThumb:Scale X/Y:Rotate",
    null);
}
```

Observing and testing the results

Build and run the project. Does it behave as you expected? If so, try rotating the textures clockwise and counterclockwise. Notice that they rotate around the center of the image, because we defined the origin or reference position of the image. You'll see more details about this important concept later in this book.

Vectors

The next concept we'll cover is *vectors*. Euclidean vectors are used across many fields of study, including mathematics, physics, computer science, and engineering. They are particularly important in games; nearly every game uses vectors in one way or another. Because they are used so extensively, this section is devoted to understanding and utilizing vectors in games.

One of the most common uses for vectors is to represent an object's displacement and direction. This can be done easily, because a vector is defined by its size and direction. Using only this small amount of information, you can represent attributes such as an object's velocity or acceleration. If you have the position of an object, its direction, and its velocity, then you have sufficient information to move it around the window without user input.

■ **Note**   A vector's size is often referred to as its length, or *magnitude*.

Vector review

Before going any further, it is important to review the concepts of a vector, starting with how you can define one. A vector can be specified using two points. For example, given the arbitrary position $P_a = (X_a, Y_a)$ and the arbitrary position $P_b = (X_b, Y_b)$, you can define the vector from P_a to P_b or (V_{ab}) as $P_b - P_a$. You can see this represented in the following equations and Figure 4-2:

$$P_a = (X_a, Y_a)$$

$$P_b = (X_b, Y_b)$$

$$V_{ab} = P_b - P_a = (X_b - X_a, Y_b - Y_a)$$

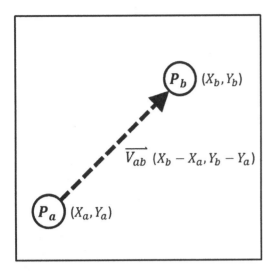

Figure 4-2. *A vector being defined by two points*

Now that you have a vector V_{ab}, you can easily ascertain its length (or size) and its direction. A vector's length is equal to the distance between the two points that created it. In this example, the length of V_{ab} is equal to the distance between P_a and P_b, while the direction of V_{ab} goes from P_a toward P_b.

In MonoGame, the Vector2 class implements the functionality of a two-dimensional (2D) vector. Conveniently, you can also use the Vector2 class to represent positions in 2D space, such as a point. In the preceding example, P_a, P_b, and V_{ab} can all be implemented as instances of the *Vector2* class; however, V_{ab} is the only mathematically defined vector. P_a and P_b represent positions, or points used to create a vector.

Recall that a vector can also be normalized. A *normalized* vector (also known as a *unit vector*) always has a size of 1. You can see a normalized vector represented in the following equation and Figure 4-3:

$$V_a = Vector2.Normalized(V_a) = (X_v, Y_v)$$

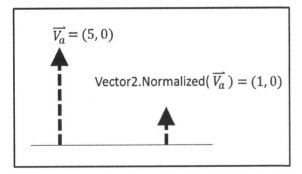

Figure 4-3. *A vector being normalized*

Vectors can also be rotated. If, for example, you have the vector $V_r = (X_r, Y_r)$ and wish to rotate it by θ (radians), then you can use the equations shown following to derive X_r and Y_r. Figure 4-4 shows the roltation of a vector being applied.

$$X_r = X_v \cos\theta + Y_v \sin\theta$$

$$Y_r = -X_v \sin\theta + Y_v \cos\theta$$

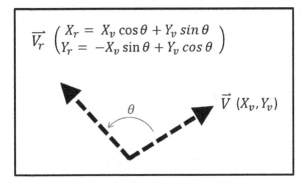

Figure 4-4. *A vector being rotated by the angle theta (in radians)*

Lastly, it is important to remember that vectors are defined by their direction and size; in other words, two vectors can be equal to each other independent of the locations of the vectors. Figure 4-5 shows two vectors (V_a and V_{bc}) that are located at different positions but have the same direction and magnitude. Because their direction and magnitude are the same, these vectors are equal to each other. In contrast, the vector V_d is not the same because its direction and magnitude are different from the others.

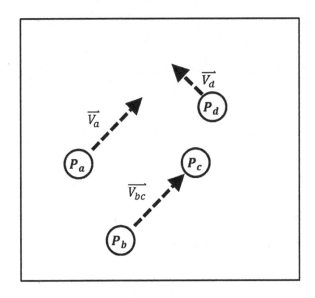

Figure 4-5. *Three valid vectors represented in 2D space with two vectors equal to each other*

The Show Vector project

This project demonstrates how to represent and manipulate vectors within the game window. You can select and manipulate each of the vectors by changing its attributes, such as direction and size. The project shows vectors being represented in three different ways. Figure 4-6 shows an example of this project running.

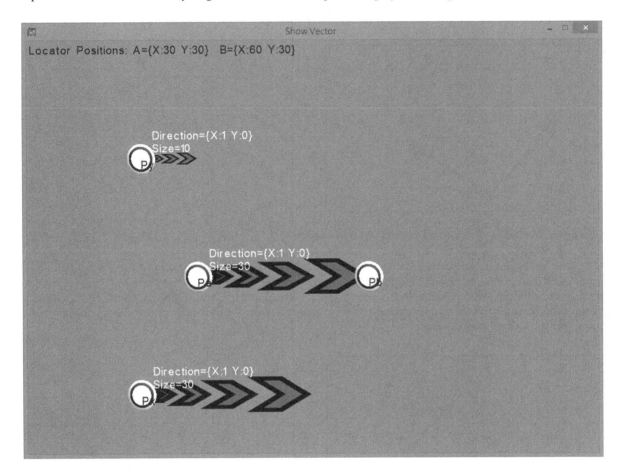

Figure 4-6. *Running the Show Vector project*

The project's controls are as follows:

- **Left thumbstick's x-axis (AD-keys)** Rotates the vector at P_y
- **Left thumbstick's y-axis (WS-keys)** Increases and decrease the length of the vector at P_y
- **Right thumbstick (arrow-keys)** Changes the currently selected locator position $(P_a, P_b, P_x, \text{ or } P_y)$
- **Button A (K-key)** Selects P_a
- **Button B (L-key)** Selects P_b
- **Button X (J-key)** Selects P_x
- **Button Y (I-key)** Selects P_y

The goals of the project are as follows:

- To understand some of the utility of vectors
- To understand how to define a vector
- To be able to define a vector at a specified position

The steps for creating the project are as follows:

1. Create the ShowVector class.
2. Modify the project's GameState class.

Add the following resource, which can be found in the Chapter04\SourceCode\ImagesAndFontsUsed folder, into your content project before you begin:

- Position.png

Creating the *ShowVector* class

1. Start by creating a new class in the GraphicsSupport folder. Name the class ShowVector.cs.

2. Add the following two static variables, which support drawing the ShowVector object. You can use a simple Texture2D type for the image and a float for the length-to-width ratio of the image.

```
protected static Texture2D sImage = null;    // Singleton for the class
private static float kLenToWidthRatio = 0.2f;
```

3. Now add a simple static function to load the image variable with the desire texture. Recall that the images used within this chapter can be found in Chapter04\ImagesAndFontsUsed.

```
static private void LoadImage()
{
    if (null == sImage)
        ShowVector.sImage = Game1.sContent.Load<Texture2D>("RightArrow");
}
```

4. You need to add a function that can correctly draw the vector to the game window. To do this, add a DrawPointVector() function that accepts two arguments. The first is the starting position and the second is the direction. Both of these arguments should be Vector2s.

```
static public void DrawPointVector(Vector2 from, Vector2 dir)
{
    ...
}
```

Because this function is a bit lengthy, let's look at each piece separately:

a. The first thing to do is load the vector image to prepare it for drawing. You can do this by using the previously created LoadImage() function:

```
LoadImage();
```

b. Next, you need to compute the correct angle of rotation for the image. This can be done by calculating the angle (theta) between the vector's direction (Vector2 dir) and the x-axis, as shown in the image that follows.

■ **Note**   The sign of the angle is positive when the rotation is counterclockwise.

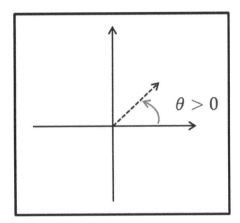

To do this, you first normalize the given vector by dividing the vector with its length. With a normalized vector, the length is the size of the hypotenuse and has a value of 1, the value of the X component is the size of adjacent, and the value of the Y component is the size of the opposite. In this way, arc cosine on the normalized vector's X value is the angle of rotation from the horizontal direction, as illustrated in the following image.

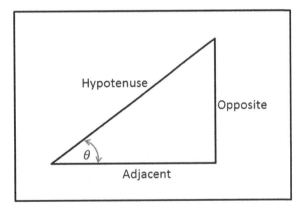

The sign of the Y value indicates if the rotation is counterclockwise (positive) or clockwise (negative). In the code that follows, you can see how the angle is found:

```
#region Step 4b. Compute the angle to rotate
float length = dir.Length();
float theta = 0f;

if (length > 0.001f)
{
    dir /= length;
    theta = (float)Math.Acos((double)dir.X);
```

```
        if (dir.X < 0.0f)
        {
            if (dir.Y > 0.0f)
                theta = -theta;
        }
        Else
        {
            if (dir.Y > 0.0f)
                theta= -theta;
        }
    }
    #endregion
```

> ■ **Note** The x-axis is used because the direction of the image used needs to be taken into account. The image used for this project points horizontally. If the image were pointed vertically, then the preceding computation would need to use the y-axis as the reference. Alternatively, you can rotate a vertically pointing image by 90 degrees before including it in the project.

    c.   Now that you know the correct rotation for the image, you can draw it. You do this by calling the Game1.sSpriteBatch.Draw() function, passing in the correct rotation angle, image, and destination rectangle, which you can calculate from the vector's position (from) and size (length). However, pay special attention to the reference point around which the image will rotate. To correctly reflect the vector's position and size, you need to rotate the image around a middle-left position (the beginning of the arrow). This is reflected in the image that follows:

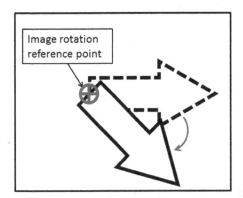

Image rotation reference point

```
    #region Step 4c. Draw Arrow
        // Define location and size of the texture to show
        Vector2 size = new Vector2(length, kLenToWidthRatio * length);
        Rectangle destRect = Camera.ComputePixelRectangle(from, size);

        // destRect is computed with respect to the "from" position
        // on the left side of the texture.
        // We only need to offset the reference
        // in the y from top left to middle left.
        Vector2 org = new Vector2(0f, ShowVector.sImage.Height/2f);
```

```
            Game1.sSpriteBatch.Draw(ShowVector.sImage, destRect, null, Color.White,
                             theta, org, SpriteEffects.None, 0f);
    #endregion
```

    d.   The last portion of this function prints out the vector's direction and size. You can achieve this using the previously created font support class's PrintStatusAt() function:

```
#region Step 4d. Print status message
    String msg;
    msg = "Direction=" + dir + "\nSize=" + length;
    FontSupport.PrintStatusAt(from + new Vector2(2, 5), msg, Color.Black);
#endregion
```

5.   Now that the DrawPointVector() function, which uses a position and direction, is complete, you need to add another function to draw a vector between two points. This is quite easy using the DrawPointVector() function you just created. The DrawFromTo() function draws a vector:

```
static public void DrawFromTo(Vector2 from, Vector2 to)
{
    DrawPointVector(from, to - from);
}
```

6.   The last function you need for the ShowVector class is a rotation function. Add a function called RotateVectorByAngle(), which accepts a vector and the desired rotation. Using the rotation angle, you can rotate the vector by implementing the vector rotation equations defined previously. After calculating the rotation, the function should return the new vector. You can see an example of this in the following code:

```
static public Vector2 RotateVectorByAngle(Vector2 v, float angleInRadian)
{
    float sinTheta = (float)(Math.Sin((double)angleInRadian));
    float cosTheta = (float)(Math.Cos((double)angleInRadian));
    float x, y;
    x = cosTheta * v.X + sinTheta * v.Y;
    y = -sinTheta * v.X + cosTheta * v.Y;
    return new Vector2(x, y);
}
```

Now that you have implemented the ShowVector class, you can modify the GameState class to support the desired vectors.

Modifying the *GameState* class

1. Add the following variables to the GameState class. These variables will be used to create your desired vectors by acting as points or locators. Remember that a vector can be defined by two points.

```
// Size of all the positions
Vector2 kPointSize = new Vector2(5f, 5f);

// Work with TexturedPrimitive
TexturedPrimitive mPa, mPb;              // The locators for showing Point A and Point B
TexturedPrimitive mPx;                   // to show same displacement can be applied to any position

TexturedPrimitive mPy;                   // To show we can rotate/manipulate vectors independently
Vector2 mVectorAtPy = new Vector2(10, 0); // Start with vector in the X direction;

TexturedPrimitive mCurrentLocator;
```

2. Modify the GameState class's constructor to initialize the locators or points with an image, position, size, and name. Also set the current locator (currently selected) to the locator mPa. You can see this reflected in the following code:

```
public GameState()
{
    // Create the primitives
    mPa = new TexturedPrimitive("Position",
        new Vector2(30, 30), kPointSize, "Pa");
    mPb = new TexturedPrimitive("Position",
        new Vector2(60, 30), kPointSize, "Pb");
    mPx = new TexturedPrimitive("Position",
        new Vector2(20, 10), kPointSize, "Px");
    mPy = new TexturedPrimitive("Position",
        new Vector2(20, 50), kPointSize, "Py");
    mCurrentLocator = mPa;
}
```

3. With the required variables declared and initialized, you can now add code to change their states in the update function. Modify the UpdateGame() function to support the following:

    a. Allow the user to change the currently selected vector by polling the gamepad's A, B, X, and Y buttons and changing mCurrentLocator to the corresponding locator:

```
#region Step 3a. Change current selected vector
    if (InputWrapper.Buttons.A == ButtonState.Pressed)
        mCurrentLocator = mPa;
    else if (InputWrapper.Buttons.B == ButtonState.Pressed)
        mCurrentLocator = mPb;
    else if (InputWrapper.Buttons.X == ButtonState.Pressed)
        mCurrentLocator = mPx;
    else if (InputWrapper.Buttons.Y == ButtonState.Pressed)
        mCurrentLocator = mPy;
#endregion
```

b. Support the movement of the currently selected vector with the gamepad's right thumbstick by changing mCurrentLocator:

```
#region Step 3b. Move Vector
    // Change the current locator position
    mCurrentLocator.Position +=
        InputWrapper.ThumbSticks.Right;
#endregion
```

c. Give the user the ability to rotate the Py vector via the left thumbstick's x-axis:

```
#region Step 3c. Rotate Vector
    // Left thumbstick-X rotates the vector at Py
    float rotateYByRadian = MathHelper.ToRadians(
        InputWrapper.ThumbSticks.Left.X);
#endregion
```

d. Give the user the ability to change the length of the Py vector via the left thumbstick's y-axis:

```
#region Step 3d. Increase/Decrease the length of vector
    // Left thumbstick-Y increase/decrease the length of vector at Py
    float vecYLen = mVectorAtPy.Length();
    vecYLen += InputWrapper.ThumbSticks.Left.Y;
#endregion
```

e. Apply the computed changes to vector Py by utilizing the ShowVector class's RotateVectorByAngle() function for the modified rotation angle, and then normalizing Py so that the new scale can be used:

```
#region Step 3e. Compute vector changes
    // Compute the rotated direction of vector at Py
    mVectorAtPy = ShowVector.RotateVectorByAngle(mVectorAtPy, rotateYByRadian);
    mVectorAtPy.Normalize(); // Normalize vectorAtPy to size of 1f
    mVectorAtPy *= vecYLen;  // Scale the vector to the new size
#endregion
```

4. As you probably have guessed, the last function you need to modify within the GameState class is the DrawGame() function. You can do this via the code provided following. As you can see, the vectors are drawn via the ShowVector class and locators are drawn using the TexturedPrimitive Draw() function.

```
public void DrawGame()
{
    // Drawing the vectors
    Vector2 v = mPb.Position - mPa.Position;   // Vector V is from Pa to Pb

    // Draw Vector-V at Pa, and Px
    ShowVector.DrawFromTo(mPa.Position, mPb.Position);
    ShowVector.DrawPointVector(mPx.Position, v);
```

```
        // Draw vectorAtPy at Py
        ShowVector.DrawPointVector(mPy.Position, mVectorAtPy);

        mPa.Draw();
        mPb.Draw();
        mPx.Draw();
        mPy.Draw();

        // Print out text message to echo status
        FontSupport.PrintStatus(
            "Locator Positions: A=" + mPa.Position +
            " B=" + mPb.Position,
            null);
    }
```

Front direction

With the basics of vectors out of the way, we can now address more vector-based game-specific concepts, starting with the idea of *front direction*. This simple idea stems from the need to understand which direction a game object is facing. For example, in a platform-style game, front direction determines which direction the hero character or enemy characters faces.

Front direction can be used to affect the gameplay or simply flip to a character's texture upon a directional change. Adding support for front direction provides you with a convenient tool for achieving many gamelike actions.

The Front Direction project

This project demonstrates how to use the concept of front direction by controlling a rocket, the direction it faces, and therefore the direction of its projectiles. The rocket can move, rotate, and fire. The user's goal is to catch a bee by hitting it with a fired projectile. If the projectile touches the bee, it causes the bee to respawn at a random position. Figure 4-7 shows an example of this project in action.

Figure 4-7. *Running the Front Direction project*

The project's controls are as follows:

- **Left thumbstick (WSAD-keys)** Changes the position of the rocket
- **Right thumbstick's x-axis (left/right-arrow-keys)** Changes the front direction of rocket by rotating it
- **Button A (K-key)** Shoots the net

The goals of the project are as follows:

- To experience front direction
- To practice traveling along a predefined direction

The steps for creating the project are as follows:

1. Modify the project's GameState class.
2. Observe the results.

Add the following resources, which can be found in the Chapter04\SourceCode\ImagesAndFontsUsed folder, into your content project before you begin:

- Insect.png
- Net.png
- Rocket.png

Modifying the *GameState* class

1. Add the following variables needed to support the desired game state. For the rocket, a TexturedPrimitive and a vector for its initial direction are all that is needed. For the projectile (the net), a TexturedPrimitive, a bool for its flight state, a vector for its velocity, and a float for its speed are needed. The bee only requires a TexturedPrimitive and a bool for its status. Lastly, a couple of variables for the game statistics are needed.

```
// Rocket support
Vector2 mRocketInitDirection = Vector2.UnitY; // This does not change
TexturedPrimitive mRocket;

// Support the flying net
TexturedPrimitive mNet;
bool mNetInFlight = false;
Vector2 mNetVelocity = Vector2.Zero;
float mNetSpeed = 0.5f;

// Insect support
TexturedPrimitive mInsect;
bool mInsectPreset = true;

// Simple game status
int mNumInsectShot;
int mNumMissed;
```

2. Next, initialize the variables to the values shown in the code that follows. This represents the game state upon the initial loading of the project.

```
public GameState()
{
    // Create and set up the primitives
    mRocket = new TexturedPrimitive("Rocket", new Vector2(5, 5), new Vector2(3, 10));
    // Initially the rocket is pointing in the positive y direction
    mRocketInitDirection = Vector2.UnitY;

    mNet = new TexturedPrimitive("Net", new Vector2(0, 0), new Vector2(2, 5));
    mNetInFlight = false; // until user press "A", rocket is not in flight
    mNetVelocity = Vector2.Zero;
    mNetSpeed = 0.5f;
```

```
    // Initialize a new insect
    mInsect = new TexturedPrimitive("Insect", Vector2.Zero, new Vector2(5, 5));
    mInsectPreset = false;

    // Initialize game status
    mNumInsectShot = 0;
    mNumMissed = 0;
}
```

3. Now the update function needs to update each individual game object. This can be done by breaking down the objects and their behaviors into different steps.

    a. First, start by updating the rocket's behavior. You can do this by rotating the rocket via the right thumbstick's x-axis and moving the rocket via the left thumbstick. You can see this reflected in the code that follows:

    ```
    mRocket.RotateAngleInRadian += MathHelper.ToRadians(InputWrapper.ThumbSticks.Right.X);
    mRocket.Position += InputWrapper.ThumbSticks.Left;
    ```

    b. Second, update the projectile's (net's) behavior by modifying its variables when the A button is pressed. You can see this achieved in the code that follows. Notice how the net uses the rocket's rotation and position when launched.

    ```
    /// Set net to flight
    if (InputWrapper.Buttons.A == ButtonState.Pressed)
    {
        mNetInFlight = true;
        mNet.RotateAngleInRadian = mRocket.RotateAngleInRadian;
        mNet.Position = mRocket.Position;
        mNetVelocity = ShowVector.RotateVectorByAngle(
            mRocketInitDirection,
            mNet.RotateAngleInRadian) * mNetSpeed;
    }
    ```

    c. The last piece that needs updating is the bee. You can easily do this by checking its alive state. If the bee does not currently exist, it should be re-created at a random position.

    ```
    if (!mInsectPreset)
    {
        float x = 15f + ((float)Game1.sRan.NextDouble() * 30f);
        float y = 15f + ((float)Game1.sRan.NextDouble() * 30f);
        mInsect.Position = new Vector2(x, y);
        mInsectPreset = true;
    }
    ```

4. The remaining portion of the update function needs to handle the interobject collision or interaction. For this project, the collisions that involve the net are what you care about. Because of this, you can check the net's flight state and update its position (based on its velocity) and its collision detections if the net is in flight. If the net touches the insect, reset the states and modify the game stats. The net misses if it collides with the border of the game window.

```
    if (mNetInFlight)
    {
        mNet.Position += mNetVelocity;

        if (mNet.PrimitivesTouches(mInsect))
        {
            mInsectPreset = false;
            mNetInFlight = false;
            mNumInsectShot++;
        }

        if ((Camera.CollidedWithCameraWindow(mNet) !=
                Camera.CameraWindowCollisionStatus.InsideWindow))
        {
            mNetInFlight = false;
            mNumMissed++;
        }
    }
}
```

5.   The last function you need to modify in the GameState class is the draw function. You can do this very simply by calling the objects' draw functions if their state is set to true. For example, the net should only be drawn if it is in flight. Also, remember to print the game status via the FontSupport class.

```
public void DrawGame()
{
    mRocket.Draw();
    if (mNetInFlight)
        mNet.Draw();

    if (mInsectPreset)
        mInsect.Draw();

    // Print out text message to echo status
    FontSupport.PrintStatus(
        "Num insects netted = " + mNumInsectShot +
        " Num missed = " + mNumMissed, null);
}
```

Observing the results

Now that you have implemented the necessary code, build and run the program. Test the program to see if it behaves as you would expect. Notice that the rocket points in the intended direction when the user uses the right thumbstick. This is because the front direction is correctly oriented with the image.

As you might have noticed when coding this project, the GameState class contains a large number of variables that belong to other objects within the game state, such as the rocket object (the TexturedPrimitive) and its initial direction vector. This is fine for demonstrating the front direction concept; however, in a real game, organizing your objects' variables within the game state is considered bad practice. You'll address this issue by creating a GameObject class in the next project.

Game objects

As you saw at the end of the last section, using the GameState class to prototype and learn new concepts can be a quick and effective way to get a project up and running. However, as a developer it is your job to design your game's architecture, which you should generally strive to make as straightforward and clean as possible, yet still maintain the ability to modify and expand it. When you include groups of related variables in the GameState class, the game's architecture can become complex and convoluted as your game grows in scale and diversity. In addition, creating similar objects becomes a tedious process, as properties for each object also need to be declared. The simplest way to solve these issues, as you may know, is to create a new class with the desired behaviors and properties.

This section combines the properties and behaviors declared in the previous project's GameState class into a new class called GameObject. These properties include front direction, velocity, and speed, and provide you with improved control over the movement of a game object.

■ **Note** Velocity can be thought of as the rate of change of the position of an object. Velocity is made up of both a direction and speed (size). If this is familiar, it is because velocity lends itself perfectly to a vector, which also has a direction and size.

The Game Object project

This project demonstrates how to control a game object by moving it around the game window. You move the game object (the rocket) by adjusting its speed and front direction. Figure 4-8 shows an example of this project running.

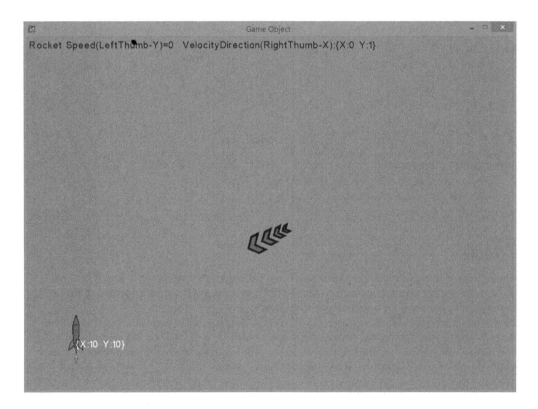

Figure 4-8. Running the Game Object project

The project's controls are as follows:

- **Left thumbstick's y-axis (AD-keys)** Controls the rocket's fly speed

- **Right thumbstick's x-axis (left/right-arrow-keys)** Changes the front direction of the rocket

The goal of the project is as follows:

- To abstract velocity and front direction into a new class

The steps for creating the project are as follows:

1. Create and understand the GameObject class.

2. Modify the game state to support the new GameObject class.

3. Observe and test the results.

Add the following resources, which can be found in the Chapter04\SourceCode\ImagesAndFontsUsed folder, into your content project before you begin:

- Arrow.png

Creating the *GameObject* class

1. Create a new class called GameObject. The GameObject class should derive from the TexturedPrimitive class so that you can take advantage of its previously defined behaviors and properties.

```
public class GameObject : TexturedPrimitive
{
    ...
}
```

2. Declare the following variables so you can support initial front direction, velocity direction, and speed:

```
// Initial front direction (when RotateAngle is 0)
protected Vector2 mInitFrontDir = Vector2.UnitY;

// GameObject behavior: velocity
protected Vector2 mVelocityDir; // If not zero, always normalized
protected float mSpeed;
```

3. To support initialization of the GameObject class, create a constructor that accepts as arguments the object's name, position, size, and label, and passes those parameters into the base class. Additionally, set the object's speed and velocity variables to their initial values.

```
protected void InitGameObject()
{
    mVelocityDir = Vector2.Zero;
    mSpeed = 0f;
}
```

```
public GameObject(String imageName, Vector2 position,
    Vector2 size, String label = null)
        : base(imageName, position, size, label)
{
    InitGameObject();
}
```

4. Create a straightforward update function for the game object that modifies its position based on its speed and velocity direction values. Notice that this is a virtual function that subclasses can override.

```
virtual public void Update()
{
    mPosition += (mVelocityDir * mSpeed);
}
```

5. Add get and set accessors for the properties of the GameObject. These will allow you to change the direction and velocity of the game object from other classes, such as the GameState class. In total, you need five functions, as described following:

   a. The first accessor you should create is InitialFrontDirection. This function allows you to get the initial front direction, as well as set the initial front direction if the incoming vector is not of zero length.

```
public Vector2 InitialFrontDirection
{
    get { return mInitFrontDir; }
    set
    {
        float len = value.Length();
        // If the input vector is well defined
        if (len > float.Epsilon)
            mInitFrontDir = value / len;
        else
            mInitFrontDir = Vector2.UnitY;
    }
}
```

   b. The next accessor is FrontDirection. This is similar to the previous accessor, except it returns a ShowVector and applies the incoming value to the rotation angle. You can see an example of the math needed to achieve this in the code and image that follow:

```
public Vector2 FrontDirection
{
    get
    {
        return ShowVector.RotateVectorByAngle(mInitFrontDir, RotateAngleInRadian);
    }
    set
    {
        float len = value.Length();
        if (len > float.Epsilon)
```

```
        {
            value *= (1f / len);
            double theta = Math.Atan2(value.Y, value.X);
            mRotateAngle = -(float)(theta-Math.Atan2(mInitFrontDir.Y, mInitFrontDir.X));
        }
    }
}
```

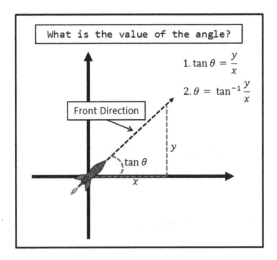

c. Now create an accessor for velocity. You can do this easily by using the code that follows. Notice how it obtains the velocity by multiplying the direction and speed together.

```
public Vector2 Velocity
{
    get { return mVelocityDir * Speed; }
    set
    {
        mSpeed = value.Length();
        if (mSpeed > float.Epsilon)
            mVelocityDir = value/mSpeed;
        else
            mVelocityDir = Vector2.Zero;
    }
}
```

d. Add a simple accessor to support Speed:

```
public float Speed
{
    get { return mSpeed; }
    set { mSpeed = value; }
}
```

e. Finally, create an accessor for VelocityDirection:

```
public Vector2 VelocityDirection
{
    get { return mVelocityDir; }
    set
    {
        float s = value.Length();
        if (s > float.Epsilon)
        {
            mVelocityDir = value / s;
        }
        else
            mVelocityDir = Vector2.Zero;
    }
}
```

Now that the GameObject class is complete and provides the necessary properties and behaviors, you can modify the GameState class to use them within the game.

Modifying the *GameState* class

1. Start by creating variables for the initial rocket position, the rocket game object, and the arrow game object:

```
Vector2 kInitRocketPosition = new Vector2(10, 10);
// Rocket support
GameObject mRocket;
// The arrow
GameObject mArrow;
```

2. Initialize the variables within the constructor with the default values shown following:

```
public GameState()
{
    mRocket = new GameObject("Rocket", kInitRocketPosition, new Vector2(3, 10));
    mArrow = new GameObject("RightArrow", new Vector2(50, 30), new Vector2(10, 4));
    // Initially pointing in the x direction
    mArrow.InitialFrontDirection = Vector2.UnitX;
}
```

3. Modify the UpdateGame() function so you can control and fly the rocket, as well as point the arrow in the rocket's direction.

    a. To control the rocket, use the gamepad's left and right thumbsticks. The right thumbstick controls the rocket's angle or front direction, while the left thumbstick's y-axis controls the rocket's speed. In addition, check and reset the rocket's position whenever it collides with the window border. Lastly, remember to call the rocket's update function. Here's the code to accomplish this:

```
#region Step 3a. Control and fly the rocket
mRocket.RotateAngleInRadian +=
    MathHelper.ToRadians(InputWrapper.ThumbSticks.Right.X);
```

```
    mRocket.Speed += InputWrapper.ThumbSticks.Left.Y * 0.1f;

    mRocket.VelocityDirection = mRocket.FrontDirection;

    if (Camera.CollidedWithCameraWindow(mRocket) !=
        Camera.CameraWindowCollisionStatus.InsideWindow)
    {
        mRocket.Speed = 0f;
        mRocket.Position = kInitRocketPosition;
    }

    mRocket.Update();
    #endregion
```

b. Set the arrow's front direction to face the rocket by finding the vector between the
    rocket's position and the arrow's position, and then apply that vector to the arrow's
    front direction property:

```
#region Step 3b. Set the arrow to point toward the rocket
Vector2 toRocket = mRocket.Position - mArrow.Position;
mArrow.FrontDirection = toRocket;
#endregion
```

4. Finally, simply draw the rocket and arrow game objects by calling their draw functions
    within DrawGame. Also remember to update the status output with the necessary
    information.

```
public void DrawGame()
{
    mRocket.Draw();
    mArrow.Draw();

    // print out text message to echo status
    FontSupport.PrintStatus(
        "Rocket Speed(LeftThumb-Y)=" + mRocket.Speed +
        " VelocityDirection(RightThumb-X):" +
        mRocket.VelocityDirection, null);
    FontSupport.PrintStatusAt(mRocket.Position, mRocket.Position.ToString(), Color.White);
}
```

Observing the results

By grouping behaviors into a new class rather than declaring multiple variables within the game state, you have
created a better-defined object and simplified your project by splitting it into more manageable pieces. You can now
instantiate several of these objects without increasing the complexity of your code drastically. In upcoming examples,
you'll see that game objects can also become quite complex; however, by isolating them within a class, you can
effectively hide much of the complexity. This makes it easier for you to use the object within the game and to modify
the object's overall behavior.

Chasers

With game objects now moving around the screen, you can now look at the more specific behavior known as chasing. Chasing behavior is useful for many tasks within games. Some of the most common are projectile-based or bullet-based behaviors and simple enemy artificial intelligence (AI).

The goal of a chasing object is usually to catch the game object that it is targeting. This requires programmatic manipulation of the chaser's front direction and velocity so it can home in on its target. However, it is generally important to avoid implementing a chaser that has perfect aim and always hits its target—because if the projectile always hits its target and characters are unable to avoid being hit, the challenge will essentially be removed from the game. However, this does not mean you should not implement a perfect chaser if your game design requires it. You'll implement a chaser in the next project.

The Chaser Object project

This project demonstrates how to control a rocket game object using both thumbsticks to control the rocket's speed and direction. Pressing the A button shoots a snake that chases the rocket. You can then manipulate the rocket and attempt to avoid being hit. Figure 4-9 shows an example of this project running.

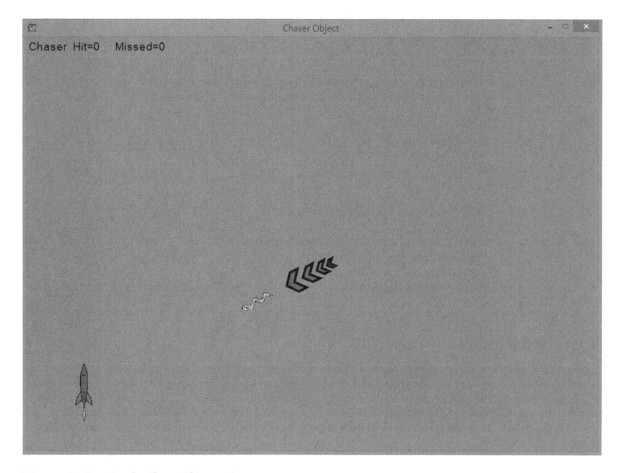

Figure 4-9. *Running the Chaser Object project*

The project's controls are as follows:

- **Left thumbstick's y-axis (WS-keys)** Controls the rocket's flying speed
- **Right thumbstick's x-axis (left/right-arrow-keys)** Changes the front direction of the rocket
- **Button A (K-key)** Shoots a snake that chases the rocket

The goals of the project are as follows:

- To review vector dot products and cross products
- To examine and implement chasing behavior

The steps for creating the project are as follows:

1. Review the concepts of dot product and cross product.

2. Create and implement the `ChaserGameObject` class.

3. Modify the `GameState` class support the new chaser class.

4. Observe and test the results.

Before digging into the implementation of chasing behavior, you'll review the mathematics required to correctly rotate or turn a game object during a chase. The two concepts you need to understand for this operation are the *dot product* and the *cross product*.

The dot product

The dot product of two normalized vectors provides you with the means to find the angle between those vectors. For example, take a look at the following statements.

Given the following:

$$V_1 = (X_1, Y_1) \text{ and } V_2 = (X_2, Y_2)$$

Then the following is true:

$$V_1 \cdot V_2 = V_2 \cdot V_1 = X_1 X_2 + Y_1 Y_2$$

■ **Note** If you need to review or refresh the concept of a dot product, refer to
`http://www.mathsisfun.com/algebra/vectors-dot-product.html`.

Additionally, if both vectors V_1 and V_2 are normalized, then $V_1 \cdot V_2 = \cos \theta$. You can see this concept reinforced in Figure 4-10.

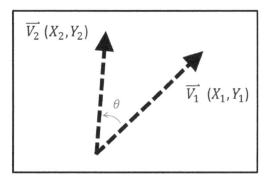

Figure 4-10. *The angle between two vectors, which can be found through the dot product*

Lastly, it is also important to recognize that if $V_1 \cdot V_2 = 0$, then the two vectors are perpendicular.

The cross product

The cross product of two vectors produces a vector that is orthogonal, or perpendicular, to both of the original vectors. In 2D games, where the 2D dimensions lie flat on the screen, the cross product results in a vector that either points inward (toward the screen) or outward (away from the screen). This may seem odd, because it's not intuitive that crossing two vectors in 2D or XY space would result in a vector that lies in the third dimension, or the Z space. However, this vector is essential for the sole purpose of determining whether the game object needs to rotate in the clockwise or counterclockwise direction. Let's take a detailed look at the following statements to clarify the mathematics involved.

Given the following:

$$V_1 = (X_1, Y_1) \text{ and } V_2 = (X_2, Y_2).$$

Then the following is true:

$$(V_1 \times V_2) \text{ is equal to a vector perpendicular to both } V_1 \text{ and } V_2.$$

■ **Note** If you need to review or refresh the concept of a cross product, refer to
http://www.mathsisfun.com/algebra/vectors-cross-product.html.

Additionally, you know that the cross product of two vectors in the XY space results in a vector in the Z direction. Lastly, when V_1 crosses $V_2 > 0$, you know that V_1 is in the clockwise direction from V_2; similarly, when $V_1 \times V_2 < 0$, you know that V_1 is in the counterclockwise direction. Figure 4-11 should help clarify this concept.

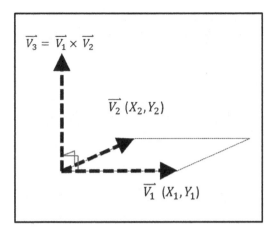

Figure 4-11. *The cross product on two vectors*

Creating the *ChaserGameObject* class

1. Create a new class named ChaserGameObject. Subclass it from the GameObject class:

```
public class ChaserGameObject : GameObject
{
    ...
}
```

2. Add the following three variables for keeping track of the target. One of these variables is the target itself. Another keeps track of whether the target has been hit, and the last one holds a value that represents how rapidly the chaser homes in on its target.

```
// The target to go toward
protected TexturedPrimitive mTarget;
// Have we hit the target yet?
protected bool mHitTarget;
// How rapidly the chaser homes in on the target
protected float mHomeInRate;
```

3. Create a constructor to initialize the variables to the following default values. Remember to use the GameObject constructor or base constructor.

```
public ChaserGameObject(String imageName, Vector2 position, Vector2 size,
    TexturedPrimitive target) : base(imageName, position, size, null)
{
    Target = target;
    mHomeInRate = 0.05f;
    mHitTarget = false;
    mSpeed = 0.1f;
}
```

4. Now, an update function is needed to adjust the chaser's direction. The following image shows an example of what you are trying to achieve. The function itself has been divided into two steps.

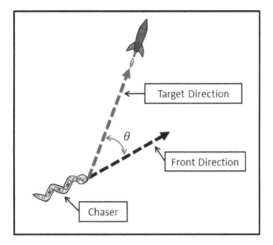

a. The first step simply checks for a null target and calls the base update function:

```
#region Step 4a.
if (null == mTarget)
    return;
// Move the GameObject in the velocity direction
base.Update();
#endregion
```

b. Next, check for collision between the target object and the chaser. If the two objects have not yet collided, then the angle between the current front direction and the target direction needs to be calculated. This is done by using the dot product. After the angle between the two vectors has been computed, the cross product is used to determine if the target direction is in the clockwise or counterclockwise direction from the front direction vector.

```
#region Step 4b.
    mHitTarget = PrimitivesTouches(mTarget);

    if (!mHitTarget)
    {
        #region Calculate angle
        Vector2 targetDir = mTarget.Position - Position;
        float distToTargetSq = targetDir.LengthSquared();

        targetDir /= (float) Math.Sqrt(distToTargetSq);
        float cosTheta = Vector2.Dot(FrontDirection, targetDir);
        float theta = (float)
        Math.Acos(cosTheta);
        #endregion
```

```
        #region Calculate rotation direction
        if (theta > float.Epsilon)
        {
            // Not quite aligned ...
            Vector3 fIn3D = new Vector3(FrontDirection, 0f);
            Vector3 tIn3D = new Vector3(targetDir, 0f);
            Vector3 sign = Vector3.Cross(tIn3D, fIn3D);

            RotateAngleInRadian += Math.Sign(sign.Z) * theta * mHomeInRate;
            VelocityDirection = FrontDirection;
        }
        #endregion
    }
    #endregion
```

5. Lastly, add the following accessors in order to allow modification or access to the instance variables of the ChaserGameObject from outside the class:

```
public float HomeInRate { get { return mHomeInRate; } set { mHomeInRate = value; } }
public bool HitTarget { get { return mHitTarget; } }
public bool HasValidTarget { get { return null != mTarget; } }
public TexturedPrimitive Target
{
    get { return mTarget; }
    set
    {
        mTarget = value;
        mHitTarget = false;
        if (null != mTarget)
        {
            FrontDirection = mTarget.Position - Position;
            VelocityDirection = FrontDirection;
        }
    }
}
```

With the ChaserGameObject now complete, all that is left is to update the GameState class to use its behavior.

Modifying the *GameState* class

1. Start by adding the following variables. One for the ChaserGameObject object itself, and two others for keeping track of the number of times the chaser has hit or miss.

```
ChaserGameObject mChaser;
// Simple game status
int mChaserHit, mChaserMissed;
```

2. In the constructor, initialize the chaser with the following values and set the hit and missed stats to zero:

```
public GameState()
{
    ...

    mChaser = new ChaserGameObject("Chaser", Vector2.Zero, new Vector2(6f, 1.7f), null);
    // Initially facing in the negative x direction
    mChaser.InitialFrontDirection = -Vector2.UnitX;
    mChaser.Speed = 0.2f;
    mChaserHit = 0;
    mChaserMissed = 0;
}
```

3. Now modify the update function with the following behavior. First, check whether there is a valid target. Then, if the target is valid, apply the chase by calling mChaser.ChaseTarget();. Increment the hit or missed variables based on whether the chaser succeeds or fails. Failure is defined by colliding with the window's edge. Also, remember to reinitialize a new chaser whenever the A button is pressed.

```
public void UpdateGame()
{
    ...

    #region 3. Check/launch the chaser!
    if (mChaser.HasValidTarget)
    {
        mChaser.ChaseTarget();

        if (mChaser.HitTarget)
        {
            mChaserHit++;
            mChaser.Target = null;
        }

        if (Camera.CollidedWithCameraWindow(mChaser) !=
                    Camera.CameraWindowCollisionStatus.InsideWindow)
        {
            mChaserMissed++;
            mChaser.Target = null;
        }
    }

    if (InputWrapper.Buttons.A == ButtonState.Pressed)
    {
        mChaser.Target = mRocket;
        mChaser.Position = mArrow.Position;
    }
    #endregion
}
```

4.   Lastly, modify the draw function to draw the chaser and print out the hit and missed stats:

```
public void DrawGame()
{
    mRocket.Draw();
    mArrow.Draw();
    if (mChaser.HasValidTarget)
        mChaser.Draw();
    // Print out text message to echo status
    FontSupport.PrintStatus("Chaser Hit=" + mChaserHit + " Missed=" + mChaserMissed, null);
}
```

Observations

Now that the project is completed, build and run the program. Test to see whether the chasing object behaves as expected. Additionally, if everything is functioning as expected, try modifying the mHomeInRate variable within the chaser to a higher or lower value. Adjusting this variable should make the chaser itself more or less accurate.

Summary

This chapter has provided basic information about working with rotating textures. You should now be familiar with positive and negative rotation directions, working with the rotation reference position (the pivot), and accomplishing specific rotation goals by manipulating the pivot position.

You also reviewed vectors in 2D space. A vector is defined by its direction and magnitude. Vectors are convenient for describing defined displacements (velocities). You reviewed some foundational vector operations, including normalization of a vector, and how to calculate dot and cross products. You worked with these operators to implement the front-facing direction capability and create simple autonomous behaviors such as pointing toward a specific object and chasing.

Lastly, and as in previous chapters, you have seen that by properly abstracting common behaviors into game objects, you can greatly reduce the complexity of your game implementation. In the next chapter, you'll continue investigating interesting game object behaviors in the form of more accurate collision determination and simple physics simulations.

Quick reference

To	Do this
Rotate a TexturedPrimitive object	Ensure the rotation is represented as radians (by calling the MathHelper.ToRadians() function to convert from degrees to radians) and set the rotation by calling TexturedPrimitive.RotateAngleInRadian.
Draw a vector from position P_a to P_b	Call ShowVector.DrawFromTo(P_a, P_b).
Draw a vector V at position P_a	Call ShowVector.DrawPointVector(P_a, V).
Visualize the rotation of a vector V by rotation theta	Once again, make sure theta is in radians, and then call ShowVector.RotateVectorByAngle(V, theta).

(continued)

To	Do this
Compute a vector from position P_a to P_b	Use `Vector2 v = P`$_b$` - P`$_a$`;`.
Compute the size of a given vector V	Use `float VectorSize = V.Length();`.
Normalize a given vector V_a	Use `V`$_a$`.Normalize();`.

Compute the angle between vectors V_a and V_b	Use the following:
	
	`V`$_a$`.Normalize();   // Remember vectors must be normalized`
	`V`$_b$`.Normalize();   // For dot product to return cosine of angle`
	`float angle = (float) Math.Acos(Vector2.dot(V`$_a$`, V`$_b$`))`

Compute the cross product between vectors V_a and V_b	Use the following:
	
	`Vector3 V`$_x$` = new Vector3(V`$_a$`, 0f); // Cross product is in 3D space`
	`Vector3 V`$_y$` = new Vector3(V`$_b$`, 0f);`
	`Vector3 crossResult = Vector3.Cross(V`$_x$`, V`$_y$`);`

Compute whether you should turn clockwise or counterclockwise to rotate from V_a to V_b	Use the following (continue from the preceding code): `if (Math.Sign(crossResult.Z) > 0)` ➜ Counterclockwise rotation `if (Math.Sign(crossResult.Z) < 0)` ➜ Clockwise rotation
Set the initial front-facing direction of a GameObject	Set `GameObject.InitialFrontDirection`.
Set or get the current front-facing direction of a GameObject	Set or get `GameObject.FrontDirection`.
Set or get the velocity of a GameObject	Set or get `GameObject.VelocityDirection` and `GameObject.Speed`.
Implement home-in chasing	Instantiate `ChaserGameObject` and set `ChaserGameObject.Target` to the appropriate target.

CHAPTER 5

■ ■ ■

Pixel-accurate collisions

After completing this chapter, you will be able to:

- Collide textured objects accurately

- Understand the efficiency concerns of pixel-accurate collision

- Program with pixel-accurate collision effectively and efficiently

- Create a new game object that follows a few simple rules of physics

As you saw in the previous chapter, by including a few mathematical concepts and some software architecture principles, you can create game objects with more advanced and interesting behaviors while maintaining the simplicity and structure of your game implementation. This chapter continues in that same vein by further enhancing game object behaviors for more specific solutions. You will see how to make collision detection between textured objects more precise and how to apply simple physics concepts to your game objects to create more natural and interesting behaviors.

You can think of both pixel-accurate collision and simple physics as attributes for your game objects. These attributes (and others that we'll cover) provide your game objects with the customized behaviors that define your game. However, adding many attributes or behaviors also has trade-offs. As you will see in this chapter, creating an object with every advanced attribute can be detrimental to your game because it can degrade performance; therefore, you should be conscious of the pros and cons of each behavior.

Pixel-accurate collision

Until now, you have handled all collisions by checking whether two primitives (or in your case, rectangles) overlap. While this is a good solution for many projects, you sometimes need more accurate collision detection. In this project, you will see how to achieve pixel-accurate collision detection between two separate textures. However, keep in mind that this is not an end-all solution. While the collision detection itself is more precise, the trade-off is that you sacrifice potential performance. This sacrifice occurs because as an image becomes larger and more complex, it also has more pixels that need to be checked for collisions (as opposed to the simple primitive calculations in you used in previous examples).

The Pixel-Accurate Collision project

This project demonstrates how to detect collision between a large and a small texture. The textures themselves vary widely in complexity. Both textures contain both transparent and nontransparent areas. A collision occurs only when the nontransparent pixels of one texture overlap those of the other texture. In this project, when a collision occurs, a soccer ball appears at the collision point. You can see an example of this project in Figure 5-1.

Figure 5-1. *Running the Pixel-Accurate Collision project*

The project's controls are as follows:

- **Right thumbstick (arrow-keys)** Moves the small texture
- **Left thumbstick (WSAD-keys)** Moves the large texture

The goals of the project are as follows:

- To demonstrate how to detect nontransparent pixel overlaps
- To understand the pros and cons of using pixel-accurate collision detection

The steps for creating the project are as follows:

1. Extend the textured primitive class to support pixel-accurate collision.
2. Modify the GameState class to use the new collision detection.

Before moving forward, let's first define the requirements needed for collision between two textured primitives. Foremost is that the texture itself needs to contain an area of transparency, in order for this type of collision detection to provide any increase in accuracy. Without transparency in the texture, you can and should use simple primitive-based collision detection. If one or both of the textures contain transparent areas, then you'll need to handle two cases of collision. The first case is to check whether the bounds of the two primitives collide. You can see this reflected in Figure 5-2. Notice how the bounds of the primitives overlap, yet none of the nontransparent colored pixels are touching.

Figure 5-2. *A large texture and small texture colliding with only their primitives*

The next case is when the colored pixels (nontransparent) of the texture overlap. Take a look at Figure 5-3. The flower texture and the target texture are clearly in contact with one another.

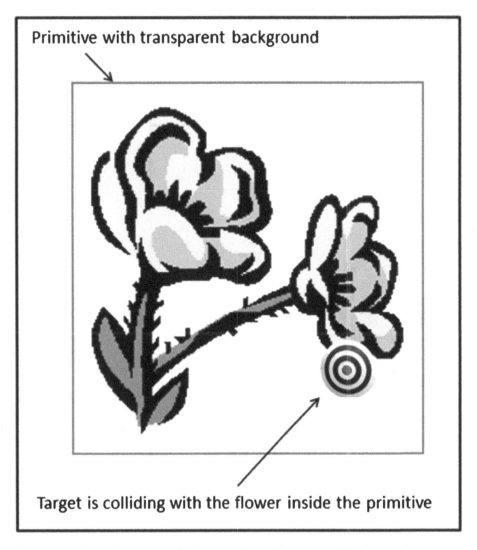

Figure 5-3. Pixel collision occurring between the small texture and the large texture

Now that the problem is clearly defined, here's the logic or pseudocode you need to achieve this type of behavior:

Given two images, Image-A and Image-B

If the bounds of the primitive of Image-A and Image-B collide then

for each Pixel-A in Image-A

pixelCameraSpace = pixel position in camera space

Transform pixelCameraSpace to Image-B space

Read Pixel-B from Image-B

If Pixel-A and Pixel-B are not both completely transparent then

A collision has occurred

The per-pixel transformation to Image-B space from pixelCameraSpace is required because collision checking must be carried out within the same coordinate space. Additionally, notice the runtime requirements for this behavior. Each pixel within Image-A must be checked, so the runtime is O(N), where N is equal to the number of pixels in Image-A, or Image-A's resolution. To mitigate some of this performance hit, you should use the smaller of the two images (the target in this case) as Image-A. However, at this point, you can probably see why the performance of pixel-accurate collision is of concern. Checking for these collisions during every update with many high-resolution textures on screen can quickly bog down performance.

Now let's take a look at how you can implement pixel-accurate collision for the TexturedPrimitive class.

Extending the *TexturedPrimitive* class

1. To begin, create a new file in the GraphicsSupport folder and name it
    TexturedPrimitivePixelCollide.cs. This class will extend the original
    TexturedPrimitive class. To do this, add the keyword partial to the
    existing TexturedPrimitive class and name the newly created class TexturedPrimitive
    so their names match within the code. You can see an example of this following:

    ```
    public partial class TexturedPrimitive
    {
        ...
    }
    ```

2. Create an array to hold the value of every pixel's color within the texture. Add a function
    to initialize the color array with the proper size and data of the image. In addition, add an
    accessor that returns the color of the specific pixel within the image:

    ```
    private Color[] mTextureColor = null;

    private void ReadColorData()
    {
        mTextureColor = new Color[mImage.Width * mImage.Height];
        mImage.GetData(mTextureColor);
    }

    private Color GetColor(int i, int j)
    {
        return mTextureColor[(j * mImage.Width) + i];
    }
    ```

3. You must call the ReadColorData() function from the InitPrimitive() function. Recall
    that the InitPrimitive() function was defined in the original TexturedPrimitive.cs file,
    and thus you must perform the modification in that file as well.

    ```
    protected void InitPrimitive(String imageName,
        Vector2 position, Vector2 size, String label = null)
    {
        ...

        ReadColorData();    // For pixel-level collision support
    }
    ```

4. Add a function for transforming indexes into the camera's coordinate space. You can see this demonstrated in the code that follows, where the index values of i and j are converted into a position in camera space and returned.

```
private Vector2 IndexToCameraPosition(int i, int j)
{
    float x = i * Width / (float)(mImage.Width - 1);
    float y = j * Height / (float)(mImage.Height - 1);

    return new Vector2(Position.X + x - (mSize.X * 0.5f),
                        Position.Y - y + (mSize.Y * 0.5f));
}
```

5. You also need a function to convert a position in camera space into the corresponding pixel index within the image. An important note for the caller of this function is that, because the camera space is often larger than the images, it is important to first check to see whether the returning position is within the bounds of the image. Take note of how the following code achieves this:

```
private Vector2 CameraPositionToIndex(Vector2 p)
{
    Vector2 delta = p - Position;
    float i = mImage.Width * (delta.X / Width);
    float j = mImage.Height * (delta.Y / Height);
    i += mImage.Width / 2;
    j = (mImage.Height / 2) - j;
    return new Vector2(i, j);
}
```

6. With the support functions completed, you can now build the primary function for pixel-accurate collision.

   a. Create a function called PixelTouches() that returns a bool and accepts a TexturedPrimitive and an out Vector2.

   ```
   public bool PixelTouches(TexturedPrimitive otherPrim, out Vector2 collidePoint)
   {
       ...
   }
   ```

■ **Note**   In C#, the keyword out is used as a parameter modifier to indicate that the argument is being passed by reference. This is similar to the argument modifier ref; however, an out argument does not need to be initialized beforehand.

---

   b. Within the function, first check whether the bounds of the two primitives overlap. If they don't, you can return false. However, when the bounds of the primitives overlap, then you need to check whether the texture pixels overlap. To do this, create while loops to iterate through every pixel within the image, transforming each to camera space. Then make sure the pixel in question is not transparent, and test whether it collides with the other image. You can see an example of this in the code that follows. Note the check that ensures the returned pixel index is within the bounds of the image.

```
bool touches = PrimitivesTouches(otherPrim);
collidePoint = Position;

if (touches)
{
    bool pixelTouch = false;

    int i=0;
    while ( (!pixelTouch) && (i<mImage.Width) )
    {
        int j = 0;
        while ( (!pixelTouch) && (j<mImage.Height) )
        {
            collidePoint = IndexToCameraPosition(i, j);
            Color myColor = GetColor(i, j);
            if (myColor.A > 0)
            {
                Vector2 otherIndex =
                    otherPrim.CameraPositionToIndex(collidePoint);
                int xMin = (int)otherIndex.X;
                int yMin = (int)otherIndex.Y;

                if ((xMin >= 0) && (xMin < otherPrim.mImage.Width) &&
                    (yMin >= 0) && (yMin < otherPrim.mImage.Height))
                {
                    pixelTouch = (otherPrim.GetColor(xMin, yMin).A > 0);
                }
            }
            j++;
        }
        i++;
    }
    touches = pixelTouch;
}
return touches;
```

7. Lastly, you need to update the PrimitivesTouches() function to perform a simple bounds check:

```
public bool PrimitivesTouches(TexturedPrimitive otherPrim)
{
    Vector2 myMin = MinBound;
    Vector2 myMax = MaxBound;
    Vector2 otherMin = otherPrim.MinBound;
    Vector2 otherMax = otherPrim.MaxBound;
    return
        ((myMin.X < otherMax.X) && (myMax.X > otherMin.X) &&
            (myMin.Y < otherMax.Y) && (myMax.Y > otherMin.Y));
}
```

Now you just need to modify the GameState class to support the new functionality of the TexturedPrimitive class.

Modifying the *GameState* class

1. Start by adding the following code to the UpdateGame() function, which is separated into two sections by the comments:

   a. The step 1a portion of the function handles primitive movement via the gamepad by mapping the primitive position to the thumbsticks.

   b. The step 1b portion of the function handles the collision detection. Note that, as prescribed earlier, the mSmallTarget.PixelTouches target is used instead of mLargeFlower.PixelTouches, because the small target contains fewer pixels than the large flower. This means that the runtime is $O(100 \times 100)$ instead of $O(2413 \times 2467)$.

```
public void UpdateGame()
{
    #region Step 1a.
    mLargeFlower.Position += InputWrapper.ThumbSticks.Left;
    mSmallTarget.Position += InputWrapper.ThumbSticks.Right;
    #endregion

    #region Step 1b.
    mPrimitiveCollide = mLargeFlower.PrimitivesTouches(mSmallTarget);
    if (mPrimitiveCollide)
    {
        Vector2 p;
        mPixelCollide = mSmallTarget.PixelTouches(mLargeFlower, out p);
        mCollidePosition.Position = p;
    }
    else
    {
        mPixelCollide = false;
    }
    #endregion
}
```

2. Lastly, draw the images via their draw functions and output the results using the FontSupport class:

```
public void DrawGame()
{
    mLargeFlower.Draw();
    mSmallTarget.Draw();

    FontSupport.PrintStatus("Primitive Collide=" +
        mPrimitiveCollide + "    PixelCollide=" + mPixelCollide, null);
    FontSupport.PrintStatusAt(mSmallTarget.Position,
        mSmallTarget.Position.ToString(), Color.Red);

    if (mPixelCollide)
        mCollidePosition.Draw();
}
```

General pixel collision

In the previous section, you saw the basic operations required to achieve pixel-accurate collision. However, as you may have noticed, the previous project applies only when the textures are aligned along their x,y-axes. This means that the function will overlook collisions between rotated images. For example, if the larger flower image was rotated the collision detection algorithm would not operate correctly.

This section explains how you can achieve pixel-accurate collision even when images are rotated. The fundamental concepts of this project are the same as in the previous project, but this version is a bit more complex, because you need some new calculations to ensure that the algorithm behaves correctly for rotated images.

The General Pixel Collision project

This project demonstrates how to detect a collision between two rotated images with pixel-level accuracy. In this project, a user can rotate each image by pressing the appropriate buttons, as detailed following. As before, when the two images collide, a soccer ball appears (as well as a test confirmation). You can see an example of this project running in Figure 5-4.

Figure 5-4. *Running the General Pixel Collision project*

The project's controls are as follows:

- **Right thumbstick (arrow-keys)** Moves the small texture
- **Left thumbstick (WSAD-keys)** Moves the large texture
- **Button A (K-key)** Rotates the large flower texture in the clockwise direction
- **Button B (L-key)** Rotates the large flower texture in the counterclockwise direction
- **Button X (J-key)** Rotates the small target texture in the clockwise direction
- **Button Y (I-key)** Rotates the small target texture in the counterclockwise direction

The goal of the project is as follows:

- To generate a pixel-accurate collision test for rotated images

The steps for creating the project are as follows:

1. Review vector decomposition.
2. Modify the `TexturedPrimitive` class's pixel-accurate collision to support rotation.
3. Modify the `GameState` class to support the new rotation behavior.

Vector review: Components and decomposition

Before continuing, here's a brief review so you can better understand vector components and how to decompose a given vector into its components. First, remember that two perpendicular directions can be used to represent the components of a vector. For example, Figure 5-5 contains two normalized vectors that can be used to represent vector $\vec{V} = (2, 3)$. The normalized vector $\hat{i} = (1, 0)$ represents the x-axis direction of vector $\vec{V}$ and the normalized vector $\hat{j} = (1, 0)$ represents the y-axis direction of vector $\vec{V}$.

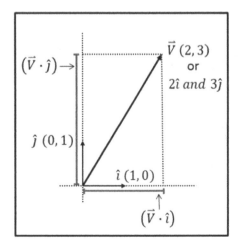

Figure 5-5. *The normalized component vectors of vector $\vec{V}$*

With that in mind, given the normalized perpendicular vectors $\hat{L}$ and $\hat{M}$ and any vector $\vec{V}$, the following formulas will always be true. You can see a representation of this principle in Figure 5-6.

$$\vec{V} = \hat{i}\left(\vec{V} \cdot \hat{i}\right) + \hat{j}\left(\vec{V} \cdot \hat{j}\right)$$

$$\vec{V} = \hat{L}\left(\vec{V} \cdot \hat{L}\right) + \hat{M}\left(\vec{V} \cdot \hat{M}\right)$$

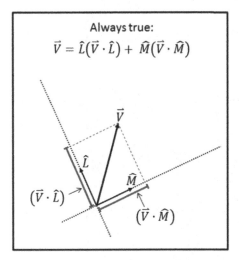

Figure 5-6. *Rotated component vectors*

A vector's components are relevant to this project because of the new challenge presented by rotating the image around its axes. Without rotation, the orthonormal set (normalized perpendicular set) simply consists of vectors along the default x-axis and y-axis. You handled this case in the previous project. You can see an example of this in Figure 5-7.

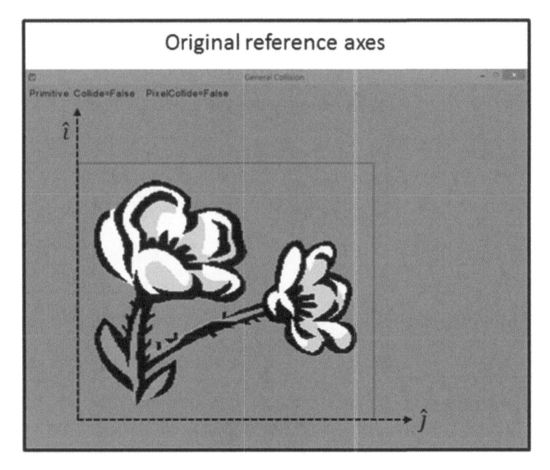

Figure 5-7. *An axis-aligned texture*

However, after the image has been rotated, the reference vector set no longer resides on the x,y-axes. Therefore, the collision computation must take into account the newly rotated axes $\hat{L}$ and $\hat{M}$, as shown in Figure 5-8.

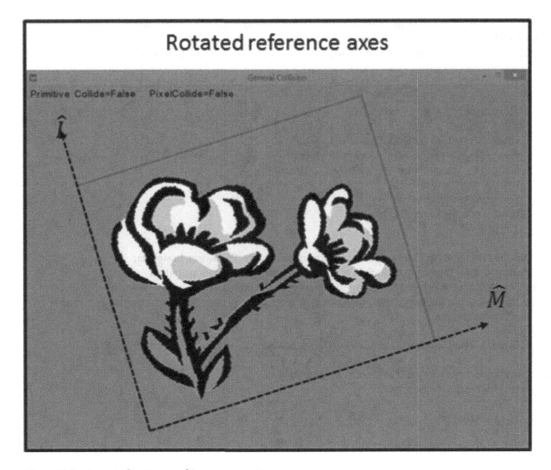

Figure 5-8. *A rotated texture and its component vectors*

In the following step, the modifications will take place in the TexturePrimitivePixelCollide.cs file, which defines part of the TexturedPrimitive class.

Modifying the *TexturedPrimitive* class

1. Start by adjusting the IndexToCameraPosition() function, taking into account the new rotated axes to compute the correct position in camera space. You do this by modifying the return values of vector *r* with the incoming vectors xDir and yDir. In this case, xDir and yDir are the $\hat{L}$ and $\hat{M}$ component vectors. You can see this in the following code:

```
private Vector2 IndexToCameraPosition(int i, int j, Vector2 xDir, Vector2 yDir)
{
    float x = i * Width / (float)(mImage.Width - 1);
    float y = j * Height / (float)(mImage.Height - 1);

    Vector2 r = Position + (x - (mSize.X * 0.5f)) * xDir - (y - (mSize.Y * 0.5f)) * yDir;

    return r;
}
```

2. Similarly, adjust the camera space-to-pixel space function by using the rotated axes. You do this by using the incoming vectors xDir and yDir to calculate the x and y offsets and then applying them to the images' width and height, as shown in the following code:

```
private Vector2 CameraPositionToIndex(Vector2 p, Vector2 xDir, Vector2 yDir)
{
    Vector2 delta = p - Position;
    float xOffset = Vector2.Dot(delta, xDir);
    float yOffset = Vector2.Dot(delta, yDir);
    float i = mImage.Width * (xOffset / Width);
    float j = mImage.Height * (yOffset / Height);
    i += mImage.Width / 2;
    j = (mImage.Height / 2) - j;
    return new Vector2(i, j);
}
```

3. Lastly, the PixelTouches() function needs some modification. Following, in step 3a, because you know the angle of rotation, and you know the initial orthonormal set (the x and y unit vectors), you can compute the rotated orthonormal set ($\hat{L}$ / $\hat{M}$). Then, in step 3b, you can use the newly computed orthonormal set to compute the offset or camera space transformations.

```
public bool PixelTouches(TexturedPrimitive otherPrim, out Vector2 collidePoint)
{
    bool touches = PrimitivesTouches(otherPrim);
    collidePoint = Position;

    if (touches)
    {
        bool pixelTouch = false;

        #region Step 3a.
        Vector2 myXDir = ShowVector.RotateVectorByAngle(Vector2.UnitX,
    RotateAngleInRadian);
        Vector2 myYDir = ShowVector.RotateVectorByAngle(Vector2.UnitY,
    RotateAngleInRadian);
        Vector2 otherXDir = ShowVector.RotateVectorByAngle(
            Vector2.UnitX, otherPrim.RotateAngleInRadian);
        Vector2 otherYDir = ShowVector.RotateVectorByAngle(
            Vector2.UnitY, otherPrim.RotateAngleInRadian);
        #endregion

        #region Step 3b.
        int i=0;
        while ( (!pixelTouch) && (i<mImage.Width) )
        {
            int j = 0;
            while ( (!pixelTouch) && (j<mImage.Height) )
            {
                collidePoint =
                    IndexToCameraPosition(i, j, myXDir, myYDir);
```

```
                    Color myColor = GetColor(i, j);
                    if (myColor.A > 0)
                    {
                        Vector2 otherIndex =
                            otherPrim.CameraPositionToIndex(
                                collidePoint,
                                otherXDir,
                                otherYDir);
                        int xMin = (int)otherIndex.X;
                        int yMin = (int)otherIndex.Y;
                        if ((xMin >= 0) && (xMin < otherPrim.mImage.Width) &&
                            (yMin >= 0) && (yMin < otherPrim.mImage.Height))
                        {
                            pixelTouch = (otherPrim.GetColor(xMin, yMin).A > 0);
                        }
                    }
                    j++;
                }
                i++;
            }
            #endregion
            touches = pixelTouch;
        }
        return touches;
    }
```

Modifying the *GameState* class

Lastly, modify the update function to support rotating both the small and large textures using the gamepad's A, B, X, and Y buttons.

```
public void UpdateGame()
{
    #region Step 1a. Select to work with PA or PB
    ...

    if (InputWrapper.Buttons.A == ButtonState.Pressed)
        mLargeFlower.RotateAngleInRadian += MathHelper.ToRadians(1f);
    if (InputWrapper.Buttons.B == ButtonState.Pressed)
        mLargeFlower.RotateAngleInRadian -= MathHelper.ToRadians(1f);
    if (InputWrapper.Buttons.X == ButtonState.Pressed)
        mSmallTarget.RotateAngleInRadian += MathHelper.ToRadians(1f);
    if (InputWrapper.Buttons.Y == ButtonState.Pressed)
        mSmallTarget.RotateAngleInRadian -= MathHelper.ToRadians(1f);
    #endregion

    ...
}
```

Simple physics

Now that you've learned a lot of the building blocks for general game object interaction, such as collision, you can now move on to more advanced game object behavior, including concepts such as acceleration, gravity (free fall), elasticity, and friction. Basic behaviors such as these are often considered pieces of a larger concept known as *physics*. While these behaviors barely scratch the surface of what can physics engines can include, they provide a good starting point for understanding how to approximate these types of behaviors in a game. It is important to note that the behaviors being implemented are *not* attempts at mimicking the real world. Rather, they only attempt to enhance gameplay by approximating behaviors that players are familiar with. Creating a realistic physics engine would require a book unto itself.

The Simple Physics project

This project demonstrates how to simulate a ball falling under gravitational pull, or free fall, while also taking into account both the elasticity and friction associated with the ball when it collides with an object. You can see an example of this project running in Figure 5-9.

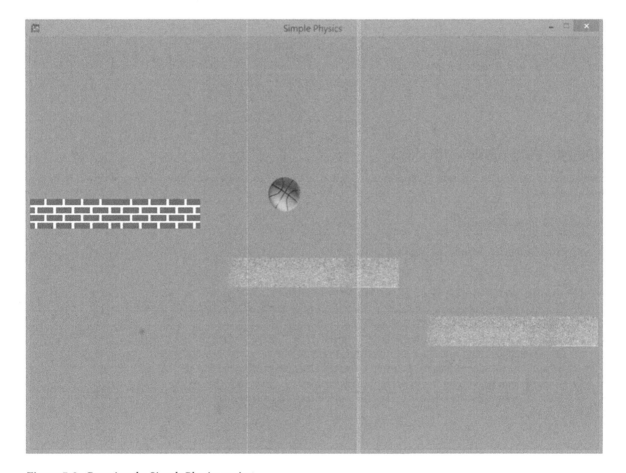

Figure 5-9. *Running the Simple Physics project*

The project's controls are as follows:

- **Hold Button A (K-key)** Respawns the ball
- **Release Button A (K-key)** Releases the ball

The goals of the project are as follows:

- To simulate the following simple physical behaviors:
- Rotational velocity
- Gravitational free fall
- Elasticity
- Friction

The steps for creating the project are as follows:

1. Gain an overview of the simple physics being implemented.

2. Review the math required to calculate the arc of a circle.

3. Add a gravity constant variable.

4. Create a `RotateObject` class for the ball.

5. Create a `Platform` class to interact with the ball object.

6. Modify the `GameState` class to include the support for the new objects.

Simple physics overview

Here's a quick overview of the basic physics concepts you'll implement in this project:

- **Velocity:** This changes the position on every update.
- **Acceleration:** This changes the velocity on each update.
- **Free fall (gravity):** This is downward acceleration for which each update decreases the y component of a velocity.
- **Friction:** This causes the slowdown of objects on horizontal surfaces. The amount that it slows is approximated by a percentage of the object's current x velocity.
- **Elasticity:** This determines how bouncy an object is after collision. The amount an object bounces is approximated by a percentage of the object's current y velocity.

Arc length review

To start, let's do a quick review of what is needed to calculate the length along part of the circumference, or arc, of a circle. More specifically, take a look at Figure 5-10. The red line, which lies upon the outer edge of the circle, is the arc of interest.

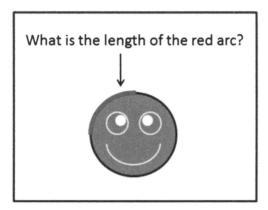

Figure 5-10. *A circle with a portion of its circumference highlighted*

Recall that the circumference of a circle is equal to $2\pi r$: the radius, r, of the circle, multiplied by the angle subscribed by the circle, 2π. In general, an arc length s is equal to r multiplied by the angular displacement, θ. You can see this in Figure 5-11.

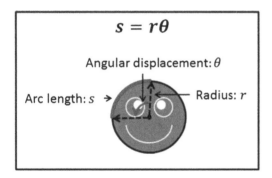

Figure 5-11. *The data needed to calculate arc on the circumference*

Now, to simulate a rolling ball, you need to rotate the texture while the ball moves. For example, if a circle were to roll across a flat surface, then the speed at which the circle is moving is defined by the object's x velocity component, which is equal to the corresponding rotational displacement, or arc length of the circle. You can see this in Figure 5-12.

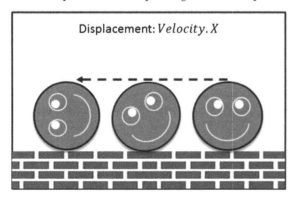

Figure 5-12. *The displacement of a circle rolling across a horizontal surface*

Now, with your knowledge of the following equation:

$$\ell = r\theta = Velocity.X$$

you can derive the following:

$$\frac{\ell}{r} = \frac{r\theta}{r} = \frac{Velocity.X}{r}$$

$$\omega = \frac{\ell}{r} = \frac{Velocity.X}{r}$$

Adding the gravity variable

Before you start adding new behavior, you first need to add the constant gravity variable into the GameState class. Make sure the variable is defined as static and public so that it can be accessed throughout the project.

```
public class GameState
{
    // Global constant for simple world physical properties
    static public float sGravity = 0.01f;

    ....
}
```

Creating the *RotateObject* class

1. Create a new class called RotateObject that inherits from the GameObject class, and include an accessor for the radius of the object.

   ```
   public class RotateObject : GameObject
   {
       public RotateObject(String image, Vector2 center, float radius)
               : base(image, center, new Vector2(radius*2f, radius*2f))
       {
       }
       public float Radius {
               get { return mSize.X / 2f; }
               set { mSize.X = 2f * value; mSize.Y = mSize.X; }
       }

       ...
   }
   ```

2. Override the `Update()` function in the new `RotateObject` class so the object's behavior can be modified. Remember to call the base update function so that the velocity is applied. Here's what happens:

   a. The velocity is modified by the gravity constant at each update to simulate a free-falling state.

   b. Then, the object is rotated in accordance with its speed in the x direction, via the implementation of the equation $\theta = \dfrac{Velocity.X}{r}$ derived earlier.

   c. Lastly, the rotation direction, clockwise or counterclockwise, is applied:

```
override public void Update()
{
    // Moves object by velocity
    base.Update();

    #region Step 2a.
    Vector2 v = Velocity;
    v.Y -= GameState.sGravity;
    Velocity = v;
    #endregion

    #region Step 2b.
    // Now rotate the object according to the speed in the x direction
    float angularDisplace = (v.X / Radius);
    #endregion

    #region Step 2c.
    // This assumes object is rolling "on top of" surfaces
    if (v.X > 0)
        mRotateAngle += angularDisplace;
    else
        mRotateAngle -= angularDisplace;
    #endregion
}
```

Now that you have a rotating object or ball, you can create a platform for it to bounce on.

Creating the *Platform* class

1. Create a new class called `Platform` that inherits from the `TexturedPrimitive` class. Have its constructor pass its parameters to the base class. Additionally, define variables and accessors for both friction and elasticity. You can see this in the code that follows:

```
public class Platform : TexturedPrimitive
{
    // Slows down by 2% at each update
    private float mFriction = 0.98f;
    // Retains 70% of velocity at each bounce
    private float mElasticity = 0.7f;
    public Platform(String image, Vector2 center, Vector2 size)
```

```
                    : base(image, center, size)
        {
        }

        public float Friction { get { return mFriction; } set { mFriction = value; } }
        public float Elasticity {  get { return mElasticity; } set { mElasticity = value; } }

        ...
    }
```

2. Now add a BounceObject() function. This function causes an object that collides with the platform to bounce, and applies friction to the object. Make the function virtual so that you can implement subclasses with varying amounts of friction and/or bounce effect. First, check to see if there is any collision, and if collision occurs, then do the following:

    a. Update the object's velocity by applying the elasticity and friction variables. Remember that friction affects the x velocity and elasticity affects the y velocity.

    b. Make sure the object does not penetrate and get stuck in the platform. Do this by checking whether the object has penetrated the platform, and if it has, push the object out.

```
virtual public void BounceObject(GameObject obj)
{
    Vector2 collidePoint;
    if (obj.PixelTouches(this, out collidePoint))
    {
        #region Step 2a.
        // Limitation: Only collide from top/bottom, not from the sides
        Vector2 v = obj.Velocity;
        v.Y *= -1 * mElasticity;
        v.X *= mFriction;
        obj.Velocity = v;
        #endregion

        #region Step 2b.
        // Make sure object is not "stuck" inside the platform
        Vector2 p = obj.Position;
        if (p.Y > Position.Y)
            p.Y = Position.Y + Size.Y * 0.5f + obj.Size.Y * 0.5f;
        else
            p.Y = Position.Y - Size.Y * 0.5f - obj.Size.Y * 0.5f;
        obj.Position = p;
        #endregion
    }
}
```

Modifying the *GameState* class

1. Return to the GameState class and add the following variables for the rotation object, platform, and position:

```
public class GameState
{
    ...

    private Vector2 kInitBallPosition = new Vector2(3f, 48f);
    // Objects in the world
    Platform mSlowStone, mBrick, mStone;
    RotateObject mBasket;

    ...
}
```

2. Next, initialize the rotation object (ball) and the three platforms within the constructor. Provide the three platforms with different textures, friction, and elasticity. You can see the default values used in the code that follows:

```
public GameState()
{
    // Create the platforms
    mBrick = new Platform("BrickPlatform", new Vector2(15, 40), new Vector2(30f, 5f));
    // How rapidly object slows down: Retains most speed
    mBrick.Friction = 0.999f;
    // How bouncy is this platform: 90%
    mBrick.Elasticity = 0.85f;

    mStone = new Platform("StonePlatform", new Vector2(50, 30), new Vector2(30, 5f));
    // How rapidly object slows down: Retains some speed
    mStone.Friction = 0.99f;
    // How bouncy is this platform: Slightly more than half: 60%
    mStone.Elasticity = 0.5f;

    mSlowStone = new Platform("StonePlatform", new Vector2(85, 20), new Vector2(30, 5));
    // How rapidly object slows down: Very rapidly
    mSlowStone.Friction = 0.9f;
    // How bouncy is this platform: Not very
    mSlowStone.Elasticity = 0.2f;

    // Both outside of the camera, so neither will be drawn
    mBasket = new RotateObject("BasketBall", new Vector2(-1, -1), 3f);
}
```

3. When the user presses the A button, you want the update function to create a ball at its initial position with a random velocity. If the ball is within the camera window, apply its update and bounce check for each platform. Here's the code:

```
public void UpdateGame()
{
    if (InputWrapper.Buttons.A == ButtonState.Pressed)
    {
        mBasket.Position = kInitBallPosition;
        Vector2 v = new Vector2((float)(0.3f + (Game1.sRan.NextDouble()) * 0.1f), 0f);
        mBasket.Velocity = v;
    }

    if (mBasket.ObjectVisibleInCameraWindow())
    {
        mBasket.Update();
        mSlowStone.BounceObject(mBasket);
        mStone.BounceObject(mBasket);
        mBrick.BounceObject(mBasket);
    }
}
```

4. Finally, draw the platforms within the DrawGame() function. Only draw the ball if it is within the camera window.

```
public void DrawGame()
{
    mSlowStone.Draw();
    mStone.Draw();
    mBrick.Draw();

  if (mBasket.ObjectVisibleInCameraWindow())
        mBasket.Draw();
}
```

Summary

This chapter showed you how to provide your game objects with more sophisticated behavior than in earlier chapters—specifically, more accurate collision detection, and basic physics to create more interesting interactions between objects. You saw some negatives and positives associated with these behaviors, so you can assess whether future game objects you create should implement these behaviors.

While implementing pixel-accurate collision, you first tackled the basic case of working with aligned textures. After that implementation, you went back and added support for collision detection between rotated textures. Tackling the easiest case first lets you test and observe the results, and helps define what you might need for the more advanced problems (rotation in this case).

The implementation of simple physics behaviors shown in this chapter prioritized functionality over realism. This type of behavior lets you create interesting behaviors that draw inspiration from the real world with relative ease. In the next chapter, you will add more specialized and unique behaviors to your game objects by creating more advanced game object states.

Quick reference

To	Do this
Detect if the boundary of two primitives overlap	Call the `PrimitivesTouches()` function.
Detect if any of the pixels of two `TexturedPrimitive` objects overlap	Call the `PixelTouches()` function. Remember, for efficiency concerns, to always call this function according to the resolution of the involved primitives: `smallTexture.PixelTrouches(largeTexture)`.
Simulate rotation	Rotate the object according to its traveling speed by $\theta = \dfrac{Speed}{r}$. For example, to simulate rotation in the horizontal direction, at each update, rotate the object by $\theta = \dfrac{Velocity.X}{r}$. Rightward motion increases the rotation angle, while leftward motion decreases the rotation angle.
Approximate gravitational free fall	Decrease the y component of a velocity by some constant at each update.
Approximate elasticity	Decrease the y component of a velocity when two objects collide.
Approximate friction	Decrease the x component of a velocity when two objects collide.

CHAPTER 6

■ ■ ■

Game object states and Semiautonomous Behaviors

After completing this chapter, you will be able to:

- Understand the uses of a finite state machine and how to implement one
- Create your own dynamic behaviors via a state machine
- Understand how to work with large groups of game objects within your game

So far, the behaviors you have added to game objects have been fairly straightforward, consisting mostly of a single state. Therefore, the game objects' behaviors have not been malleable to conditions that would modify their initial behaviors. In this chapter, we will show you how to create more complex and dynamic behaviors for your game objects. These include common game behaviors that react autonomously to outside conditions or triggers, such as player input or timers. To implement these malleable behaviors, each game object will need to implement its own finite state machine.

Review of finite state machines

A finite state machine can be thought of as a model or functionality added to an object—or in your case, a game object. By definition, a finite state machine has a limited or finite number of states and can exist in only one state at a time. The transition between states is dependent upon the behavior desired for the state machine and is triggered by some condition.

For example, take a look at the generalized state machine in Figure 6-1. This finite state machine can be reduced to three primary states and their transitions. If you look closely at the figure, you can see that each state is outlined and exists as a separate entity. A condition generally must be met to cause a transition between states. This transition condition is often (but does not necessarily need to be) unique for each state within the finite state machine. It is also important to notice that this state machine contains several illegal transitions. For example, there's no way to transition from state 2 back to state 1 in this example. If a state is not connected to the state machine via at least one transition condition, then it does not exist within the state machine and should be removed.

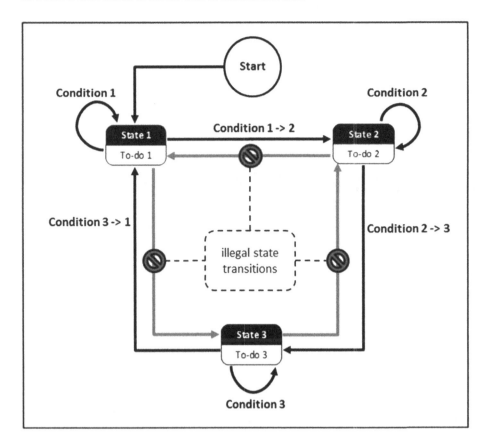

Figure 6-1. *A basic finite state machine diagram with three states*

Creating a spinning arrow

The first finite state machine you will implement centers around a simple spinning arrow. The arrow in this project demonstrates three distinct states, as well as the conditions required to transition from one state to the next. For the purposes of this project, each state can transition to only one other state. This means that a condition or trigger is associated with each of the three states. The transition between states can occur if and only if the condition has been met.

The Spinning Arrow project

This project lets you control a hero by moving it around the screen. The project contains an arrow that spins until the hero enters the arrow's detection range; when that occurs, the arrow points toward the hero. The project also displays the arrow's current state in the top-left corner of the window. You can see an example of this project running in Figure 6-2.

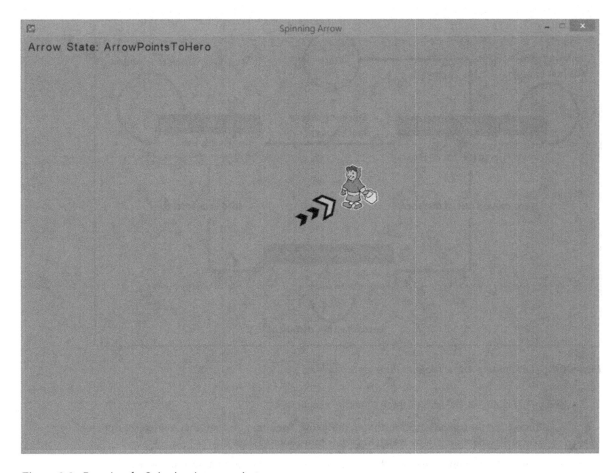

Figure 6-2. *Running the Spinning Arrow project*

The arrow's finite state machine

The only new concept introduced in this project from the previous chapter's projects is the arrow's finite state machine; because of this, let's take a closer look at the specifics involved. The arrow itself starts by spinning up to the maximum speed. It continues to spin at its maximum speed until it detects that the hero character is within range. When the hero character is detected, the arrow will stop spinning and point in the direction of the hero. After the hero leaves the arrow's detection range, the arrow begins spinning again, thereby returning to its starting state. You can see this reflected in Figure 6-3. Notice that once the arrow's state machine has started, it cannot break away from its state loop and must be within one of its three states.

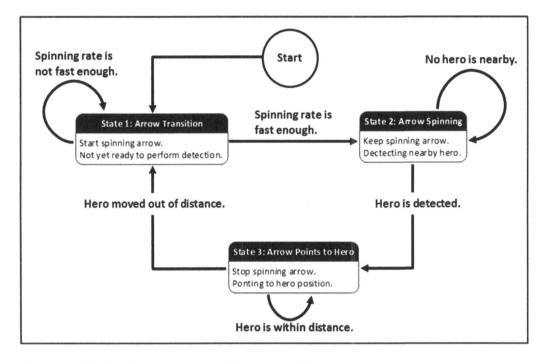

Figure 6-3. The Spinning Arrow project's finite state machine

As shown in Figure 6-3, the arrow's three states are as follows:

- **State 1: Arrow transition** Starts to spin the arrow. The spin rate continues to increase until it reaches its maximum, after which the arrow transitions to state 2.

- **State 2: Arrow spinning** Keeps the arrow spinning at its maximum rate until the hero is detected, at which point it then transitions to state 3.

- **State 3: Arrow points to hero** Stops the arrow from spinning and points it in the direction of the hero. When the hero has moved out of detection range, it transitions back to state 1.

This project has one control, as follows:

- **Left thumbstick (WSAD-keys)** Moves the hero

The goals of the project are as follows:

- To implement a simple finite state machine

- To dynamically reload textures

The steps for creating the project are as follows:

1. Create a SpinningArrow class.

2. Create a PlayerControlHero class.

3. Modify the GameState class.

Add the following resources, which can be found in the Chapter06\SourceCode\Resources folder, into your content project before you begin:

- KidLeft.png

- KidRight.png

- RightArrow.png

The SpinningArrow class will contain all the behavior and functionality of the arrow. This includes the three possible states and the current state of the arrow, as well as the spinning behavior.

Creating the *SpinningArrow* class

1. Create a new class called SpinningArrow that inherits from the GameObject class:

```
public class SpinningArrow : GameObject
{
    ...
}
```

2. Define an enum type that contains each possible state of the arrow. Because you know the three states already, this is straightforward.

```
public enum SpinningArrowState
{
    ArrowTransition,
    ArrowSpinning,
    ArrowPointsToHero
};
```

3. Add the following variables for keeping track of the arrow's current state and its current spin rate. Additionally, add the constants needed to define the arrow's trigger distance from the hero, its maximum spin rate, and its rate of spin change:

```
private SpinningArrowState mArrowState = SpinningArrowState.ArrowTransition;
private float mSpinRate = 0f;

#region Constants
private const float kHeroTriggerDistance = 15f;
private const float kMaxSpinRate = (float) Math.PI / 10f;
private const float kDeltaSpin = kMaxSpinRate / 200f;
#endregion
```

4. Next, add the constructor to initialize the arrow by using the GameObject base class and the arrow's initial front direction. In addition, add a simple public accessor that returns the arrow's current state:

```
public SpinningArrow(Vector2 position) :
    base("RightArrow", position, new Vector2(10, 4))
{
    InitialFrontDirection = Vector2.UnitX;
}
```

```
public SpinningArrowState ArrowState
{
    get { return mArrowState; }
}
```

■ **Note**   Vector2.UnitX is a default provided for a unit vector of (1, 0).

---

5.   Create the function that spins the arrow. You can do this easily by increasing the arrow's rotation angle incrementally during each update. Make sure to check whether the angle is greater than 2π. If so, subtract 2π from the arrow's rotation angle. Doing this imposes a limit so the angle stays between zero and 2π.

```
private void SpinTheArrow()
{
    RotateAngleInRadian += mSpinRate;
    if (RotateAngleInRadian > (2 * Math.PI))
        RotateAngleInRadian -= (float)(2 * Math.PI);
}
```

6.   Create a main update function that is responsible for calling the proper update method depending upon the arrow's current state. A switch statement works perfectly for this. In the code that follows are three update functions, each called for one of the three states. To create these specific update functions, follow the subsequent steps:

```
public void UpdateSpinningArrow(TexturedPrimitive hero)
{
    switch (mArrowState)
    {
        case SpinningArrowState.ArrowTransition:
            UpdateTransitionState();
            break;
        case SpinningArrowState.ArrowSpinning:
            UpdateSpinningState(hero);
            break;
        case SpinningArrowState.ArrowPointsToHero:
            UpdatePointToHero(hero.Position - Position);
            break;
    }
}
```

a.   Create the update function for the arrow-transition state. In this function, apply the arrow's spin and then test whether the arrow has reached its maximum spin rate. If so, change the current state to ArrowSpinning; if not, increase the current spin rate.

```
private void UpdateTransitionState()
{
    SpinTheArrow();

    if (mSpinRate < kMaxSpinRate)
        mSpinRate += kDeltaSpin;
```

```
        else
            // Transition to Spin state
            mArrowState = SpinningArrowState.ArrowSpinning;
    }
```

b. Next, create the update function for the spinning state. In this update, apply the
    arrow's spin and then check whether the hero's position has entered the arrow's
    detection range. If so, reset the current spin rate and change the current state to
    ArrowPointsToHero. Note that this condition triggers a call to the update function for
    the ArrowPointsToHero state. This call provides an immediate reaction.

```
private void UpdateSpinningState(TexturedPrimitive hero)
{
    SpinTheArrow();

    Vector2 toHero = hero.Position - Position;
    if (toHero.Length() < kHeroTriggerDistance)
    {
        mSpinRate = 0f;
        mArrowState = SpinningArrowState.ArrowPointsToHero;
        UpdatePointToHero(toHero);
    }
}
```

c. You need one last update function for the ArrowPointsToHero state. In this function,
    you continue pointing the arrow toward the hero as long as the hero's position is
    within kHeroTriggerDistance. If the hero moves out of the detection range, you
    change the state back to ArrowTransition.

```
private void UpdatePointToHero(Vector2 toHero)
{
    float dist = toHero.Length();
    if (dist < kHeroTriggerDistance)
    {
        FrontDirection = toHero;
    }
    else
        mArrowState = SpinningArrowState.ArrowTransition;
}
```

Now you can create the class used to control the hero. The PlayerControlHero class will provide the simple
behavior of moving the hero when the left thumbstick is used. Additionally, the hero's image is swapped depending
on which direction it moves.

Creating the *PlayerControlHero* class

1. Create a new class named PlayerControlHero that inherits from the GameObject class:

```
public class PlayerControlHero : GameObject
{
    ...
}
```

2. Create a constructor to initialize the hero's image, position, and size using the `GameObject` base class:

```
public PlayerControlHero(Vector2 position) :
        base("KidLeft", position, new Vector2(7f, 8f))
{
    ...
}
```

3. Lastly, add an update function. In this function, use the gamepad's left thumbstick to modify the hero's current position. Additionally, you can use this function to change the direction that the hero is facing by detecting whether the thumbstick's x-axis is positive or negative. This is possible because MonoGame caches the textures the first time they are loaded.

```
public void UpdateHero()
{
    Vector2 delta = InputWrapper.ThumbSticks.Left;
    Position += delta;

    if (delta.X > 0)
        mImage = Game1.sContent.Load<Texture2D>("KidRight");
    else
        mImage = Game1.sContent.Load<Texture2D>("KidLeft");
}
```

All that remains is to use the new classes in the `GameState` class.

Modifying the *GameState* class

1. Start by creating variables for the arrow and the hero and initializing them within the constructor with the values shown in the following code:

```
PlayerControlHero mHero;
SpinningArrow mArrow;

public GameState()
{
    mArrow = new SpinningArrow(new Vector2(50, 40));
    mHero = new PlayerControlHero(new Vector2(5, 5));
}
```

2. Now modify the update function so it calls the corresponding updates for the hero and the arrow:

```
public void UpdateGame()
{
    mHero.UpdateHero();
    mArrow.UpdateSpinningArrow(mHero);
}
```

3. Lastly, as usual, use the draw function to draw your game objects. Remember to print the project's current status via the FontSupport class.

```
public void DrawGame()
{
    mHero.Draw();
    mArrow.Draw();
    FontSupport.PrintStatus("Arrow State: " + mArrow.ArrowState.ToString(), null);
}
```

Adding many spinning arrows

With your finite state machine for the SpinningArrow project complete, you will now increase the number of arrows within the project from 1 to 20. The state functionality for each arrow remains the same; however, you will add visual feedback for each of the arrow's states. By increasing the number of arrows in the project, you increase the project's complexity rather drastically. Adding many arrows should also serve to reinforce the benefits of taking an object-oriented approach when creating your game objects.

The Many Spinning Arrows project

As before, this project lets a user control a hero by moving it around the screen. The project contains a set of arrows that spin until the hero has entered an arrow's detection range, at which time the arrows stop and point toward the hero. The project also reflects the arrow states by changing their color when the state changes. The colors for each state are as follows: gray for state 1 (arrow transition), green for state 2 (arrow spinning), and red for state 3 (arrow points to hero). In addition, each arrow has smaller black arrows equal to its current state number. You can see an example of this project running in Figure 6-4.

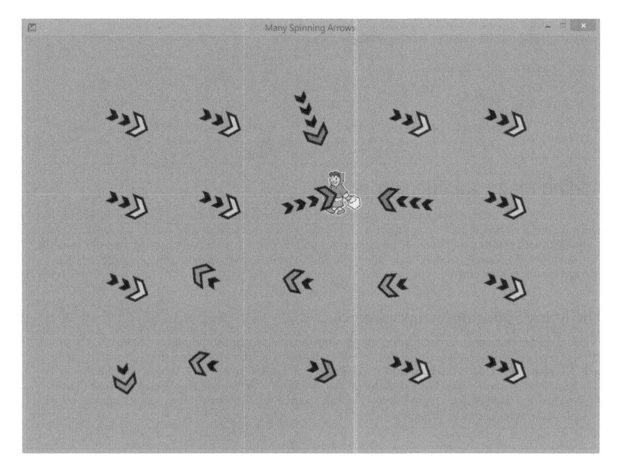

Figure 6-4. *Running the Many Spinning Arrows project*

The project has one control, as follows:

- **Left thumbstick (WSAD-keys)** Moves the hero

The goals of the project are as follows:

- To increase complexity by increasing the number of game objects
- To load textures at run time

The steps for creating the project are as follows:

1. Modify the SpinningArrow class to reflect the changes in its state.
2. Create a SpinningArrowSet class in order to properly handle the arrows.
3. Modify the GameState class to use the new functionality.

Add the following resources, which can be found in the Chapter06\SourceCode\Resources folder, into your content project before you begin:

- TransientArrow.png

- PointingArrow.png

You first need to add the visual indicators for state changes by swapping to the appropriate image when the changes occur. You can achieve this by modifying the SpinningArrow class.

Modifying the *SpinningArrow* class

1. If you recall the state diagram from the previous section, you will remember that the arrow starts within the ArrowTransition state. Support this by replacing the image in the constructor with TransientArrow.png:

```
public SpinningArrow(Vector2 position) :
        base("TransientArrow", position, new Vector2(10, 4))
{
    // Arrow initially facing postive x direction
    InitialFrontDirection = Vector2.UnitX;
}
```

2. The ArrowSpinning state is transitioned to from the ArrowTransition state. Therefore, modify the update of ArrowTransition to use the RightArrow.png image when changing states, as shown here:

```
private void UpdateTransitionState()
{
    ...

    // Transition to Spin state
    mArrowState = SpinningArrowState.ArrowSpinning;
    mImage = Game1.sContent.Load<Texture2D>("RightArrow");

    ...
}
```

3. The next state is ArrowPointsToHero, which is transitioned to from the ArrowSpinning state. Therefore, modify the ArrowSpinning update to use the PointingArrow.png image when changing states.

```
private void UpdateSpinningState(TexturedPrimitive hero)
{
    ...

    // Transition to ArrowPointsToHero state
    mSpinRate = 0f;
    mArrowState = SpinningArrowState.ArrowPointsToHero;
    mImage = Game1.sContent.Load<Texture2D>("PointingArrow");

    ...
}
```

4. Finally, because the state machine is a loop, the next state is `ArrowTransition`, which is transitioned to from the `ArrowPointsToHero` state. Therefore, modify the `ArrowPointsToHero` update to use the `TransientArrow.png` image when changing states.

```
private void UpdatePointToHero(Vector2 toHero)
{
    ...

        // Go back to TransitionState for spinning up the arrow
        mArrowState = SpinningArrowState.ArrowTransition;
        mImage = Game1.sContent.Load<Texture2D>("TransientArrow");

    ...
}
```

Now it is time to create the arrows. Rather than creating each arrow separately or creating an array, a better approach is to create a separate class for the array of arrows and instantiate it once within the `GameState` class. You can think of the `SpinningArrowSet` class as you would a deck of cards. To create a deck of cards, you would create a card class and a deck class that holds an array or set of 52 cards.

Creating the *SpinningArrowSet* class

1. Create a new class called `SpinningArrowSet`. Add a constant variable for the number of rows and columns of arrows, as well as a list to hold the entire arrow set:

```
public class SpinningArrowSet
{
    private const int kNumRows = 4;
    private const int kNumColumns = 5;
    private List<SpinningArrow> mTheSet = new List<SpinningArrow>();

    ...
}
```

2. Next, add the constructor to initialize the arrows on the screen with a consistent spacing between them. To do this, create a nested loop that creates the arrows, incrementing the x and y positions and adding each arrow to the set for each iteration.

```
public SpinningArrowSet()
{
    Vector2 min = Camera.CameraWindowLowerLeftPosition;
    Vector2 max = Camera.CameraWindowUpperRightPosition;
    Vector2 size = max - min;
    float deltaX = size.X / (float)(kNumColumns + 1);
    float deltaY = size.Y / (float)(kNumRows + 1);

    for (int r = 0; r < kNumRows; r++)
    {
        min.Y += deltaY;
        float useDeltaX = deltaX;
```

```
        for (int c = 0; c < kNumColumns; c++)
        {
            Vector2 pos = new Vector2(min.X + useDeltaX, min.Y);
            SpinningArrow arrow = new SpinningArrow(pos);
            mTheSet.Add(arrow);
            useDeltaX += deltaX;
        }
    }
}
```

3. Lastly, you need to create the update and draw functions for the set of arrows. You can do this easily by using a simple foreach loop to call the corresponding update function and draw function for the set. Remember to include the hero parameter for the update function.

```
public void UpdateSpinningSet(TexturedPrimitive hero)
{
    foreach (var arrow in mTheSet)
        arrow.UpdateSpinningArrow(hero);
}

public void DrawSet()
{
    foreach (var arrow in mTheSet)
        arrow.Draw();
}
```

Now you can use the SpinningArrowSet class you just created within the GameState class instead of the SpinningArrow class.

Modifying the *GameState* class

1. Start by creating variables for the set of arrows and the hero, and initializing them within the constructor with the values shown in the code that follows. Notice that the GameState class's complexity remains the same.

```
PlayerControlHero mHero;
SpinningArrowSet mArrows;

public GameState()
{
    mArrows = new SpinningArrowSet();
    mHero = new PlayerControlHero(new Vector2(5, 5));
}
```

2. Now modify the UpdateGame() function to call the update function for the hero and the set of arrows:

```
public void UpdateGame()
{
    mHero.UpdateHero();
    mArrows.UpdateSpinningSet(mHero);
}
```

3. Lastly, use the DrawGame() function to draw your game objects by calling their corresponding draw methods:

```
public void DrawGame()
{
    mHero.Draw();
    mArrows.DrawSet();
}
```

Creating a patrol enemy

The Patrol Enemy project serves as another example of a finite state machine. As in the previous project, the patrol enemy loops through its states until a specific condition is met; however, the states themselves become more sophisticated in this project.

The Patrol Enemy project

In this project, the user again controls a hero by moving it around the screen. The game window contains a rocket that patrols different designated areas or regions. The hero does not affect the rocket's state. You can see an example of this project running in Figure 6-5.

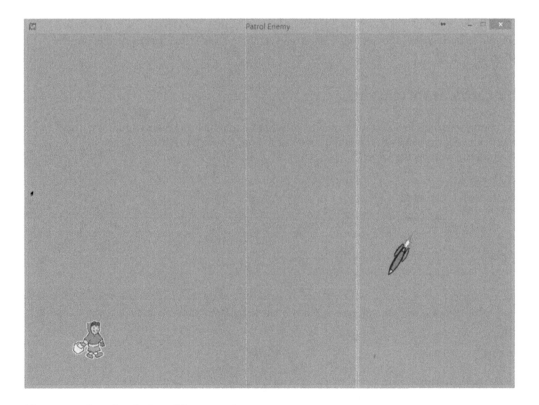

Figure 6-5. *Running the Patrol Enemy project*

The project has one control, as follows:

- **Left thumbstick (WSAD-keys)** Moves the hero

The goals of the project are as follows:

- To implement a more complex example of a finite state machine

- To work with randomness and understand its applications

- To understand how to define regions

The steps for creating the project are as follows:

1. Gain an understanding of the finite state machine needed.

2. Create the `PatrolEnemy` class, which contains the state machine.

3. Modify the `GameState` class to use the `PatrolEnemy` class.

Add the following resource, which can be found in the `Chapter06\SourceCode\Resources` folder, into your content project before you begin:

- `PatrolEnemy.png`

The patrol enemy's state machine

The patrol enemy starts by randomly selecting a location within a random region in which to spawn; after spawning, the enemy transitions to its next state. When it spawns at a random point of interest within a region, its state-change condition of being close enough to its target destination is immediately met, and it must therefore target a new random point of interest. You can see an example of this in Figure 6-6. The rocket spawns in the bottom-left region and then selects its new target within the top-left region.

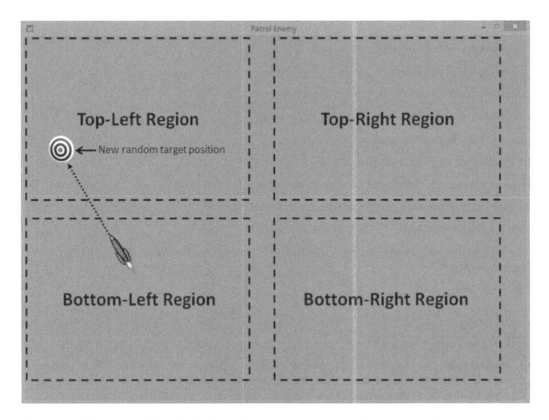

Figure 6-6. *The regions defined in the Patrol Enemy project and a random target position*

After completing its spawning behavior, the rocket continues to move toward its new target until it is close enough that it must find a new target. In Figure 6-7, you can see an example of this behavior in the finite state machine that the patrol enemy uses. As you can see, the states themselves are quite similar: move toward your target until you reach it, and then find a new target within the next region to move toward.

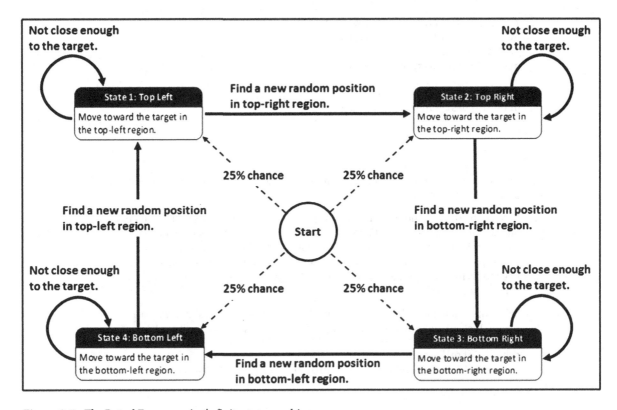

Figure 6-7. *The Patrol Enemy project's finite state machine*

Now that you have an understanding of the state machine, you can begin creating your patrolling enemy. The PatrolEnemy class is self-contained since includes its finite state machine as well as its random region and random target functionality.

Creating the *PatrolEnemy* class

1. Create a new class called PatrolEnemy that inherits from the GameObject class. Additionally, create an enum that contains each possible PatrolEnemy state, a variable for its current state, and the other variables shown in the following code for the target position, patrol speed, and range from the target position for triggering a new state.

```
public class PatrolEnemy : GameObject
{
    protected enum PatrolState {
        TopLeftRegion,
        TopRightRegion,
        BottomLeftRegion,
        BottomRightRegion
    }
```

```
    // Target position we are moving toward
    private Vector2 mTargetPosition;
    // Current state
    private PatrolState mCurrentState;

    private const float kPatrolSpeed = 0.3f;
    private const float kCloseEnough = 1f;


    ...
}
```

2. Add a constructor that initializes the front direction, target position, and position for this
    PatrolEnemy. Remember to use the GameObject base class.

    a. In the constructor, randomly select a region, call its corresponding update function,
        and set the enemy's position to the new randomly generated target position. You
        can see this in the following code. Notice that Game1.sRan.NextDouble(); is used
        to compute a random state. The function returns a number between 0 and 1; all you
        need to do is divide the states into fourths. This gives each state a 25 percent chance
        of being selected.

    b. Take note that the function lacks a randomly generated target position within a
        region. Instead, this is handled in the update function, which you will see later.

```
public PatrolEnemy() :
    base("PatrolEnemy", Vector2.Zero, new Vector2(5f, 10f))
{
    InitialFrontDirection = Vector2.UnitY;

    // Causes update state to always change to a new state
    mTargetPosition = Position = Vector2.Zero;

    #region Generate a random state to begin
    double initState = Game1.sRan.NextDouble();
    if (initState < 0.25)
    {
        UpdateBottomLeftState();
    }
    else if (initState < 0.5)
    {
        UpdateBottomRightState();
    }
    else if (initState < 0.75)
    {
        UpdateTopLeftState();
    }
    else
    {
        UpdateTopRightState();
    }
    Position = mTargetPosition;
    #endregion
}
```

3. You can now create your main update function. This function is used to call the corresponding update depending upon the enemy's current state. Remember to call base.Update() as well.

```
public void UpdatePatrol()
{
    // Operation common to all states ...
    base.Update(); // Moves game object by velocity

    switch (mCurrentState)
    {
        case PatrolState.BottomLeftRegion:
            UpdateBottomLeftState();
            break;

        case PatrolState.BottomRightRegion:
            UpdateBottomRightState();
            break;

        case PatrolState.TopRightRegion:
            UpdateTopRightState();
            break;

        case PatrolState.TopLeftRegion:
            UpdateTopLeftState();
            break;
    }
}
```

4. It is now time to create each state's update function. Each update function is applied if the enemy's position is close enough to the target position. This is simply done by using the Pythagorean theorem to find the distance between the two positions. In the code, the function LengthSquared() is used to accomplish this. You can see an example of this in the image that follows.

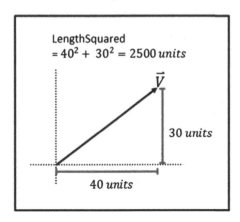

$$LengthSquared = 40^2 + 30^2 = 2500 \; units$$

$\vec{V}$

30 *units*

40 *units*

5. If the target is close enough, you transition to the next state, generate the target's new random position in the next state's region, and compute the new position and velocity. Remember from the state diagram that the states transition in a clockwise direction.

```
private void UpdateBottomLeftState()
{
    if ((Position - mTargetPosition).LengthSquared() < kCloseEnough)
    {
        mCurrentState = PatrolState.TopLeftRegion;
        mTargetPosition = RandomBottomRightPosition();
        ComputePositionAndVelocity();
    }
}

private void UpdateBottomRightState()
{
    if ((Position - mTargetPosition).LengthSquared() < kCloseEnough)
    {
        mCurrentState = PatrolState.BottomLeftRegion;
        mTargetPosition = RandomTopRightPosition();
        ComputePositionAndVelocity();
    }
}

private void UpdateTopRightState()
{
    if ((Position - mTargetPosition).LengthSquared() < kCloseEnough)
    {
        mCurrentState = PatrolState.BottomRightRegion;
        mTargetPosition = RandomTopLeftPosition();
        ComputePositionAndVelocity();
    }
}

private void UpdateTopLeftState()
{
    if ((Position - mTargetPosition).LengthSquared() < kCloseEnough)
    {
        mCurrentState = PatrolState.TopRightRegion;
        mTargetPosition = RandomBottomLeftPosition();
        ComputePositionAndVelocity();
    }
}
```

6. Now add a function that computes the enemy's position and velocity. First, the speed of the object is randomized to be between 80 and 120 percent of kPatrolSpeed. Then the vector to the next position is assigned to the velocity direction and front direction.

```
private void ComputePositionAndVelocity()
{
    Speed = kPatrolSpeed * (0.8f + (float)(0.4 * Game1.sRan.NextDouble()));
    Vector2 toNextPosition = mTargetPosition - Position;
    VelocityDirection = toNextPosition;
    FrontDirection = VelocityDirection;
}
```

7. Lastly, you need to add the functions that generate the random positions within each region. The image that follows shows where the top-left, top-right, bottom-right, and bottom-left regions are defined. The steps provided will guide you through the process of creating these regions.

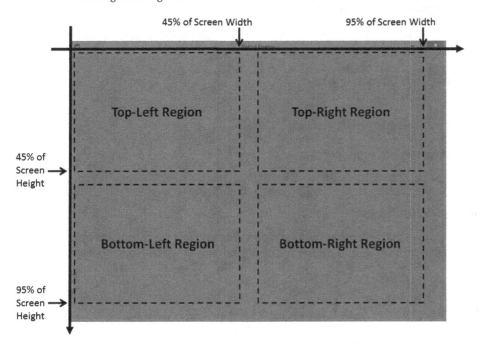

a. Start by creating a ComputePoint() function that accepts a region and returns a position within it, as shown in the code that follows. Notice that each region is 45 percent of the window size, so you obtain a random position by getting a random position within that 45 percent and then adding the region's offset.

```
private const float sBorderRange = 0.45f;

private Vector2 ComputePoint(double xOffset, double yOffset)
{
    Vector2 min = Camera.CameraWindowLowerLeftPosition;
    Vector2 max = Camera.CameraWindowUpperRightPosition;
```

```
            Vector2 size = max - min;
            float x = min.X + size.X * (float)(xOffset + (sBorderRange * Game1.sRan.NextDouble()));
            float y = min.Y + size.Y * (float)(yOffset + (sBorderRange * Game1.sRan.NextDouble()));
            return new Vector2(x, y);
        }
```

b.   Now add the randomness functions for the four regions by passing in the correct region offset:

```
private Vector2 RandomBottomRightPosition()
{
    return ComputePoint(0.5, 0.0);
}

private Vector2 RandomBottomLeftPosition()
{
    return ComputePoint(0.0, 0.0);
}

private Vector2 RandomTopRightPosition()
{
    return ComputePoint(0.5, 0.5);
}

private Vector2 RandomTopLeftPosition()
{
    return ComputePoint(0.0, 0.5);
}
```

Modifying the *GameState* class

All that you need now is to modify the GameState class. Add a variable for the hero and the enemy, and instantiate them within the constructor. Call the hero and patrol's update and draw functions correspondingly, as shown following:

```
public class GameState
{
    PlayerControlHero mHero;
    PatrolEnemy mEnemy;

    public GameState()
    {
        mEnemy = new PatrolEnemy();
        mHero = new PlayerControlHero(new Vector2(5, 5));
    }

    public void UpdateGame()
    {
        mHero.UpdateHero();
        mEnemy.UpdatePatrol();
    }
```

```
    public void DrawGame()
    {
        mHero.Draw();
        mEnemy.Draw();
    }
}
```

Implementing smooth turning

After running the previous project, you may have noticed that the rocket or patrolling enemy abruptly changes directions when transitioning between states. This can be a jarring effect—especially when it occurs in quick succession. This project is devoted to smoothing out the sudden change in front direction so that the patrolling enemy's movement becomes more fluid.

The Smooth Turning Patrol project

As before, you control a hero by moving it around the screen. The game window contains a rocket that patrols different designated areas or regions. The hero character does not affect the rocket's state. You can see an example of this project running in Figure 6-8.

Figure 6-8. *Running the Smooth Turning Patrol project*

The project has one control, as follows:

- **Left Thumbstick (WSAD-keys)** Moves the hero

The goal of this project is as follows:

- To integrate home-in functionality to gradually turn the patrol object toward the final destination.

The project will be completed in one step, as follows:

1. Modify the PatrolEnemy class for smooth turning behavior.

When considering object-oriented programming, it is generally good practice to make the behaviors a game object has as self-contained as possible. This reduces the amount potential bugs and the complexity of your project, as well as increases its scalability. Due to the object-oriented structure you have implemented thus far, you need to modify only the PatrolEnemy class to add smooth turning behavior to your patrolling enemy.

Modifying the *PatrolEnemy* class

1. Start by adding the following variables. Assuming that the update is being called 60 times per second, then kStateTimer is equal to 5 seconds. mStateTimer is used for counting down. Remember to initialize mStateTimer within the constructor.

```
public class PatrolEnemy : GameObject
{
    ...

    private const int kStateTimer = 60 * 5;
    private int mStateTimer;

    public PatrolEnemy() :
        base("PatrolEnemy", Vector2.Zero, new Vector2(5f, 10f))
    {
        mStateTimer = kStateTimer;

        ...
    }

    ...
}
```

2. Next, modify the UpdatePatrol() function so that it decreases the timer during each update in addition to computing the new front direction.

```
public void UpdatePatrol()
{
    base.Update();
    mStateTimer--;

    Vector2 toTarget = mTargetPosition - Position;
    float distToTarget = toTarget.Length();
    toTarget /= distToTarget;
    ComputeNewDirection(toTarget);
```

```
            switch (mCurrentState)
            {
                ...
            }
        }
}
```

3. Now implement the `ComputeNewDirection()` function, which calculates the new front
    direction. You do this by first calculating the angle between the current front direction and
    the target direction, as shown in the image that follows. Recall that you use the dot product
    to find this angle. If the angle between the two directions is not zero (`float.Epsilon`), then
    you update the front direction by using the cross product to find which direction to rotate
    and then rotating by a percentage (in this case 3 percent) of the total angle needed to face
    the target direction.

▪ **Note**   Because these calculations work with floating-point numbers, it is often difficult or impossible to hit zero
exactly. To account for this, you use `float.Epsilon`, because it is the smallest single value greater than zero.

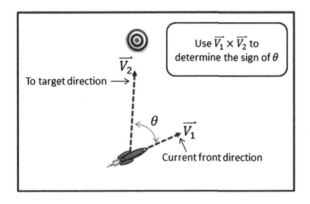

```
private void ComputeNewDirection(Vector2 toTarget)
{
    double cosTheta = Vector2.Dot(toTarget, FrontDirection);
    float theta = (float)Math.Acos(cosTheta);
    if (theta > float.Epsilon)
    {
        Vector3 frontDir3 = new Vector3(FrontDirection, 0f);
        Vector3 toTarget3 = new Vector3(toTarget, 0f);
        Vector3 zDir = Vector3.Cross(frontDir3, toTarget3);
        RotateAngleInRadian -= Math.Sign(zDir.Z) * 0.03f * theta;
        VelocityDirection = FrontDirection;
    }
}
```

4. In each state's corresponding update function, add a new condition to check for the expiration of the timer (it counts toward zero). If the timer expires (reaches zero), then you change the state.

```
private void UpdateBottomLeftState(float distToTarget)
{
    if ((mStateTimer < 0) || (distToTarget < kCloseEnough))
    {
        mCurrentState = PatrolState.BottomRightRegion;
        mTargetPosition = RandomBottomRightPosition();
        ComputeNewSpeedAndResetTimer();
    }
}

private void UpdateBottomRightState(float distToTarget)
{
    if ((mStateTimer < 0) || (distToTarget < kCloseEnough))
    {
        mCurrentState = PatrolState.TopRightRegion;
        mTargetPosition = RandomTopRightPosition();
        ComputeNewSpeedAndResetTimer();
    }
}

private void UpdateTopRightState(float distToTarget)
{
    if ((mStateTimer < 0) || (distToTarget < kCloseEnough))
    {
        mCurrentState = PatrolState.TopLeftRegion;
        mTargetPosition = RandomTopLeftPosition();
        ComputeNewSpeedAndResetTimer();
    }
}

private void UpdateTopLeftState(float distToTarget)
{
    if ((mStateTimer < 0) || (distToTarget < kCloseEnough))
    {
        mCurrentState = PatrolState.BottomLeftRegion;
        mTargetPosition = RandomBottomLeftPosition();
        ComputeNewSpeedAndResetTimer();
    }
}
```

5. Finally, add a new function to compute the patrol speed and reset the timer:

```
private void ComputeNewSpeedAndResetTimer()
{
    Speed = kPatrolSpeed * (0.8f + (float)(0.4 * Game1.sRan.NextDouble()));
    mStateTimer = (int) (kStateTimer * (0.8f + (float)(0.6 * Game1.sRan.NextDouble())));
}
```

Patrol that chases

The Patrol That Chases project is similar to the previous projects in that it contains a rocket that patrols around the game window. However, additional functionality has been added to the patrolling game object in the form of a new state. This additional state determines whether the rocket game object is patrolling or chasing.

The Patrol That Chases project

This project lets you control a hero character by moving it around the window. The game window also contains a patrolling rocket game object. The rocket will begin to chase the hero when the hero has entered its *aggro range* (the radius in which a monster will attack the player). After the chasing state has been activated, the patrolling object will continue to chase until it has touched the hero or until the chase timer expires. The game records the number of times the hero has been caught by the rocket in the upper-left corner. You can see an example of this project running in Figure 6-9.

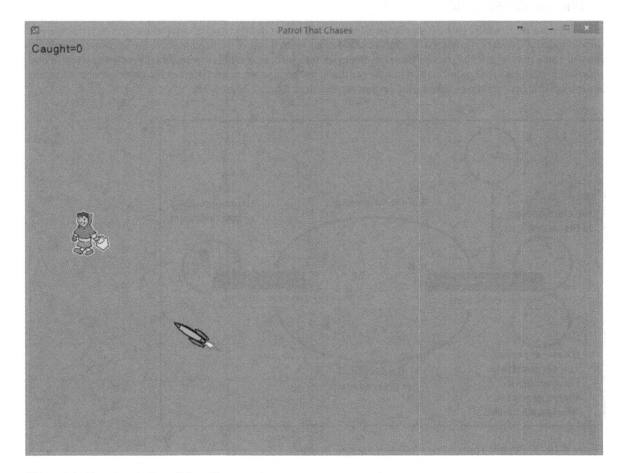

Figure 6-9. *Running the Patrol That Chases project*

The project has one control, as follows:

- **Left thumbstick (WSAD-keys)** Moves the hero

The goal of the project is as follows:

- To integrate home-in functionality to gradually turn and move the patrol object toward the hero

The steps for creating the project are as follows:

1. Add a new chase state in addition to the existing state.

2. Modify the `PatrolEnemy` class to implement the new chase state.

3. Modify the `GameState` class to use the new functionality.

Adding the chase state

In the previous projects, the patrol state contained several states that defined the behavior of the rocket. These states corresponded to different regions that the rocket could move to. In this project, in addition to the previous behavior, you will add a chase state. The chase state exists alongside the patrol states. This means that the rocket must be in one of these states. If it is in the patrol state, it behaves as in the previous projects, and if it is in the chase state, it chases the hero object until its conditions are met. For further clarification, refer to Figure 6-10.

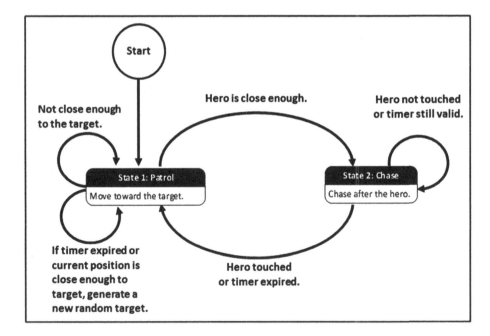

Figure 6-10. *The Patrol That Chases project's finite state machine*

It is now time to add the chasing functionality to the enemy patrol object.

Modifying the *PatrolEnemy* class

1. Start by modifying the `PatrolState` enum to reflect the two states:

```
protected enum PatrolState
{
    PatrolState,
    ChaseHero
}
```

2. Add a new constant variable named `kDistToBeginChase`; this is the distance that will trigger patrol enemy to chase the hero.

```
private const float kDistToBeginChase = 15f;
```

3. Because you're adding a new state alongside the patrol state, the generation of the next random target will be needed more than once; therefore, you should separate its logic into a new function. Name the function RandomNextTarget. In this function, you will set the current state to PatrolState, and then, as shown previously in the constructor, choose a random region in which to begin.

```
private void RandomNextTarget()
{
    mStateTimer = kStateTimer;
    mCurrentState = PatrolState.PatrolState;
    // Generate a random begin state
    double initState = Game1.sRan.NextDouble();
    if (initState < 0.25)
        mTargetPosition = RandomBottomRightPosition();
    else if (initState < 0.5)
        mTargetPosition = RandomTopRightPosition();
    else if (initState < 0.75)
        mTargetPosition = RandomTopLeftPosition();
    else
        mTargetPosition = RandomBottomLeftPosition();

    ComputeNewSpeedAndResetTimer();
}
```

4. In the constructor, remove the lines of code responsible for generating the next random target and replace them with a call to RandomNextTarget. This is done in the code that follows:

```
public PatrolEnemy() :
    base("PatrolEnemy", Vector2.Zero, new Vector2(5f, 10f))
{
    InitialFrontDirection = Vector2.UnitY;

    // Causes update state to always change into a new state
    mTargetPosition = Position = Vector2.Zero;

    RandomNextTarget();
    Position = mTargetPosition;
}
```

5. Modify the UpdatePatrol() function to include the two base states: patrolling and chasing. In addition, include a Boolean variable that becomes true when the hero has been caught:

```
public bool UpdatePatrol(GameObject hero)
{
    bool caught = false;

    base.Update();
    mStateTimer--;

    Vector2 toTarget = mTargetPosition - Position;
    float distToTarget = toTarget.Length();
    toTarget /= distToTarget;
    ComputeNewDirection(toTarget);

    switch (mCurrentState)
    {
        case PatrolState.PatrolState:
            UpdatePatrolState(hero, distToTarget);
            break;

        case PatrolState.ChaseHero:
            caught = UpdateChaseHeroState(hero, distToTarget);
            break;
    }
    return caught;
}
```

6. Create a new function called DectectHero that determines whether the hero has come within range of the rocket. Begin the function by finding the vector between the rocket's position and the hero's position. If that vector's length is less than the distance that triggers the chase state, then you will set the timer to 120 percent of kStateTimer, increase the rocket's moving speed, and change the current state to chasing. Additionally, you set the target position to the hero's position and change the texture to reflect the change in state.

```
private void DetectHero(GameObject hero)
{
    Vector2 toHero = hero.Position - Position;
    if (toHero.Length() < kDistToBeginChase)
    {
        mStateTimer = (int)(kStateTimer * 1.2f); // 1.2 times as much time for chasing
        Speed *= 2.5f;   // 2.5 times the current speed!
        mCurrentState = PatrolState.ChaseHero;
        mTargetPosition = hero.Position;
        mImage = Game1.sContent.Load<Texture2D>("AlertEnemy");
    }
}
```

7. Now you can add the function responsible for updating when the patrol state is active. As before, first check whether the timer has expired or the object is close enough to its target position. If either of these conditions is met, generate a new random target using the function you created, and then recompute the speed and reset the timer via the ComputeNewSpeedAndResetTimer() function. Additionally, call the DetectHero() function during each update.

```
private void UpdatePatrolState(GameObject hero, float distToTarget)
{
    if ((mStateTimer < 0) || (distToTarget < kCloseEnough))
    {
        RandomNextTarget();
        ComputeNewSpeedAndResetTimer();
    }
    DetectHero(hero);
}
```

8. Now add a function to update the hero when the chasing state is active. The UpdateChaseHeroState() function uses pixel-accurate collision to detect whether the hero has been touched by the rocket. You can see this reflected in the code that follows. If the PixelTouches() function returns true or the timer has expired, then a new random target is chosen that changes the current state back to patrolling. Again, a new image is loaded to reflect the change in state.

```
private bool UpdateChaseHeroState(GameObject hero, float distToHero)
{
    bool caught = false;
    Vector2 pos;
    caught = PixelTouches(hero, out pos);
    mTargetPosition = hero.Position;

    if (caught || (mStateTimer < 0))
    {
        RandomNextTarget();
        mImage = Game1.sContent.Load<Texture2D>("PatrolEnemy");
    }
    return caught;
}
```

Modifying the *GameState* class

The only modification you need to make to the GameState class is to track the number of times the hero has been caught. In the code that follows, the variable mNumCaught has been added, incremented in the update function, and printed in the draw function:

```
public class GameState
{
    PlayerControlHero mHero;
    PatrolEnemy mEnemy;
    int mNumCaught = 0;
```

```
    public GameState()
    {
        mEnemy = new PatrolEnemy();
        mHero = new PlayerControlHero(new Vector2(5, 5));
    }

    public void UpdateGame()
    {
        mHero.UpdateHero();
        if (mEnemy.UpdatePatrol(mHero))
            mNumCaught++;
    }

    public void DrawGame()
    {
        mHero.Draw();
        mEnemy.Draw();
        FontSupport.PrintStatus("Caught=" + mNumCaught.ToString(), null);
    }
}
```

Creating many enemies

The project in this section is similar to the Many Spinning Arrows project in that it increases the number of objects that can chase the hero. As with the Many Spinning Arrows project, this increases the overall complexity; however, the functionality of the enemies remains the same as in the previous project.

The Many Enemies project

As before, in this project you control the hero character by moving it around the window. The game window contains many patrolling rocket game objects. The rockets will begin to chase the hero when the hero enters any rocket's aggro range. Once the chasing state for a rocket has been activated, that rocket will continue to chase until it touches the hero or the chase timer expires. The game records the number of times the hero has been caught in the upper-left corner. You can see an example of this project running in Figure 6-11.

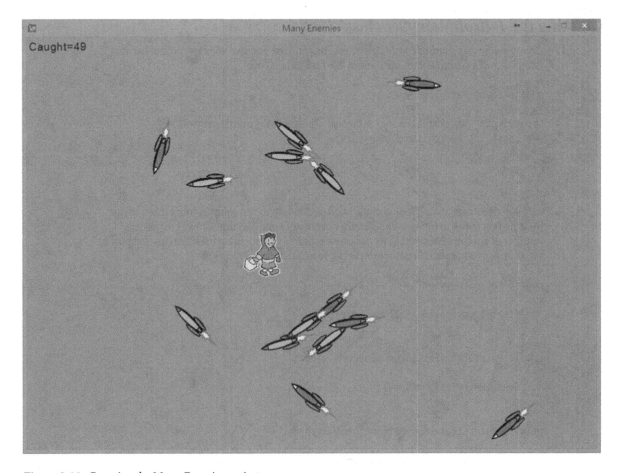

Figure 6-11. *Running the Many Enemies project*

The project has one control, as follows:

- **Left thumbstick (WSAD-keys)** Moves the hero

The goal of the project is as follows:

- To increase complexity by increasing the number of game objects.

The steps for creating the project are as follows:

1. Create a PatrolEnemySet class in order to handle the group of enemies.

2. Modify the GameState class to use the new set class.

Since this project is functionally identical to the previous project, all that you need to do is create a PatrolEnemySet class, which handles generating many enemies at once.

Creating the *PatrolEnemySet* class

1. Create a new class named PatrolEnemySet. Include the variable mTheSet for the list of enemies and a constant variable named kDefaultNumEnemy.

```
public class PatrolEnemySet
{
    private List<PatrolEnemy> mTheSet = new List<PatrolEnemy>();
    const int kDefaultNumEnemy = 15;

    ...
}
```

2. Add two constructors that loop through and instantiate the enemies, adding them to the list. The first constructor creates a default number of enemies; the second creates the number of enemies specified in its parameter. Notice that the loop itself is extracted into a separate function called CreateEnemySet() to avoid code duplication.

```
public PatrolEnemySet()
{
    CreateEnemySet(kDefaultNumEnemy);
}

public PatrolEnemySet(int numEnemy)
{
    CreateEnemySet(numEnemy);
}

private void CreateEnemySet(int numEnemy)
{
    for (int i = 0; i < numEnemy; i++)
    {
        PatrolEnemy enemy = new PatrolEnemy();
        mTheSet.Add(enemy);
    }
}
```

3. Add the UpdateSet() function for updating all the enemy objects. Remember to return a count variable to keep track of the number of times the hero has been caught.

```
public int UpdateSet(GameObject hero)
{
    int count = 0;
    foreach (var enemy in mTheSet)
    {
        if (enemy.UpdatePatrol(hero))
            count++;
    }
    return count;
}
```

4. Finally, include a DrawSet() function to loop through each enemy and call its draw function.

```
public void DrawSet()
{
    foreach (var enemy in mTheSet)
        enemy.Draw();
}
```

Modifying the *GameState* class

The only change you need to implement in the GameState class is to use the new PatrolEnemySet class instead of the PatrolEnemy class. In the following code, mEnemies uses the PatrolEnemySet constructor, update, and draw functions in place of the PatrolEnemy functions.

```
public class GameState
{
    PlayerControlHero mHero;
    PatrolEnemySet mEnemies;
    int mNumCaught = 0;

    public GameState()
    {
        mEnemies = new PatrolEnemySet();
        mHero = new PlayerControlHero(new Vector2(5, 5));
    }

    public void UpdateGame()
    {
        mHero.UpdateHero();
        mNumCaught += mEnemies.UpdateSet(mHero);
    }

    public void DrawGame()
    {
        mHero.Draw();
        mEnemies.DrawSet();
        FontSupport.PrintStatus("Caught=" + mNumCaught.ToString(), null);
    }
}
```

Summary

In this chapter, you learned how to use a finite state machine to create autonomous behavior for your game objects. By breaking down the game objects' behavior into a set of rules formulated as state and transition conditions, you can apply the techniques described here to implement any number of behaviors.

You also learned how to increase the complexity of the project by increasing the number of game objects within the GameState class. You achieved this by creating a set of objects that increase the project's complexity while minimizing the additional code needed, letting you manage a group of objects in the GameState class as if they were a single entity.

Finally, you learned how to implement several gamelike behaviors, including distance triggers, patrolling, and chasing. By combining these concepts, you can create sophisticated and interesting games.

Quick reference

To	Do this
Support semiautonomous behavior of game objects	Define a finite state machine, as follows:
	1. Determine the behaviors of the machine.
	2. Group distinct behaviors into separate states.
	3. Define what triggers the transitions between states, as well as how and when they're triggered.
Implement a finite state machine	1. Define a new class to encapsulate the behavior.
	2. Define an enum for each of the states.
	3. Define an update function with a switch or case statement for each of the states.
	4. Define a separate state service function for each state.
Introduce unpredictability to a finite state machine	Include randomness in, for example, positional computation or duration of states.
Support many instances of objects with finite state machine behavior	1. Define a new class with a collection of the finite state machine object.
	2. Implement Update() and Draw() functions in the new class to iterate through and call the corresponding Update() and Draw() functions of the finite state machine objects in the collection. For example, the SpinningArrowSet class has a collection of SpinningArrow objects, and the Update() and Draw() functions of the SpinningArrowSet class iterate through and call the corresponding Update() and Draw() functions of the SpinningArrow objects in the collection.
Patrol across regions or areas	1. Identify regions of patrol as states.
	2. Randomly generate a position in each region.
	3. Move the patrol object toward a new region until sufficiently close to the border.
	4. Transition to the new state or region.
Include unpredictability in patrolling	Include randomness when generating target positions for each region, and when computing the next state.
Smooth transitioning between patrol regions	Integrate home-in functionality to gradually turn patrol objects toward a destination position:
	1. Compute the vector from the patrol object to the destination position.
	2. Compute the dot product between the computed vector and the patrol's front direction.
	3. Turn the patrol clockwise or counterclockwise depending on the sign of the cross product between the two vectors.
Ensure a patrolling enemy does not orbit a target position	Include a countdown timer to force a transition to a new state.
Make a patrolling enemy chase a hero	Support a state that uses the hero's location as the target position. In this case, it is important to remember to transition out of the hero-chasing state the when hero is sufficiently far away.
Create many patrolling enemies	Define an enemy patrol set to include a collection of patrolling enemies.

CHAPTER 7

■ ■ ■

Sprites, Camera, Action!

After completing this chapter, you will be able to:

- Understand the components of sprite sheet animation

- Create your own animation using a sprite sheet

- Manipulate the game camera

- Add audio to a game project for both music and sound effects

This chapter covers many of the additional concepts that are commonly needed to create full-featured and complete game projects, but were not introduced in previous chapters. These concepts include animation via sprite sheets, in-game camera manipulation, and audio for background music and cue effects. Animation, camera manipulation, and audio are often unnecessary for creating core game mechanics; however, including them creates a richer experience for end users by providing them with customized feedback for specific actions within your game.

Sprite animation

In games, you often want to have your characters or game objects appear as if they are in motion. While the previous chapters explained how to move game objects around the screen to create movement, because the images themselves were static they probably felt somewhat lifeless. To address this problem, you can use animation. As you may know, you create an animation by rapidly displaying related images in succession to create a sense of motion—and animation is no different in games. Typically, you use animation for simple motions such as walking and running, as well as more complex motions such as fighting strikes or dance moves. This section shows how you can add motion to your objects by using a sequence of images and a sprite sheet.

The Sprite Animation project

This project demonstrates how to move two animated characters around the screen. You are able to adjust the animation speed of each character in order to create a more fluid sense of movement across the screen. You can see an example of this project running in Figure 7-1.

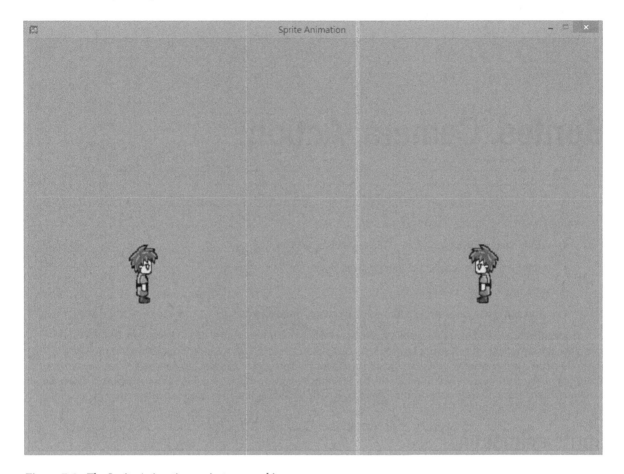

Figure 7-1. *The Sprite Animation project, zoomed in*

The project's controls are as follows:

- **Right thumbstick (arrow-keys)** Moves the character around
- **Left thumbstick's x-axis (AD-keys)** Controls the animation speed
- **Button A (K-key)** Selects the left character
- **Button B (L-key)** Selects the right character

The goals of the project are as follows:

- To experience components involved in sprite animation
- To understand the support MonoGame SpriteBatch provides for sprite animation

The steps for creating the project are as follows:

1. Gain an overview of sprite sheets.
2. Create a `SpritePrimitive` class.
3. Modify the `GameState` class to include the newly created sprite functionality.

Add the following resource, which can be found in the Chapter07\SourceCode\Resources folder, into your content project before you begin:

- SimpleSpriteSheet.png

Overview of sprite sheets

To achieve animation, games often use what are known as sprites, or more specifically, *sprite sheets*. A *sprite sheet* is an image that contains an animation separated into one or more rows and columns ($R \times C$). For example, in Figure 7-2 you can see a 4×2 sprite sheet that contains two separate animations. The animations depict a character walking right and left. In this example, the animations are separated into separate rows; however, this is not always the case. The organization of a sprite sheet is generally handled by its creator.

Figure 7-2. *The individual frames needed to depict a game character walking right and left*

For a more specific example, take a look at the top row of the sprite sheet in Figure 7-2. The images in this row depict the character walking to the right. To achieve this effect, each character image must to be displayed from left to right, in the sequence 1, 2, 3, 4. After the last character image has been displayed, the animation is looped back to the first image in the row. You can see an example of this in Figure 7-3.

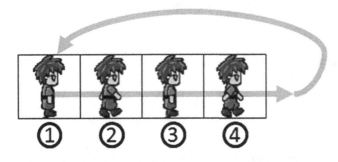

Figure 7-3. *A sprite animation sequence that loops*

Now that you know the general usage that sprite sheets can provide, here's a quick look at the math you need to achieve this type of behavior. Given that the sprite sheet is 4×2 and the image has a resolution of 256×128 pixels, you can deduce that each sprite has a resolution of 256/4×128/2 or 64×64 pixels.

While that works great for this particular sprite sheet example, you'll need a more generalized equation to implement a class that can handle sprite sheets that contain varying numbers of sprites and resolutions.

However, this is still fairly simple to calculate. Given that the pixel resolution of the sprite sheet is equal to $P \times Q$, where P represents the pixel width and Q represents the pixel height, then each sprite's resolution within the sprite sheet is equal to $P/R \times Q/C$, where R and C represent the numbers of rows and columns, respectively.

For example, if a sprite sheet has a pixel resolution of 256×256 and its rows and columns are 4×4, then each sprite has a resolution of 256/4×256/2, or 64×64 pixels. In general, sprite sheets are composed of sprites of equal size to allow easy targeting of each individual sprite. Sprite sheets with varying-size sprites do exist; however, you then need a more sophisticated calculation to single out each sprite.

With the basic knowledge of sprite sheets under your belt, you can now tackle the creation of a sprite class.

Creating the *SpritePrimitive* class

1. Begin by creating a new class called SpritePrimitive that inherits from GameObject. Add instance variables for rows, columns, padding, and the sprite sheet's width and height. The padding variable is used to define the space between each frame or sprite if necessary.

■ **Note** The padding of a sprite sheet depends upon its creator. Generally, a sprite sheet contains consistent padding around all sides.

```
public class SpritePrimitive : GameObject
{
    private int mNumRow, mNumColumn, mPaddings;
    private int mSpriteImageWidth, mSpriteImageHeight;

    #region Per Animation setting
    ...
    #endregion


    ...
}
```

2. Now create the following variables to provide support for sprite animation:

```
private int mUserSpecifedTicks;
private int mCurrentTick;
private int mCurrentRow, mCurrentColumn;
private int mBeginRow, mEndRow;
private int mBeginCol, mEndCol;
```

- mUserSpecifedTicks keeps track of the number of machine ticks before changing to the next frame.

- mCurrentTick is for keeping track of the number of ticks since the current frame started to be displayed.

- mCurrentRow and mCurrentColumn are for displaying the current frame's row and column.

- mBeginRow, mEndRow, mBeginCol, and mEndCol are used to keep track of which frame you start and end on.

3. Add a constructor to initialize the variables to the default values. Make sure to support parameters for the file name, position, and size, as well as the amount of rows, columns, and padding that the sprite sheet contains.

```
public SpritePrimitive(String image, Vector2 position, Vector2 size,
    int rowCounts, int columnCount, int padding) :
    base(image, position, size)
{
    mNumRow = rowCounts;
    mNumColumn = columnCount;
    mPaddings = padding;
    mSpriteImageWidth = mImage.Width / mNumRow;
    mSpriteImageHeight = mImage.Height / mNumColumn;

    mUserSpecifedTicks = 1;
    mCurrentTick = 0;
    mCurrentRow = 0;
    mCurrentColumn = 0;
    mBeginRow = mBeginCol = mEndRow = mEndCol = 0;
}
```

4. Now create get and set accessors for the variables, as shown in the code that follows:

```
public int SpriteBeginRow
{
    get { return mBeginRow; }
    set { mBeginRow = value; mCurrentRow = value; }
}
public int SpriteEndRow
{
    get { return mEndRow; }
    set { mEndRow = value; }
}
public int SpriteBeginColumn
{
    get { return mBeginCol; }
    set { mBeginCol = value; mCurrentColumn = value; }
}
public int SpriteEndColumn
{
    get { return mEndCol; }
    set { mEndCol = value; }
}
public int SpriteAnimationTicks
{
    get { return mUserSpecifedTicks; }
    set { mUserSpecifedTicks = value; }
}
```

5. Next, create a public method that allows you to set the beginning and ending frames for the animation. To do this, you must know which row and column the beginning frame resides in. Additionally, you allow for the modification of the tick interval, which specifies how often the animation should change frames. The smaller the tick interval, the faster the animation will be.

```
public void SetSpriteAnimation(int beginRow, int beginCol, int endRow, int endCol,
int tickInterval)
{
    mUserSpecifedTicks = tickInterval;
    mBeginRow = beginRow;
    mBeginCol = beginCol;
    mEndRow = endRow;
    mEndCol = endCol;

    mCurrentRow = mBeginRow;
    mCurrentColumn = mBeginCol;
    mCurrentTick = 0;
}
```

6. Create the Update() function. During each update, increment the current tick and check whether or not the tick time is up. If so, reset the current tick and move to next sprite frame. When the current frame is equal to the last frame in the row, set the current frame back to the first frame in the row.

```
public override void Update()
{
    base.Update();

    mCurrentTick++;
    if (mCurrentTick > mUserSpecifedTicks)
    {
        mCurrentTick = 0;
        mCurrentColumn++;
        if (mCurrentColumn > mEndCol)
        {
            mCurrentColumn = mBeginCol;
            mCurrentRow++;

            if (mCurrentRow > mEndRow)
                mCurrentRow = mBeginRow;
        }
    }
}
```

7. Now it is time to create the Draw() function. First and foremost, you need to create the destination rectangle where the image will be displayed by calling the Camera class's ComputePixelRectangle() function. Then add a source rectangle that specifies the frame on the sprite sheet that will be mapped to the destination rectangle. This is done using the position of the desired frame's top-left corner (taking padding into account) and the sprite image's width and height. Finally, define the origin of rotation and draw the destination rectangle using the Game1.sSpriteBatch.Draw() function call.

```
public override void Draw()
{
    // Define location and size of the texture
    Rectangle destRect = Camera.ComputePixelRectangle(Position, Size);

    int imageTop = mCurrentRow * mSpriteImageWidth;
    int imageLeft = mCurrentColumn * mSpriteImageHeight;
    // Define the area to draw from the spriteSheet
    Rectangle srcRect = new Rectangle(
        imageLeft + mPaddings,
        imageTop + mPaddings,
        mSpriteImageWidth, mSpriteImageHeight);

    // Define the rotation origin
    Vector2 org = new Vector2(mSpriteImageWidth/2, mSpriteImageHeight/2);

    // Draw the texture
    Game1.sSpriteBatch.Draw(
        mImage,
        destRect,            // Area to be drawn in pixel space
        srcRect,             // Rect on the spriteSheet
        Color.White,         //
        mRotateAngle,        // Angle to rotate (clockwise)
        org,                 // Image reference position
        SpriteEffects.None, 0f);

    if (null != Label)
        FontSupport.PrintStatusAt(Position, Label, LabelColor);
}
```

Now you'll modify the GameState class to use the SpritePrimitive class.

Modifying the *GameState* class

1. Start by adding variables for sprite animation speed, the hero primitives, and the currently selected hero primitive.

    ```
    const int kSpriteSpeedFactor = 10;    // Value of 1 maps to updates of 10 ticks
    SpritePrimitive mHero, mAnotherHero;
    SpritePrimitive mCurrent;
    ```

2. Now modify the constructor to initialize the instance variables with the values shown in the code that follows:

    ```
    public GameState()
    {
        mHero = new SpritePrimitive(
            "SimpleSpriteSheet",
            new Vector2(20, 30), new Vector2(10, 10),
    ```

```
        4,  // Number of rows
        2,  // Number of columns
        0); // Padding between images

mAnotherHero = new SpritePrimitive(
    "SimpleSpriteSheet",
    new Vector2(80, 30), new Vector2(10, 10),
    4,  // Number of rows
    2,  // Number of columns
    0); // Padding between images

// Start mHero by walking left and mAnotherHero by walking right
mHero.SetSpriteAnimation(0, 0, 0, 3, 10);       // Slowly
mAnotherHero.SetSpriteAnimation(1, 0, 1, 3, 5); // Twice as fast
mCurrent = mAnotherHero;
}
```

3. Remember, mHero.SetSpriteAnimation(0, 0, 0, 3, 10); means the animation will start from frame 0, 0 and continue to frame 0, 3. The 10 used indicates the number of ticks before changing to the next frame. The following image provides a visual representation of the frame-numbering system.

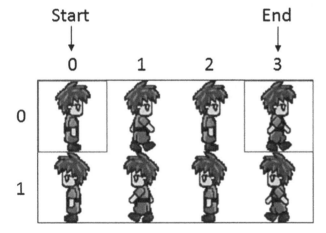

4. Next, in the UpdateGame() function, perform the following steps:

   a. Update both heroes by calling their Update() functions:

```
public void UpdateGame()
{
    mHero.Update();
    mAnotherHero.Update();

    UserControlUpdate();
}
```

b. Implement the UserControlUpdate() function by doing the following:

- Changing the currently selected hero via the A and B buttons

- Rotating the image when the X or Y button is pressed

- Mapping the current hero's position to the right thumbstick for movement

- Mapping the left thumbstick to the animation speed of the hero

```
private void UserControlUpdate()
{
    #region Selecting Hero
    if (InputWrapper.Buttons.A == ButtonState.Pressed)
        mCurrent = mHero;
    if (InputWrapper.Buttons.B == ButtonState.Pressed)
        mCurrent = mAnotherHero;
    mCurrent.Position += InputWrapper.ThumbSticks.Right;
    #endregion

    #region Specifying rotation
    if (InputWrapper.Buttons.X == ButtonState.Pressed)
        mCurrent.RotateAngleInRadian += MathHelper.ToRadians(1);
    if (InputWrapper.Buttons.Y == ButtonState.Pressed)
        mCurrent.RotateAngleInRadian += MathHelper.ToRadians(-1);
    #endregion

    #region spriteSheet Update
    if (InputWrapper.ThumbSticks.Left.X == 0)
    {
        mCurrent.SpriteEndColumn = 0;  // Stops the animation
    }
    Else
    {
        float useX = InputWrapper.ThumbSticks.Left.X;
        mCurrent.SpriteEndColumn = 3;
        if (useX < 0)
        {
            mCurrent.SpriteBeginRow = 1;
            mCurrent.SpriteEndRow = 1;
            useX *= -1f;
        }
        else
        {
            mCurrent.SpriteBeginRow = 0;
            mCurrent.SpriteEndRow = 0;
        }
        mCurrent.SpriteAnimationTicks = (int)((1f - useX) * kSpriteSpeedFactor);
    }
    #endregion
}
```

5. Finally, modify the DrawGame() function so it draws both heroes:

```
public void DrawGame()
{
    mHero.Draw();
    mAnotherHero.Draw();
}
```

Sprite collision

In the preceding project, you saw how to use the principles of sprite sheets to create animations. However, if you use textures in various stages of the animation the pixel-accurate collision-detection function you created earlier will no longer function correctly. This is because your pixel collision-detection function assumes the textures being used are static. In this section, you will see how to implement pixel-accurate collision for animated sprites.

The Sprite Collision project

This project demonstrates how to move a character around the screen and collide it with pixel accuracy with several other objects. The character itself will be animated via a sprite sheet. The project displays the current collision status in the top-left corner of the screen. You can see an example of this project running in Figure 7-4.

Figure 7-4. *Running the Sprite Collision project; the project accurately detects collisions, even for sprite characters*

The project's controls are as follows:

- **Right thumbstick (arrow-keys)** Moves the selected object
- **Left thumbstick (WSAD-keys)** Moves the hero
- **Right and left triggers (M and N keys)** Rotates the selected object
- **Button A (K-key)** Selects the flower
- **Button B (L-key)** Selects the lower-left plane (the rocketlike object)

The goals of the project are as follows:

- To implement per-pixel collision for sprite images
- To use an efficient storage system for color, which is used for sharing images

The steps for creating the project are as follows:

1. Modify the TexturedPrimitive class to add new accessors.
2. Modify the SpritePrimitive class to add new accessors.
3. Modify the TexturedPrimitivePixelCollide partial class to support per-pixel collision.
4. Modify the GameState class to use the changes made to the project.

Add the following resources, which can be found in the Chapter07\SourceCode\Resources folder, into your content project before you begin:

- Flower.png
- Target.png

Modifying the *TexturedPrimitive* class

To support pixel-accurate collision detection for sprites, you'll need to modify the TexturedPrimitive class. You do this by adding accessors for the sprite's position and size on the sprite sheet. Set the accessors to the top-left corner of the image and sprite sheet size by default. Notice that in the following code, the accessors are defined as virtual. By defining these as virtual, you allow those classes that inherit from the TexturedPrimitive class to override the accessors to return their desired values.

```
protected virtual int SpriteTopPixel { get { return 0; } }
protected virtual int SpriteLeftPixel { get { return 0; } }
protected virtual int SpriteImageWidth { get { return mImage.Width; } }
protected virtual int SpriteImageHeight { get { return mImage.Height; } }
```

Modifying the *SpritePrimitive* class

Override the parent accessors to return the proper top-left position and size of the current sprite within the sprite sheet:

```
#region override to support per-pixel collision
protected override int SpriteTopPixel
{
    get { return mCurrentRow * mSpriteImageHeight; }
}
```

```
protected override int SpriteLeftPixel
{
    get { return mCurrentColumn * mSpriteImageWidth; }
}
protected override int SpriteImageWidth
{
    get { return mSpriteImageWidth; }
}
protected override int SpriteImageHeight
{
    get { return mSpriteImageHeight; }
}
#endregion
```

Next, you'll modify the TexturedPrimitivePixelCollide partial class, which you created earlier to handle pixel-accurate collision for textures, so it can accommodate varying sprites.

Modifying the *TexturedPrimitivePixelCollide* partial class

1. Modify the PixelTouches() function to use the newly created SpriteImageWidth and SpriteImageHeight variables. You can see this achieved in the code that follows. The rest of the function remains the same.

    ```
    public bool PixelTouches(TexturedPrimitive otherPrim, out Vector2 collidePoint)
    {
        ...

        if (touches)
        {
            ...

            int i = 0;
            while ( (!pixelTouch) && (i<SpriteImageWidth) )
            {
                int j = 0;
                while ( (!pixelTouch) && (j<SpriteImageHeight) )
                {
                    ...
                }

                ...
            }
        }

        ...
    }
    ```

2. Now, in the GetColor() function, you need to find the correct pixel location for the current sprite frame within the sprite sheet in order to return the correct color. To achieve this, use SpriteTopPixel and SpriteLeftPixel, as shown in the code that follows:

```
private Color GetColor(int i, int j)
{
    return mTextureColor[((j+SpriteTopPixel) * mImage.Width) + i + SpriteLeftPixel];
}
```

3. Next, you need to change how you convert between coordinate spaces. The overall purpose of this conversion remains the same; however, because you no longer need the entire image, you can reference the sprite size instead of the image size. You can see this reflected in the code that follows:

```
private Vector2 IndexToCameraPosition(int i, int j, Vector2 xDir, Vector2 yDir)
{
    float x = i * Width / (float)(SpriteImageWidth - 1);
    float y = j * Height / (float)(SpriteImageHeight- 1);

    Vector2 r = Position
        + (x - (mSize.X * 0.5f)) * xDir
        - (y - (mSize.Y * 0.5f)) * yDir;

    return r;
}

private Vector2 CameraPositionToIndex(Vector2 p, Vector2 xDir, Vector2 yDir)
{
    Vector2 delta = p - Position;
    float xOffset = Vector2.Dot(delta, xDir);
    float yOffset = Vector2.Dot(delta, yDir);
    float i = SpriteImageWidth * (xOffset / Width);
    float j = SpriteImageHeight * (yOffset / Height);
    i += SpriteImageWidth / 2;
    j = (SpriteImageHeight / 2) - j;
    return new Vector2(i, j);
}
```

4. In order to share the same color data for multiple images, use a dictionary data structure. By using a dictionary data structure, multiple instances of the same image can share the same color information, which reduces some of the performance impact of adding multiple instances of the same game object.

■ **Note**   A *dictionary* is a data structure that contains a unique key for every value, thus providing fast lookups when looking for a specific value.

In the function that follows, you can see that along with the dictionary (sTextureData), the LoadColorInfo() function returns the necessary image data (an array of colors) depending upon the input parameters.

```
public partial class TexturedPrimitive
{
    ...

    #region Static support for sharing color data across same image
    static Dictionary<String, Color[]> sTextureData =
            new Dictionary<string, Color[]>();

    static private Color[] LoadColorInfo(String imageName, Texture2D image)
    {
        Color[] imageData = new Color[image.Width * image.Height];
        image.GetData(imageData);
        sTextureData.Add(imageName, imageData);
        return imageData;
    }
    #endregion

    ...
}
```

5. Lastly, modify the ReadColorData() function to use the newly created dictionary and the LoadColorInfo() function:

```
private void ReadColorData()
{
    if (sTextureData.ContainsKey(mImageName))
        mTextureColor = sTextureData[mImageName];
    else
        mTextureColor = LoadColorInfo(mImageName, mImage);
}
```

Finally, you'll modify the GameState class to use the newly created sprite collision.

Modifying the *GameState* class

1. First, add the variables for the hero sprite, the flower texture, the four texture planes, the currently selected texture, and the variables needed to display the collision status and position. You can see this reflected in the code that follows:

```
public class GameState
{
    const int kSpriteSpeedFactor = 10;  // Value of 1 maps to updates of 10 ticks
    SpritePrimitive mHero;              // Hero sprite
    const int kNumPlanes = 4;
    TexturedPrimitive[] mPlane;         // The planes
    TexturedPrimitive mFlower;          // The large background
    TexturedPrimitive mCurrentPrim;     // Refer to either plane or flower
```

```
        // Support for displaying of collision
        TexturedPrimitive mHeroTarget;        // Where latest hero pixel collision happened
        bool mHeroPixelCollision;             // If there is a pixel collision for the hero
        bool mHeroBoundCollision;             // If there is an image-bound collision for the hero

        public GameState()
        {
            ...
        }

        ...
}
```

2. Next, initialize the variables within the constructor with the default values shown following:

```
public GameState()
{
    // Set up the flower ...
    mFlower = new TexturedPrimitive("Flower", new Vector2(50, 35), new Vector2(60, 60));

    // Planes
    mPlane = new TexturedPrimitive[kNumPlanes];
    mPlane[0] =
        new TexturedPrimitive("PatrolEnemy", new Vector2(10, 15), new Vector2(5, 10));
    mPlane[1] =
        new TexturedPrimitive("PatrolEnemy", new Vector2(90, 15), new Vector2(5, 10));
    mPlane[2] =
        new TexturedPrimitive("PatrolEnemy", new Vector2(90, 55), new Vector2(5, 10));
    mPlane[3] =
        new TexturedPrimitive("PatrolEnemy", new Vector2(10, 55), new Vector2(5, 10));

    mHeroTarget = new TexturedPrimitive("Target", new Vector2(0, 0), new Vector2(3, 3));
    mCurrentPrim = mPlane[0];
    mHeroBoundCollision = false;
    mHeroPixelCollision = false;

    mHero = new SpritePrimitive(
        "SimpleSpriteSheet",
        new Vector2(20, 30), new Vector2(10, 10),
        4,  // Number of rows
        2,  // Number of columns
        0); // Padding between images

    // Start Hero by walking left and AnotherHero by walking right
    mHero.SetSpriteAnimation(0, 0, 0, 3, 10);
}
```

3. In the update function, call the upcoming `CollisionUpdate()` function:

```
public void UpdateGame()
{
    mHero.Position += InputWrapper.ThumbSticks.Left;
    mHero.Update();

    CollisionUpdate();
    UserControlUpdate();
}
```

4. Now create the `CollisionUpdate()` function to handle all the collisions between the various objects in the game. Notice that even though the hero uses a loop to detect the collision between itself and a plane, the logic inside the loop is essentially the same as the logic used for the flower collision.

```
private void CollisionUpdate()
{
    Vector2 pixelCollisionPosition = Vector2.Zero;

    #region Collide the hero with the flower
    mHeroBoundCollision = mHero.PrimitivesTouches(mFlower);
    mHeroPixelCollision = mHeroBoundCollision;
    if (mHeroBoundCollision)
    {
        mHeroPixelCollision =
            mHero.PixelTouches(mFlower, out pixelCollisionPosition);
        if (mHeroPixelCollision)
            mHeroTarget.Position = pixelCollisionPosition;
    }
    #endregion

    #region Collide the hero with planes
    int i = 0;
    while ((!mHeroPixelCollision) && (i < kNumPlanes))
    {
        mHeroBoundCollision = mPlane[i].PrimitivesTouches(mHero);
        mHeroPixelCollision = mHeroBoundCollision;
        if (mHeroBoundCollision)
        {
            mHeroPixelCollision =
                mPlane[i].PixelTouches(mHero, out pixelCollisionPosition);
            if (mHeroPixelCollision)
                mHeroTarget.Position = pixelCollisionPosition;
        }
        i++;
    }
    #endregion
}
```

5. You can now modify the UserControlUpdate() function to account for hero selection and rotation of the hero and flower. In this function, you map the controls for the hero and the flower. Remember to include buttons that swap between currently selected objects.

```
private void UserControlUpdate()
{
    #region Selecting Hero
    if (InputWrapper.Buttons.A == ButtonState.Pressed)
        mCurrentPrim = mFlower;
    if (InputWrapper.Buttons.B == ButtonState.Pressed)
        mCurrentPrim = mPlane[0];
    mCurrentPrim.Position += InputWrapper.ThumbSticks.Right;
    #endregion

    #region Specifying hero rotation
    if (InputWrapper.Buttons.X == ButtonState.Pressed)
        mHero.RotateAngleInRadian += MathHelper.ToRadians(1);
    if (InputWrapper.Buttons.Y == ButtonState.Pressed)
        mHero.RotateAngleInRadian += MathHelper.ToRadians(-1);
    #endregion

    #region Specifying flower rotation
    mCurrentPrim.RotateAngleInRadian += MathHelper.ToRadians(
        InputWrapper.Triggers.Left);
    mCurrentPrim.RotateAngleInRadian -= MathHelper.ToRadians(
        InputWrapper.Triggers.Right);
    #endregion

    #region Sprite Sheet Update
    ...
    #endregion
}
```

6. Finally, in the DrawGame() function, call each game object's corresponding Draw() function and print the hero's current collision status to the screen:

```
public void DrawGame()
{
    mFlower.Draw();
    mHero.Draw();
    foreach (var p in mPlane)
        p.Draw();

    if (mHeroPixelCollision)
        mHeroTarget.Draw();

    FontSupport.PrintStatus("Collisions Bound(" + mHeroBoundCollision +
        ") Pixel(" + mHeroPixelCollision + ")", null);
}
```

Moving and zooming the camera

In the example games you've built thus far, the camera view has remained in a static position and at a static zoom level. In this section, you will learn how to add zoom-and-move features to your Camera class. By creating a more fully featured Camera class, you will be able to reproduce common camera effects seen in many 2D games. For example, zooming lets users focus their attention on a particular portion of the screen. Additionally, you can employ zoom to create a zoom-out effect that lets players see more of your game world on the screen at one time. Moving the camera provides the ability to pan to points of interest and attach the camera to your hero character or game object. By attaching the camera to your hero character, you can easily reproduce the first-person point of view commonly seen in side-scrolling games and top-down adventure games.

The Camera Zoom Move project

This project demonstrates how to manipulate the camera's position and zoom level using the gamepad. You'll see how the camera can move relative to both a large texture and a hero character. You control the hero character. The camera will chase the hero character to keep it within the game window. You can see an example of this project running in Figure 7-5.

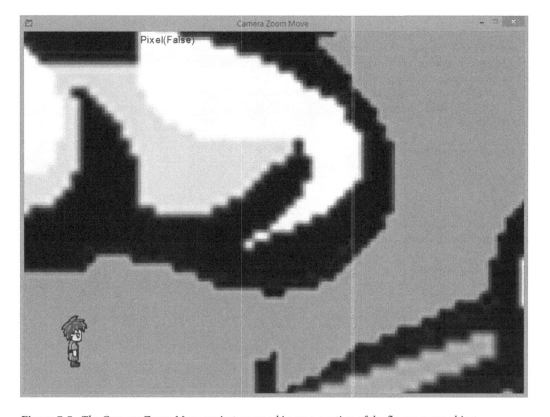

Figure 7-5. *The Camera Zoom Move project, zoomed in on a portion of the flower game object*

The project's controls are as follows:

- **Right thumbstick (arrow-keys)** Moves the camera window
- **Left thumbstick (WSAD-keys)** Moves the hero
- **Button A (K-key)** Zooms out
- **Button B (L-key)** Zooms in
- **Buttons X and Y (J and I keys)** Rotate the hero

The goals of the project are as follows:

- To implement moving and zooming functionality in the Camera class
- To understand how to keep a game object of interest within the camera's window

The steps for creating the project are as follows:

1. Modify the Camera class to account for the new functionality.
2. Modify the GameState class to use the camera's new functionality.

Modifying the *Camera* class

1. To begin, in your Camera class, add a static move-camera function that accepts a change in position and applies it to the camera's origin:

```
static public void MoveCameraBy(Vector2 delta)
{
    sOrigin += delta;
}
```

2. Now you can create the camera's zoom function. Start by considering the image shown following. The image shows the variables you need to achieve a zoom-out effect by increasing the size of the camera window.

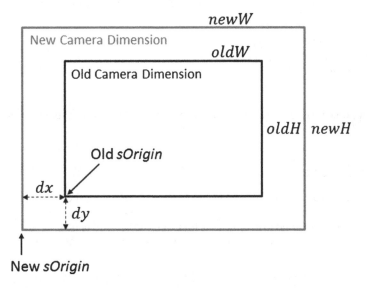

Notice that the inner black rectangle is defined by variables labeled *old*—more specifically, an old origin, width, and height. To define the outer red rectangle, you must calculate all new values. You can calculate the new width and height easily by adding the change in width and height to the camera's old width and height. In the image, this change is defined as *dx* and *dy* in the image. However, because the rectangle is centered, the total change is *2dx* and *2dy*. With that new information in hand, you can deduce the following:

$$newW = oldW + 2 \cdot \Delta x$$

$$newH = oldH + 2 \cdot \Delta y$$

Therefore, the following is true:

$$\Delta x = \frac{(newW - oldW)}{2}$$

$$\Delta y = \frac{(newH - oldH)}{2}$$

3. Now that you have an understanding of the mathematics needed, you can create a zoom function for the camera. Do this by passing in the desired change, saving the old width and height, calculating the new width and height, and then applying the changes to the origin. You can achieve this by following the process defined in the code that follows:

```
static public void ZoomCameraBy(float deltaX)
{
    float oldW = sWidth;
    float oldH = sHeight;

    sWidth = sWidth + deltaX;
    sRatio = -1f;
    cameraWindowToPixelRatio();

    float dx = 0.5f * (sWidth - oldW);
    float dy = 0.5f * (sHeight - oldH);
    sOrigin -= new Vector2(dx, dy);
}
```

Now that your Camera class supports the required manipulation, you can take advantage of the camera's new functionality within the GameState class.

Modifying the *GameState* class

1. Begin by modifying the constructor to initialize your game objects with the values shown following. Notice that the flower game object is used as a reference so you can see changes to the camera. The plane objects are used to demonstrate how game objects will behave offscreen. Finally, the hero provides the camera with a target that it should keep on the screen.

```
public GameState()
{
    // Set up the flower ...
    mFlower = new TexturedPrimitive("Flower",
        new Vector2(50, 35), new Vector2(350, 350));

    // Planes
    mPlane = new TexturedPrimitive[kNumPlanes];
    mPlane[0] = new TexturedPrimitive("PatrolEnemy",
        new Vector2(20, -80), new Vector2(20, 40));
    mPlane[1] = new TexturedPrimitive("PatrolEnemy",
        new Vector2(150, -100), new Vector2(20, 40));
    mPlane[2] = new TexturedPrimitive("PatrolEnemy",
        new Vector2(150, 120), new Vector2(20, 40));
    mPlane[3] = new TexturedPrimitive("PatrolEnemy",
        new Vector2(20, 170), new Vector2(20, 40));

    mHeroTarget = new TexturedPrimitive("Target", new Vector2(0, 0), new Vector2(3, 3));
    mHeroBoundCollision = false;
    mHeroPixelCollision = false;

    mHero = new SpritePrimitive(
        "SimpleSpriteSheet",
        new Vector2(10, 10),
        new Vector2(10, 10),
        4,  // Number of rows
        2,  // Number of columns
        0); // Padding between images

    // Start Hero by walking left and AnotherHero by walking toward right
    mHero.SetSpriteAnimation(0, 0, 0, 3, 10); // Slowly
}
```

2. With the objects properly initialized, add the following changes to the update function. The following code shows that the update function has been subdivided into several service functions (to prevent the function from becoming too large and unreadable).

    a. Start by using the gamepad's left thumbstick in order to change the hero's current position.

    b. Detect any collision between the hero and the flower and between the hero and the planes. You do this using the pixel-accurate collision functions you created earlier.

    c. Apply the camera manipulations you created in the Camera class by binding them to the gamepad's A and B buttons (to zoom in and out) and the right thumbstick (to change the position).

    d. You want to make sure that the hero character always stays within the camera's window. To do this, you need to move the camera whenever the hero reaches the edge of the screen. The previously created camera window collision states work great for this. By detecting which camera border the hero character has collided with, you can move the camera's position in the proper direction to keep the hero on the screen.

     e. Lastly, remember to support hero rotation and apply the correct sprite animation
      depending upon the hero character's direction of movement.

```
public void UpdateGame()
{
    // Change the hero position by thumbstick
    Vector2 heroMoveDelta = InputWrapper.ThumbSticks.Left;
    mHero.Position += heroMoveDelta;
    mHero.Update();

    CollisionUpdate();

    // Back hero out of the collision!
    if (mHeroPixelCollision)
        mHero.Position -= heroMoveDelta;

    HeroMovingCameraWindow();
    UserControlUpdate();
}

private void HeroMovingCameraWindow()
{
    Camera.CameraWindowCollisionStatus status = Camera.CollidedWithCameraWindow(mHero);
    Vector2 delta = Vector2.Zero;
    Vector2 cameraLL = Camera.CameraWindowLowerLeftPosition;
    Vector2 cameraUR = Camera.CameraWindowUpperRightPosition;
    const float kChaseRate = 0.05f;
    float kBuffer = mHero.Width * 2f;
    switch (status)
    {
        case Camera.CameraWindowCollisionStatus.CollideBottom:
            delta.Y = (mHero.Position.Y - kBuffer - cameraLL.Y) * kChaseRate;
            break;
        case Camera.CameraWindowCollisionStatus.CollideTop:
            delta.Y = (mHero.Position.Y + kBuffer - cameraUR.Y) * kChaseRate;
            break;
        case Camera.CameraWindowCollisionStatus.CollideLeft:
            delta.X = (mHero.Position.X - kBuffer - cameraLL.X) * kChaseRate;
            break;
        case Camera.CameraWindowCollisionStatus.CollideRight:
            delta.X = (mHero.Position.X + kBuffer - cameraUR.X) * kChaseRate;
            break;
    }
    Camera.MoveCameraBy(delta);
}

private void UserControlUpdate()
{
    #region Specifying hero rotation
    ...
    #endregion
```

```
#region Sprite Sheet Update
...
#endregion

#region Camera Control
// Zooming in/out with buttons A and B
if (InputWrapper.Buttons.A == ButtonState.Pressed)
    Camera.ZoomCameraBy(5);
if (InputWrapper.Buttons.B == ButtonState.Pressed)
    Camera.ZoomCameraBy(-5);

// Move the camera with right thumbstick
Camera.MoveCameraBy(InputWrapper.ThumbSticks.Right);
#endregion
}
```

3. Finally, modify the DrawGame() function to draw each of the game objects and output the current collision status to the screen.

```
public void DrawGame()
{
    mFlower.Draw();
    foreach (var p in mPlane)
        p.Draw();
    mHero.Draw();

    if (mHeroPixelCollision)
        mHeroTarget.Draw();

    FontSupport.PrintStatus("Collisions Bound(" +
            mHeroBoundCollision + ") Pixel(" +
            mHeroPixelCollision + ")", null);
}
```

Adding audio

In general, audio effects used in games fall into two categories. The first category is *background audio*, which includes music or ambient effects, and is often used to bring atmosphere or emotion to different portions of the game. The second category is *sound effects*. Sound effects are useful for all sorts of things, from notifying users of game actions to hearing the footfalls of your hero character. Usually, sound effects represent a specific action, triggered either by the user or by the game itself. Such sound effects are often thought of as an *audio cue*.

One important difference between these two types of audio is how you control them. Sound effects or cues cannot be stopped or have their volume adjusted once they have started; therefore, cues are generally very short. On the other hand, background audio can be started and stopped at will, and you can adjust the volume during playback. These capabilities are useful for fading background audio in or out depending on the current GameState class, or for stopping the background track completely and starting another one.

The Audio project

In this project, as in the previous one, you can move the hero character as well as the camera; however, this version triggers sound effects as various actions are performed. Additionally, a background track will be played at the start of the project. You can see an example of this project running in Figure 7-6.

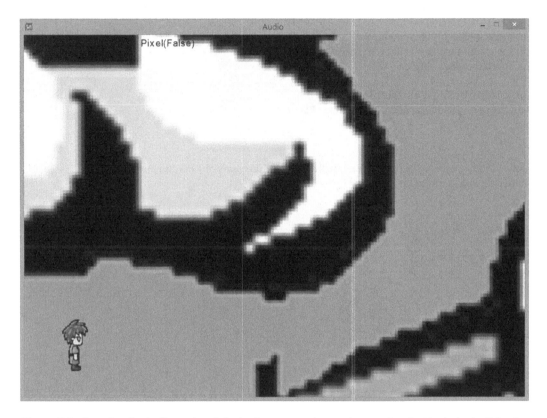

Figure 7-6. *Running the Audio project; it looks the same as the previous project, but includes both background music and audio cues*

The project's controls are as follows:

- **Right thumbstick (arrow-keys)** Moves the camera window
- **Left thumbstick (WSAD-keys)** Moves the hero
- **Button A (K-key)** Zooms out
- **Button B (L-key)** Zooms in
- **Buttons X and Y (J and I keys)** Rotate the hero

The goals of the project are as follows:

- To understand how to implement audio into your game project
- To understand the difference between the two types of audio used

The steps for creating the project are as follows:

1. Create an AudioSupport class in order to provide the new audio functionality needed.

2. Modify the GameState class to include the newly added audio.

Like Font resources, as covered in Chapter 3, audio files must first be converted into xnb format before they can be included in a MonoGame project. Once again, we can use the XNAFormatter program to convert the following resources found in the Chapter07\SourceCode\Resources folder:

- Bounce.wav

- Mind_Meld.mp3

- Wall.wav

Once converted, the corresponding xnb files can be included in the MonoGame project. Right click over the Content folder and go to Add ➤ Existing Items, or simply drag and drop the xnb files into the Content folder.

■ **Note**   Like with images and fonts, if you choose to drag and drop the files into the Content folder, you must remember to bring up the Properties window of each audio resource and change the Build Action field to Content, and Copy to Output Directory to Copy if newer.

Creating the *AudioSupport* class

1. Create a new class called AudioSupport. Make the class static so you can access it easily throughout the project. Create a dictionary data structure to store all the sound effects or cues. Finally, create an instance variable to keep track of the background audio.

```
static public class AudioSupport
{
    // Audio effect files
    private static Dictionary<String, SoundEffect> sAudioEffects =
        new Dictionary<string,SoundEffect>();
    // Constant background audio
    private static SoundEffectInstance sBackgroundAudio = null;

    ...
}
```

2. Add a method so you can find a desired audio clip. You do this by searching the dictionary data structure for the desired audio clip by name. If the clip is found within the data structure, the code should return it, otherwise it should first load the missing clip into the dictionary and then return it.

```
static private SoundEffect FindAudioClip(String name)
{
    SoundEffect sound = null;
    if (sAudioEffects.ContainsKey(name))
        sound = sAudioEffects[name];
```

```
        else
        {
            sound = Game1.sContent.Load<SoundEffect>(name);
            if (null != sound)
                sAudioEffects.Add(name, sound);
        }
        return sound;
    }
```

3. Now you can create a function to play an audio cue. To do this, you first find the audio cue
    using the function you just created, and then call its Play() function.

```
static public void PlayACue(String cueName)
{
    SoundEffect sound = FindAudioClip(cueName);
    if (null != sound)
        sound.Play();
}
```

4. Add functionality to start and stop the background audio. To start the clip, find the
    background audio and initialize your background audio instance variable by creating a
    new instance of the clip. Additionally, modify its settings and call the Play() function.
    To stop background audio, call its Pause() and Stop() functions, reset its volume to zero,
    and then delete the clip by calling its Dispose() function.

```
static private void StartBg(String name, float level)
{
    SoundEffect bgm = FindAudioClip(name);
    sBackgroundAudio = bgm.CreateInstance();
    sBackgroundAudio.IsLooped = true;
    sBackgroundAudio.Volume = level;
    sBackgroundAudio.Play();
}

static private void StopBg()
{
    if (null != sBackgroundAudio)
    {
        sBackgroundAudio.Pause();
        sBackgroundAudio.Stop();
        sBackgroundAudio.Volume = 0f;

        sBackgroundAudio.Dispose();
    }
    sBackgroundAudio = null;
}
```

5. Next, add a function to play the background audio. This function is used to stop any
    existing background audio and then start a new background audio file at a desired volume
    level. This is easily done by utilizing the functions you just created.

```
    static public void PlayBackgroundAudio(String bgAudio, float level)
    {
        StopBg();
        if (("" != bgAudio) || (null != bgAudio))
        {
            level = MathHelper.Clamp(level, 0f, 1f);
            StartBg(bgAudio, level);
        }
    }
}
```

Now that the audio support class is finished, you can use it within the GameState class by playing effects for various actions.

Modifying the *GameState* class

1. Start the background audio when the game initializes. You do this by calling the PlayBackgroundAudio() function within the constructor:

```
public GameState()
{
    ...

    // Begin background audio
    AudioSupport.PlayBackgroundAudio("Mind_Meld", 0.4f);
}
```

2. To play the Bounce.wav audio cue when the hero character collides with the flower, call AudioSupport.PlayACue("Bounce") whenever a flower-to-hero collision occurs:

```
public void UpdateGame()
{
    ...

    // Collide the hero with the flower
    mHeroBoundCollision = mHero.PrimitivesTouches(mFlower);
    mHeroPixelCollision = mHeroBoundCollision;
    if (mHeroBoundCollision)
    {
        mHeroPixelCollision = mHero.PixelTouches(mFlower, out pixelCollisionPosition);
        if (mHeroPixelCollision)
        {
            AudioSupport.PlayACue("Bounce");
        }
    }

    ...
}
```

3. Similarly, to play the Wall.wav cue when the hero character collides with a rocket, call AudioSupport.PlayACue("Wall") whenever a hero-to-rocket collision occurs:

```
public void UpdateGame()
{
    ...

    int i = 0;
    while ((!mHeroPixelCollision) && (i < kNumPlanes))
    {
        mHeroBoundCollision = mPlane[i].PrimitivesTouches(mHero);
        mHeroPixelCollision = mHeroBoundCollision;
        if (mHeroBoundCollision)
        {
            mHeroPixelCollision =
                mPlane[i].PixelTouches(mHero, out pixelCollisionPosition);
            if (mHeroPixelCollision)
            {
                AudioSupport.PlayACue("Wall");
            }
        }
        i++;
    }

    ...
}
```

Summary

In this chapter, you have seen how to add animation, camera manipulation, and audio to your game project. By implementing these concepts, you can provide players with an enriched experience as they interact with your game. Animation lets you give motion and add realism to your game objects by iterating through a sequence of images. Animation gives visual feedback to the user for things such as player movements and actions.

Additionally, by implementing camera manipulation, you are able to create larger and more interesting game worlds, as well as direct the player's attention to specific game elements. You accomplish this with basic move and zoom functionality.

Finally, you saw how to implement two different types of audio: background music and audio cues (or sound effects). You can use background music to set the mood or atmosphere of the game, and you control its playback at run time. You use audio cues or sound effects to augment a specific action of the player or the game. Audio cues, once started, cannot be modified.

Quick reference

To	Do this
Create simple animation for an object	Identify the corresponding begin and end (row, column) positions on the sprite sheet.
Instantiate a SpritePrimitive object	1. Identify and include the desired sprite sheet image in your project, making sure you take note of the file name.
	2. Instantiate a SpritePrimitive game object with the corresponding file name.
	3. Define the size and position of the game object.
	4. Configure the game object to correspond to the amount of rows, columns, and padding on the sprite sheet.
Define a sprite animation with SpritePrimitive	Call the SetSpriteAnimation() function, as follows:
	1. Identify the beginning and end (row, column) of the animation.
	2. Define the speed of the animation as a function of the number of Update() function calls.
Ensure sprite animation is shown	Call the Update() function of the SpritePrimitive object in GameState.UpdateGame().
Support pixel-accurate collision for an animated sprite	Override the texture size and position functions of the TexturedPrimitive class to return the corresponding information for one sprite. Having the TexturedPrimitivePixelCollide class refer to these new definitions results in pixel-accurate collision support for individual sprites.
Move a camera	Call Camera.MoveCameraBy(deltaMovement), where deltaMovement describes the amount that the camera position will be moved in the x and y directions.
Zoom the camera in or out	Call Camera.ZoomCameraBy(deltaSize), where a positive deltaSize causes the camera to zoom out (see more of the game window), and a negative value causes the camera to zoom into the game window.
Have the camera follow an object	Continuously detect the collisions between the object and the camera (by calling Camera.CollidedWithCameraWindow()) and move the camera position accordingly. Refer to Chapter 3 for the details of Camera.CollidedWithCameraWindow().
Start background audio	Call AudioSupport.PlayBackgroundAudio("file name", level).
Stop background audio	Call AudioSupport.PlayBackgroundAudio(null, 0).
Play an audio cue	Call AudioSupport.PlayACue("cueName").

CHAPTER 8

■ ■ ■

Particle Systems

After completing this chapter, you will be able to:

- Understand how to create simple explosion or fire-like effects with particle systems

- Differentiate between alpha and additive blending effects when working with particles

- Understand when and how to implement a particle emitter

This chapter shows you how to implement your own basic particle system so you can create various particle effects. In games, particle systems are used for various purposes, such as displaying fire, showing a spell or explosion effect, or creating a trail for a game object. In the example projects in this chapter, the particle system will be triggered by collisions; however, that does not need to be the only case. For example, in an underwater game, you might implement a particle system that attaches to a hero character and emits bubbles over time. The implementation in this chapter is intended to function as a basic example; however, the particle system you'll implement is flexible enough that you should be able to customize it for your own games.

Particle systems

In this section, you will create a particle system that includes the basic functionality you need to achieve common effects, such as explosions and spell effects. Additionally, you can initialize your effect at a specific location or add it to a game object and trigger it when needed. Your implementation will also include the ability to use blending effects that display more smoothly.

The Particle System project

The gameplay functionality of this project is identical to that from the previous chapter. Here, however, you'll add particle effects that appear at points of collision. You can see an example of this project running in Figure 8-1.

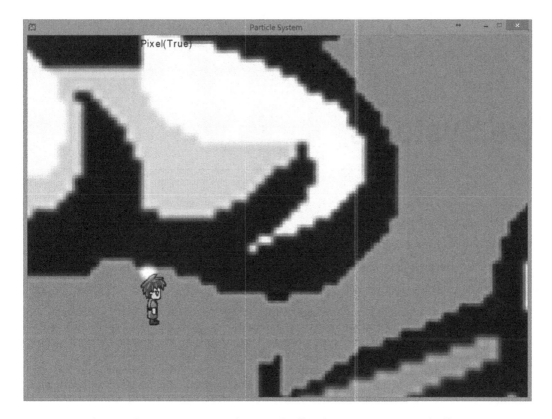

Figure 8-1. *The Particle System project, with a particle effect showing at the point of collision*

The project's controls are as follows:

- **Right thumbstick (arrow-keys)** Moves the camera window
- **Left thumbstick (WSAD-keys)** Moves the hero
- **Button A (K-key)** Zooms out
- **Button B (L-key)** Zooms in
- **Buttons X and Y (J and I keys)** Rotate the hero

The goals of this project are as follows:

- To create a primitive object that represents a single particle
- To implement randomness
- To understand alpha and additive blending
- To understand and create a particle system
- To initialize and maintain the particle collection
- To create and draw particles when desired

The steps for creating the project are as follows:

1. Learn about the components of the particle system.

2. Modify the TexturedPrimitive class to support tint color.

3. Create the ParticlePrimitive class to support a single particle.

4. Create the ParticleSystem class to support a collection of ParticlePrimitive objects.

5. Modify the GameState class to include the new particle system.

Add the following resource, which can be found in the Chapter08\SourceCode\Resources folder, into your content project before you begin:

- ParticleImage.png

Understanding particle systems

In its simplest form, a particle system is a collection of primitives. The primitives within a particle system are known as *particles*. All the particles in a particle system have a common set of properties, such as life span, size, rate of change in size, and speed. By manipulating these properties in different ways, you can achieve various effects. In general, each particle executes a behavior based on its properties until its life span is over.

Another important aspect for a particle system is randomness. To create an effect such as an explosion, game developers often use random values to initialize a particle's properties. Without a random factor, patterns often become apparent as the particle system executes. Overall, you can think of a particle system as a group or collection of particles. By randomizing each particle's properties, you can achieve engaging effects for a variety of purposes.

With the basic understanding of the components of a particle system, you are ready to begin adding support for the upcoming particle classes. The first modification you need to make is adding color-tinting support within the TexturedPrimitive class. Adding this allows you to tint your images.

Modifying the *TexturedPrimitive* class

1. In TexturedPrimitive.cs, add the mTintColor variable and initialize it within the InitPrimitive() function:

```
protected Color mTintColor;

protected void InitPrimitive(String imageName, Vector2 position, Vector2 size, String
label = null)
{
    ...

    mTintColor = Color.White;

    ...
}
```

2. In the Draw() function, locate the SpriteBatch.Draw call and modify it to include the tint color:

```
Game1.sSpriteBatch.Draw(mImage,
                destRect,            // Area to be drawn in pixel space
                null,                //
                mTintColor,          //
                mRotateAngle,        // Angle to rotate (clockwise)
                org,                 // Image reference position
                SpriteEffects.None, 0f);
```

Creating the *ParticlePrimitive* class

1. Create a new folder named ParticleSupport. Then create a new class called ParticlePrimitive that inherits from the GameObject class, and save it in the new ParticleSupport folder you just created. Add the instance variables shown following to the ParticlePrimitive class to support life span, size change, and randomness:

```
public class ParticlePrimitive : GameObject
{
    private float kLifeSpanRandomness = 0.4f;
    private float kSizeChangeRandomness = 0.5f;
    private float kSizeRandomness = 0.3f;
    private float kSpeedRandomness = 0.1f;

    // Number of updates before a particle disappear
    private int mLifeSpan;
    // How fast does the particle changes size
    private float mSizeChangeRate;

    ...
}
```

2. Next, create a constructor that accepts a position, size, and life span for the particle. For this example, pass the ParticleImage.png image name in the base constructor call. Lastly, set the particle properties to the default values shown in the following code:

```
public ParticlePrimitive(Vector2 position, float size, int lifeSpan) :
    base("ParticleImage", position, new Vector2(size, size))
{
    mLifeSpan =(int)(lifeSpan * Game1.RandomNumber(-kLifeSpanRandomness,
                                    kLifeSpanRandomness));

    mVelocityDir.X = Game1.RandomNumber(-0.5f, 0.5f);
    mVelocityDir.Y = Game1.RandomNumber(-0.5f, 0.5f);
    mVelocityDir.Normalize();
    mSpeed = Game1.RandomNumber(kSpeedRandomness);

    mSizeChangeRate = Game1.RandomNumber(kSizeChangeRandomness);
```

```
    mSize.X *= Game1.RandomNumber(1f-kSizeRandomness, 1+kSizeRandomness);
    mSize.Y = mSize.X;
}
```

3. You need to override the existing update function within the base class. In the update function, first call the base class's update, and then decrement the life span, adjust the particle's size, and modify its tint color:

```
public override void Update()
{
    base.Update();
    mLifeSpan--;    // Continue to approach expiration

    // Change its size
    mSize.X += mSizeChangeRate;
    mSize.Y += mSizeChangeRate;

    // Change the tintcolor randomly
    Byte[] b = new Byte[3];
    Game1.sRan.NextBytes(b);
    mTintColor.R += b[0];
    mTintColor.G += b[1];
    mTintColor.B += b[2];
}
```

4. Finally, create an accessor called Expired to return the particle's current life status. Returning false indicates that the particle life span is over.

```
public bool Expired { get { return (mLifeSpan < 0); } }
```

Now that you have created the class for a particle, you can create the particle system itself.

Creating the *ParticleSystem* class

1. Create a new class called ParticleSystem within the ParticleSupport folder. Add a collection of particles to the particle system using a list data structure. Don't forget to initialize the list of particles within the constructor.

```
public class ParticleSystem
{
    // Collection of particles
    private List<ParticlePrimitive> mAllParticles;

    public ParticleSystem()
    {
        mAllParticles = new List<ParticlePrimitive>();
    }

    ...
}
```

2. Now add a function that creates a particle at a specific position. You can do this easily by passing in the desired position of the particle, creating a particle, and adding it to the collection.

```
public void AddParticleAt(Vector2 pos)
{
    ParticlePrimitive particle = new ParticlePrimitive(pos, 2f, 50);
    mAllParticles.Add(particle);
}
```

3. Next, create a function to update each particle within the collection. This function should iterate through each particle in the list, calling its update function. Additionally, check to see whether the particle has expired; if so, remove it from the list.

```
public void UpdateParticles()
{
    int particleCounts = mAllParticles.Count;
    for (int i = particleCounts- 1; i >= 0; i--)
    {
        mAllParticles[i].Update();
        if (mAllParticles[i].Expired)
            mAllParticles.RemoveAt(i);   // Remove expired ones
    }
}
```

4. Finally, create a function to draw the particle system. You do this by drawing each particle within the list. Additionally, you can apply a blend state of Additive and AlphaBlend to the particles. The details of both blend states are shown following.

```
public void DrawParticleSystem()
{
    // 1. Switch blend mode to "Additive"
    Game1.sSpriteBatch.End();
    Game1.sSpriteBatch.Begin(SpriteSortMode.Immediate, BlendState.Additive);

    // 2. Draw all particles
    foreach (var particle in mAllParticles)
        particle.Draw();

    // 3. Switch blend mode back to AlphaBlend
    Game1.sSpriteBatch.End();
    Game1.sSpriteBatch.Begin(SpriteSortMode.Immediate, BlendState.AlphaBlend);
}
```

Understanding alpha and additive blending

Blending is a process of mixing overlapping colors to produce a new color. The blending process consists of three key components. First is the *source color*, which is the overlaying or top color. Second is the *destination color*, which is the bottom color—the color underneath the source color. The last color is the *blended color*, which is a color calculated from the source color and the destination color. Alpha blending and additive blending are two different ways of calculating a blended color.

Typically, alpha blending is achieved with the following equation:

$$Output\_Color = Source\_Alpha * Source\_Color + (1 - Source\_Alpha) * Destination\_Color$$

By inspecting this equation, you can see that when the source's alpha is equal to 1, the Output_Color equals the Source_Color. Alternatively, when the source's alpha is equal to 0, the Output_Color equals the Destination_Color. Logically this makes sense. If the source is completely opaque (has an alpha of 1), then the background color will not show through. However, if the source is completely transparent (has an alpha of 0), then the background color will show through unchanged. An alpha value between 0 and 1 will compute an output color that is a linear combination (blend) of the source and destination colors.

MonoGame achieves additive blending using the following equation:

$$Output\_Color = Source\_Alpha * Source\_Color * Tint\_Color + Destination\_Color$$

By inspecting this equation, you can see that the approach to additive blending is similar to alpha blending; however, there are some differences. The first difference is that Tint_Color is included along with Source_Alpha. Secondly, the destination color is added without the reference to Source_Alpha. This means the bottom color is added to the top or overlaying color.

In addition to alpha and additive blending, there are other types, such as multiplicative blending. The type of blending you should use within your games depends upon the effect you're trying to achieve. Figure 8-2 shows examples of the effects that alpha and additive blending produce.

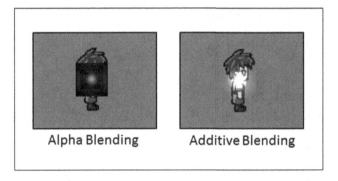

Figure 8-2. *The difference between alpha and additive blending*

You can now add the GameState class modifications necessary to use the particle system within your game.

Modifying the *GameState* class

1. Start by adding an instance variable for the particle system and initializing it within the constructor:

```
ParticleSystem mParticleSystem;

public GameState()
{
    ...

    mParticleSystem = new ParticleSystem();
}
```

2. Next, call the particle system's update within the game state's update function. Additionally, create particles at the point of collision when a collision is detected. Do this by calling the AddParticleAt() function when a collision occurs. Remember that the collision detection logic has been separated into its own CollisionUpdate() function.

```
public void UpdateGame()
{
    ...

    mParticleSystem.UpdateParticles();
}

private void CollisionUpdate()
{
    ...

    #region Collide the hero with the flower

    ...

    if (mHeroPixelCollision)
    {
        mParticleSystem.AddParticleAt(pixelCollisionPosition);
    }

    ...

    #endregion

    #region Collide the hero with planes

    ...

    if (mHeroPixelCollision)
    {
        mParticleSystem.AddParticleAt(pixelCollisionPosition);
    }

    ...

    #endregion
}
```

3. Lastly, simply draw the particle system by calling its function within the game state's draw function:

```
public void DrawGame()
{
    mFlower.Draw();
    foreach (var p in mPlane)
```

```
            p.Draw();
        mHero.Draw();

        mParticleSystem.DrawParticleSystem();

        ...
    }
```

Particle emitters

The particle system you just created works great for creating particles; however, useful particle systems should include the ability to control the duration of particle creation, the location where particles are created, and the behaviors of the created particles. This is where the *particle emitter* comes in. With control over the duration, location, and behaviors of emitted particles, you can create interesting effects such as fire, explosions, and trails by simply modifying the way particles are emitted.

The Particle Emitter project

This project allows you to implement particle emitter for your particle system. The functionality of this project is identical to that in the previous section; however, you'll use particle emitter to control the emission of particles after creating the particle system. You can see an example of this project running in Figure 8-3.

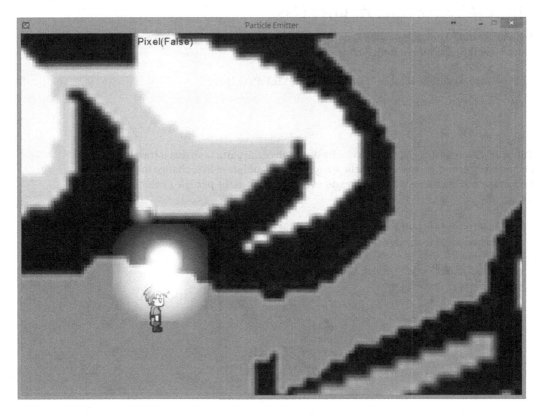

Figure 8-3. *The Particle Emitter project with a large particle emission at the point of collision*

The project's controls are as follows:

- **Right thumbstick (arrow-keys)** Moves the camera window
- **Left thumbstick (WSAD-keys)** Moves the hero
- **Button A (K-key)** Zooms out
- **Button B (L-key)** Zooms in
- **Buttons X and Y (J and I keys)** Rotate the hero

The goals of this project are as follows:

- To create a new particle type called ReddishParticlePrimitive
- To allow continuous particle emission from the ParticleSystem class

The steps for creating the project are as follows:

- Create the ReddishParticlePrimitive class.
- Create the ParticleEmitter class to support continuous particle emission.
- Modify the ParticleSystem class to support the particle emitter.
- Modify the GameState class to support the newly created emitter.

Creating the *ReddishParticlePrimitive* class

1. Begin by creating a new class called ReddishParticlePrimitive in the ParticleSupport folder. Have the class inherit from ParticlePrimitive.

```
public class ReddishParticlePrimitive : ParticlePrimitive
{
    ...
}
```

2. Within the class constructor, set the velocity direction of the particle so that it travels in an upward direction, increase the particle's speed by a multiple of five, change the size of the particle and the rate at which it changes over time, and set the particle's color to dark orange:

```
public ReddishParticlePrimitive(Vector2 position, float size, int lifeSpan) :
        base(position, size, lifeSpan)
{
    mVelocityDir.Y = 5f * Math.Abs(mVelocityDir.Y);
    mVelocityDir.Normalize();
    mSpeed *= 5.25f;
    mSizeChangeRate *= 1.5f;
    mSize.X *= 0.7f;
    mSize.Y = mSize.X;

    mTintColor = Color.DarkOrange;
}
```

3. Next, override the update function so you can modify the tint color over time. The code following modifies the RGB values individually during each update:

```
public override void Update()
{
    base.Update();

    Color s = mTintColor;
    if (s.R < 255)
        s.R += 1;
    if (s.G != 0)
        s.G -= 1;
    if (s.B != 0)
        s.B -= 1;
    mTintColor = s;
}
```

Now it is time to create the ParticleEmitter class. The emitter class gives you the ability to emit particles with a specific type of movement behavior over a finite amount of time.

Creating the *ParticleEmitter* class

1. Begin by creating a class called ParticleEmitter within the ParticleSupport folder. Include instance variables that control the minimum number of particles emitted each cycle, the emitter's position, and the number of particles that remain to be emitted.

```
public class ParticleEmitter
{
    const int kMinToEmit = 5;
    protected Vector2 mEmitPosition;
    protected int mNumRemains;


    ...
}
```

2. Now initialize the variables within the constructor and provide an accessor so you can determine whether there are any remaining particles to be emitted:

```
public ParticleEmitter(Vector2 pos, int n)
{
    mNumRemains = n;
    mEmitPosition = pos;
}

public bool Expired { get { return (mNumRemains <= 0); } }
```

3. Next, create a function called EmitParticles(). This function determines the number and type of particles that need to be emitted.

a. The function begins by computing how many particles should be emitted. This is accomplished by checking whether all the remaining particles should be emitted (true when the remaining number is less than the minimum) or whether some random percentage of the remaining particles should be emitted. After this number is determined, the particles are emitted to the input allParticles particle list.

b. Having calculated the number of particles to emit, this example next creates either a reddish-colored or normal (unmodified) particle; these have a 40 and 60 percent chance of being created, respectively. This adds a bit of randomness to the particle generation and results in a more interesting appearance.

```
public void EmitParticles(List<ParticlePrimitive> allParticles)
{
    int numToEmit = 0;
    if (mNumRemains < kMinToEmit)
    {
        // If only a few are left, emits all of them
        numToEmit = mNumRemains;
    }
    else
    {
        // Otherwise, emits about 20% of what's left
        numToEmit = (int)Game1.RandomNumber(0.2f * mNumRemains);
    }
    // Left for future emitting.
    mNumRemains -= numToEmit;

    for (int i = 0; i < numToEmit; i++)
    {
        ParticlePrimitive particle;
        // 40% chance emitting simple particle,
        // 60% chance emitting the new reddish particle
        if (Game1.RandomNumber(1.0f) > 0.6f)
            particle = new ParticlePrimitive(mEmitPosition, 2f, 30);
        else
            particle = new ReddishParticlePrimitive(mEmitPosition, 2f, 80);
        allParticles.Add(particle);
    }
}
```

Modifying the *ParticleSystem* class

1. Now modify the ParticleSystem class by adding a particle emitter list and initializing it within the constructor:

```
private List<ParticleEmitter> mAllEmitters;

public ParticleSystem()
{
    ...

    mAllEmitters = new List<ParticleEmitter>();
}
```

2. Remove the AddParticleAt() function and replace it with the AddEmitterAt() function.
By doing this, you can now generate a range of particles that will emit from a desired
position. The code following generates some number of particles between 50 and 100:

```
public void AddEmitterAt(Vector2 pos)
{
    ParticleEmitter e = new ParticleEmitter(pos, (int) Game1.RandomNumber(50, 100));
    mAllEmitters.Add(e);
}
```

3. Next, you need to modify the UpdateParticles() function to account for the newly added
emitters. Do this by iterating through the emitter list, emitting each particle, and removing
the expired emitters:

```
public void UpdateParticles()
{
    int emittersCount = mAllEmitters.Count;
    for (int i = emittersCount - 1; i >= 0; i--)
    {
        mAllEmitters[i].EmitParticles(mAllParticles);
        if (mAllEmitters[i].Expired)
            mAllEmitters.RemoveAt(i);
    }

    ...
}
```

Finally, you can make a quick modification to the GameState class so you can use the new ParticleEmitter class.

Modifying the *GameState* class

1. Modify the CollisionUpdate() function by replacing the AddParticleAt() function calls
with your new AddEmitterAt() function. Now, when a collision occurs, an emitter will
create particles for a set amount of time before disappearing.

```
private void CollisionUpdate()
{
    ...

    #region Collide the hero with the flower

    ...

    if (mHeroPixelCollision)
    {
        mParticleSystem.AddEmitterAt(pixelCollisionPosition);
    }
    ...

    #endregion
```

```
        #region Collide the hero with planes

        ...

        if (mHeroPixelCollision)
        {
            mParticleSystem.AddEmitterAt(pixelCollisionPosition);
        }

        ...

        #endregion
    }
```

Summary

In this chapter, you saw how to implement a particle system in your game. This particle system consists of a collection of particles, each of which contains properties that determine its behavior over a specifiable life span. Additionally, you saw how you can apply blending effects to your particles to give a customized appearance to your particle system. Specifically, you were shown how to implement alpha and additive blending.

Finally, you learned how to implement a particle emitter to support continued particle emission. Continuous emission is useful for fire and other effects that need to exist for an extended period of time.

Quick reference

To	Do this
Create an instantaneous bursting effect	Instantiate a ParticleSystem class and call the AddParticleAt() function to create the particle effect at the desired location.
Create a longer-lasting effect, such as fire or an explosion	Instantiate a ParticleEmitter class with the desired number of particles to be emitted and duration upon which to emit. Then add the emitter to the ParticleSystem class.
Create your own particle effect	1. Subclass from the ParticlePrimitive class (as in the case of ReddishParticlePrimitive class) and implement customized initialization and update behavior to the color, travel direction, velocity, life span, and so on.
	2. Create your own emitter class (for example, by subclassing from the ParticleEmitter class) and customize the creation and emitting behaviors.

■ ■ ■

CHAPTER 9

Building Your First 2D Game

After completing this chapter, you will be able to:

- Begin the designing of a 2D game

- Enumerate and specify functionality of elements in your game

- Translate the gaming element specification into C# classes

- Appreciate and work with the accuracy supported by the GameTime class

- Synthesize the preceding elements into a final fun game

- Approach the evaluation of your own game

- Begin investigation into the procedures to publish your final game

This chapter covers the process and implementation details of creating your own simple game using the concepts and techniques discussed throughout this book. It will demonstrate how you can leverage the code you have already produced in implementing simple games, such as the one described in this chapter, with straightforward efforts. In fact, the game described in this chapter was created over one weekend. This type of rapid development allows you to create quick prototypes of your ideas or simply focus on creating a fun and challenging experience for your target audience. Finally, at the end of this chapter is a discussion of some considerations for publishing your games with some relevant references for further investigations.

Simple Game: Fish Food

In this game, the player plays as a fish that swims along the seabed in an attempt to travel as far as it can. As it travels, the fish will encounter several enemy fish. The player will have to avoid these fish in order to continue traveling along the seabed. The fish will also encounter worms while traveling that it can consume in order to grow in size. If the player's fish is caught, it will lose a size and if it is of size one the game will end and the distance it traveled will be displayed. The player's fish can also shoot bubbles at the enemy fish in order to stun them for a few seconds in its attempt to avoid them.

The Fish Food project

This project demonstrates how to create a simple game by utilizing and modifying the content from this book. In the game, the player controls a hero character and attempts to travel as far as possible before getting caught by enemies. You can see the initial splash screen of this project running in Figure 9-1.

Figure 9-1. *Running the Fish Food game*

The project's controls are as follows:

- **Left thumbstick (WSAD keys)** Moves that hero character
- **Button A (K key)** Fires a bubble or starts the game

The goals of this project are as follows:

- To experience the entire game development process with a non-trivial game
- To experience mapping of gameplay description to specifications of game elements
- To iterate and specify all elements in a non-trivial game
- To experience the coding and modification of classes for each gaming element
- To synthesize all gaming elements in the GameState class to support gameplay

The first step in building a complete game is actually not about programming; rather, it is all about design. For the Fish Food game, we begin by specifying the complete functionality of the game, followed by enumerating the functionality of every element in the game, including game window, environment, hero, food, enemies, and camera behaviors. This complete specification of the game is referred to as the game design documentation. This documentation should completely describe how the game will be played. It is vital that this documentation be in a consistent state before you begin the actual programming. This is because it is much easier to change the behaviors of gaming elements by modifying the description than by changing programming code.

After the enumeration of the game design, the steps for creating the project are as follows:

1. Building the object with the most straightforward behavior, in this case the BubbleShot class.

2. Create the Hero class to represent the fish that the player will control.

3. Modify the PatrolEnemy class to allow enemies the ability to utilize sprite sheets and other customized behaviors.

4. Create the enemies: JellyFish, BlowFish, and FightingFish classes.

5. Create the PatrolEnemySet class to allow convenient working with collections of enemies.

6. Create the FishFood class for feeding the hero fish.

7. Create the EnvironmentGenerator class to furnish the gaming environment.

8. Modify the GameState class to incorporate all of the preceding elements in implementing the final game.

Add the following resources, which can be found in the Chapter9\SourceCode\Resources folder, into your content project before you begin:

- Break.xnb
- Bubble.xnb
- BUBBLE_1.xnb
- Chomp.xnb
- Eat.xnb
- ENEMY_1.xnb
- ENEMY_2.xnb
- ENEMY_3.xnb
- GAMEOVERSCREEN_1.xnb
- GROUND_1.xnb
- HERO_1.xnb
- Hit.xnb
- MindMeld.xnb
- SEAWEEDSMALL_1.xnb
- SEAWEEDTALL_1.xnb
- SIGN_1.xnb
- SPLASHSCREEN_1.xnb
- Stun.xnb
- Touch.xnb
- WORM_1.xnb

Fish Food Game Design

Before creating or implementing a game or prototype, it is always a good idea to write down the game's concept and functionality. This document can then become the foundation for your game's design document. It is generally important to have a design document when developing your game, as it provides you with an overview of the game objects and their interactions or behaviors among each other. This is especially important for larger projects or projects with multiple team members. For the purposes of this simple game project, because of its limited size and scope, a small summary and outline of the base functionality will suffice as the design document.

■ **Note**　Please refer to `GameDesignDocTemplate.doc`, located in Chapter 9 of the source code, for an example of what a full-fledged game design documentation template might look like.

Game functionality outline

Goals and Objectives:

- Travel as far as you can

- Avoid being caught by other fish

- Consume food to increase the hero's size

Game

- Side-scrolling to the right endlessly

- Increases in difficulty the further you travel by spawning more fish

- Displays distance traveled and size of the hero

- Provides a starting and ending splash screen

Environment

- Generates a simplistic endless terrain by repeating a seabed and a few pieces of seaweed as the camera pans right

- Generates a sign displaying the distance traveled at fixed intervals

Hero, under player control

- Can be moved up, down, left and right

- Can shoot a projectile to stun enemies

- Can change in size

Food

- Periodically falls to the seabed at semi-random intervals

- Can be eaten by the hero to increase its size

Enemies

- Jellyfish: can patrol in all directions and stun the hero when they touch

- Blowfish: patrols in the vertical direction and decreases hero size when touched

- Fighting Fish: patrols in the horizontal direction and decreases hero size when touched except when hero is larger in size

- All enemies chase the hero when approached

Camera

- Bounds the hero to the screen

- Pans to the right when the hero crosses the center of the screen

You can start by creating the simplest object. The preceding design outline states that the hero character can shoot a projectile. The projectile or bubble shot is quite basic and derives all of its behaviors from the base class.

Creating the *BubbleShot* class

1. Begin by creating a new class called BubbleShot that inherits from GameObject. As you may remember, the GameObject class you implemented earlier provides behavior for game objects. Add a constant variable for its size and speed. Initialize the proper variables and use the bubble image provided.

```
public class BubbleShot : GameObject
{
    private const float kBubbleShotWidth = 7f;
    private const float kBubbleShotHeight = 7f;
    private const float kBubbleShotSpeed = 1.8f;

    public BubbleShot(Vector2 position, int facing)
        : base("BUBBLE_1", position,
                new Vector2(kBubbleShotWidth, kBubbleShotHeight), null)
    {
        Speed = kBubbleShotSpeed;
        mVelocityDir = new Vector2(facing, 0);
    }
}
```

2. Now simply add a function that returns whether the BubbleShot is currently on screen by utilizing your previously made Camera class.

```
public bool IsOnScreen()
{
    // take advantage of the camera window bound check
    Camera.CameraWindowCollisionStatus status = Camera.CollidedWithCameraWindow(this);
    return (Camera.CameraWindowCollisionStatus.InsideWindow == status);
}
```

Creating the *Hero* class

1. Create a new class called Hero that inherits from SpritePrimitive. Add the following variables and functions in order to enable the Hero with particle support.

```
public class Hero : SpritePrimitive
{
  #region Particle Stuff
  private const float kCollideParticleSize = 4f;
  private const int kCollideParticleLife = 20;

  ParticleSystem mCollisionEffect = new ParticleSystem();
  // to support particle system
  private ParticlePrimitive CreateParticle(Vector2 pos)
  {
    return new ParticlePrimitive(pos, kCollideParticleSize, kCollideParticleLife);
  }
  #endregion
  ...
}
```

2. Next, add the following constants for the hero size, the time between shots, the offset position for the shots, the time that hero can be stunned, and the maximum growth size of the hero. Also add the following instance variables. Note that the hero size accessor also performs the size recalculation.

```
//Constants
private const float kHeroWidth = 20f;
private const float kTimeBetweenBubbleShot = 1.5f;     // number of seconds between shots
private const float kBubbleShotOffset = 0.35f * kHeroWidth;
private const float kStunTimer = 1.5f;
private const int kMaxHeroSize = 2;
private float mTimeSinceLastShot = 0;
private float mStunTimer;
private int mHeroCurrentSize;
public int HeroSize
{
    get { return mHeroCurrentSize; }
    set
    {
        mHeroCurrentSize = value;
        this.Size = new Vector2(
                kHeroWidth + kHeroWidth * (mHeroCurrentSize - 1) / 3,
                kHeroWidth + kHeroWidth * (mHeroCurrentSize - 1) / 3);
    }
}
```

3. Now create an enum for the hero's current state and add a list and accessor for the BubbleShot.

```
private enum HeroState
{
    Playing,
    Stunned,
    Unstunnable,
    Lost
}
private HeroState mCurrentHeroState;
private List<BubbleShot> mBubbleShots;
public List<BubbleShot> AllBubbleShots() { return mBubbleShots; }
```

4. You can now create a constructor in order to initialize the needed instance variables. Remember to pass in the proper sprite sheet and initialize it to the starting frame.

```
public Hero(Vector2 position)
    : base("HERO_1", position, new Vector2(kHeroWidth, kHeroWidth), 2, 2, 0)
{
    mHeroCurrentSize = 1;
    mStunTimer = 0;
    mCurrentHeroState = HeroState.Playing;
    mBubbleShots = new List<BubbleShot>();
    mTimeSinceLastShot = kTimeBetweenBubbleShot;

    SetSpriteAnimation(0, 0, 1, 1, 10);
    SpriteCurrentRow = 1;
}
```

5. For the update function, create a switch statement that updates according to the hero's current state as shown in the following.

```
public void Update(GameTime gameTime, Vector2 delta, bool shootBubbleShot)
{
    switch(mCurrentHeroState)
    {
        case HeroState.Playing:
            UpdatePlayingState(gameTime, delta, shootBubbleShot);
            break;
        case HeroState.Stunned:
            UpdateStunnedState(gameTime);
            break;
        case HeroState.Unstunnable:
            UpdateUnstunnableState(gameTime);
            UpdatePlayingState(gameTime, delta, shootBubbleShot);
            break;
```

```
            case HeroState.Lost:
                mCurrentHeroState = HeroState.Lost;
                break;
            default:
                break;
        }
    }
```

6. For HeroState.Playing, create and call a function that

   - bounds the hero to the screen

   - applies player input to the hero's position

   - faces the sprite and BubbleShot in the correct direction

   - updates the particles

   - calculates the time between shots and shoots the bubble when able

   - updates all the bubbles that have been shot

```
public void UpdatePlayingState(GameTime gameTime, Vector2 delta, bool shootBubbleShot)
{
    base.Update();
    // take advantage of the camera window bound check
    BoundObjectToCameraWindow();

    // Player control
    mPosition += delta;

    // Sprite facing direction
    if (delta.X > 0)
        SpriteCurrentRow = 1;
    else if (delta.X < 0)
        SpriteCurrentRow = 0;

    // BubbleShot direction
    int bubbleShotDir = 1;
    if (SpriteCurrentRow == 0)
        bubbleShotDir = -1;

    mCollisionEffect.UpdateParticles();

    float deltaTime = gameTime.ElapsedGameTime.Milliseconds;
    mTimeSinceLastShot += deltaTime / 1000;

    // Can the hero shoot a BubbleShot?
    if (mTimeSinceLastShot >= kTimeBetweenBubbleShot)
    {
        if (shootBubbleShot)
        {
            BubbleShot j = new BubbleShot(
                        new Vector2(Position.X + kBubbleShotOffset * bubbleShotDir,
                         Position.Y), bubbleShotDir);
```

```
                mBubbleShots.Add(j);
                mTimeSinceLastShot = 0;
                AudioSupport.PlayACue("Bubble");
            }
        }

        // now update all the BubbleShots out there ...
        int count = mBubbleShots.Count;
        for (int i = count - 1; i >= 0; i--)
        {
            if (!mBubbleShots[i].IsOnScreen())
            {
                // outside now!
                mBubbleShots.RemoveAt(i);
            }
            else
                mBubbleShots[i].Update();
        }
    }
```

7. For HeroState.Stunned, create and call a function that implements the stun timer. This is easily done by incrementing the timer by the elapsed time each update. The action of stunning the hero comes from the fact that this update is being called rather than the UpdatePlayingState() function.

```
public void UpdateStunnedState(GameTime gameTime)
{
    float deltaTime = gameTime.ElapsedGameTime.Milliseconds;
    mStunTimer += deltaTime / 1000;
    if (mStunTimer >= kStunTimer)
    {
        mStunTimer = 0;
        mCurrentHeroState = HeroState.Unstunnable;
    }
}
```

8. For HeroState.Unstunnable, create and call a function that transitions the hero from the stunned state to the playing state. This state is required to ensure that the hero is not stunned permanently. This can be accomplished by reusing the stun timer as shown in the following code.

```
public void UpdateUnstunnableState(GameTime gameTime)
{
    float deltaTime = gameTime.ElapsedGameTime.Milliseconds;
    mStunTimer += deltaTime / 1000;
    if (mStunTimer >= kStunTimer)
    {
        mStunTimer = 0;
        mCurrentHeroState = HeroState.Playing;
    }
}
```

■ **Note**   The update functions have used a parameter type of GameTime. This is provided via the base update function. Up until now for all time-based calculations, you have used the concept of update ticks. That is the number of update function calls between particular actions. While this works well, it is not always ideal due to the fact that the time between each update function call can vary. GameTime remedies the variable duration in-between update function calls by providing you with the ability to get the ElapsedGameTime to accurately account for time between update function calls. For more information on GameTime refer to http://msdn.microsoft.com/library/microsoft.xna.framework. gametime(v=xnagamestudio.40).aspx.

9. You can now implement Draw() by overriding the base draw function and draw the hero, the bubbles, and the particles.

```
public override void Draw()
{
    base.Draw();
    foreach (var j in mBubbleShots)
        j.Draw();
    mCollisionEffect.DrawParticleSystem();
}
```

10. Last, functions are needed to provide simple functionality such as adjusting size of the hero, stunning the hero, checking whether the player has lost or not, and feeding the hero. The implementation of these functions is straightforward, as you can see in the following code. Remember to set the current hero's state to lost when its size becomes less than one.

```
public void AdjustSize(int incAdjustment)
{
    if (incAdjustment + HeroSize > kMaxHeroSize)
        return;
    HeroSize += incAdjustment;
    MathHelper.Clamp(HeroSize, 0, 3);
    if (HeroSize <= 0)
    {
        mCurrentHeroState = HeroState.Lost;
    }
}

public void StunHero()
{
    if (mCurrentHeroState != HeroState.Unstunnable && mCurrentHeroState != HeroState.
Stunned)
    {
        mCurrentHeroState = HeroState.Stunned;
        AudioSupport.PlayACue("Stun");
        AdjustSize(-1);
    }
}
```

```
public bool HasLost()
{
    if (mCurrentHeroState == HeroState.Lost)
        return true;
    else
        return false;
}

public void Feed()
{
    AdjustSize(1);
    AudioSupport.PlayACue("Chomp");
}
```

With the hero completed, you can now begin working on the base class for the enemies. In the design outline for the game, each enemy has their own patrolling style; because of this commonality, a heavily modified PatrolEnemy class can be used as the base class. The extensiveness of the modifications is to allow enemies the ability to utilize sprite sheets and other customized behavior. Due to the variety of changes, we will provide a quick breakdown of the entire class.

Modifying the *PatrolEnemy* class

1. Recall that the PatrolEnemy class was introduced in Chapter 6 to support semiautonomous behaviors. Here we start by changing the PatrolEnemy class to inherit from the SpritePrimitive class. Then, add a new state called StunState to the PatrolState enum. Also create a new enum called PatrolType.

    ```
    public class PatrolEnemy : SpritePrimitive
    {
        protected enum PatrolState
        {
            PatrolState,
            ChaseHero,
            StuntState
        }

        protected enum PatrolType
        {
            FreeRoam,
            LeftRight,
            UpDown
        }
        ...
    }
    ```

2. Now add the following constants and color variables shown in the following code for keeping track of the enemies' various properties such as speed, aggro radius, and size.

    ```
    // Constants  ...
    private const float kPatrolSpeed = 0.2f;
    private const float kCloseEnough = 20f;     // distance to trigger next patrol target
    ```

```
                    private const float kDistToBeginChase = 40f; // distance to trigger patrol chasing of hero
                    private const int kStateTimer = 60 * 5;    // this is about 5 seconds
                    private const int kStunCycle = kStateTimer / 2; // half of regular state timer
                    private const float kChaseSpeed = 0.3f;
                    protected const float kEnemyWidth = 10f;
                    protected const int kInitFishSize = 1;

                    private Color kPatrolTint = Color.White;
                    private Color kChaseTint = Color.OrangeRed;
                    private Color kStuntTint = Color.LightCyan;
```

3. You can now add the instance variables and successors for the state timer, destroy flag, and
    fish size.

```
                    private Vector2 mTargetPosition;            // Target position we are moving towards
                    private PatrolState mCurrentState;          // Current State
                    protected PatrolType mCurrentPatrolType;    // Current Patrol Type
                    protected EnemyType mCurrentEnemyType;
                    protected bool mAllowRotate;

                    private int mStateTimer;    // interestingly, with "gradual" velocity changing, we cannot
                                               // guarantee that we will ever reach the mTargetPosition
                                               // (we may ended up orbiting the target), so we set a timer
                                               // when timer is up, we transit

                    private bool mDestoryFlag;
                    public bool DestoryFlag { get { return mDestoryFlag; } }

                    protected int mFishSize;
                    public int FishSize
                    {
                        get { return mFishSize; }
                        set
                        {
                            mFishSize = value;
                            this.Size = new Vector2(mFishSize * kEnemyWidth + kEnemyWidth,
                                                    mFishSize * kEnemyWidth + kEnemyWidth);
                        }
                    }
```

4. Next is the constructor and parameter support for initializing the sprite sheet by
    utilizing the base class and for initializing the variables to their default values as shown
    in the following code. Do not forget to set the sprite sheets' current frame and tick rate.
    Additionally, many of the values shown will be overridden by classes that inherit from
    PatrolEnemy.

```
public PatrolEnemy(String image, Vector2 position, Vector2 size, int rowCounts, int
columnCount, int padding) :
        base(image, position, size, rowCounts, columnCount, padding)
    {
        // causes update state to always change into a new state
        mTargetPosition = Position = Vector2.Zero;
```

```
            Velocity = Vector2.UnitY;
            mTintColor = kPatrolTint;
            mCurrentPatrolType = PatrolType.FreeRoam;
            Position = RandomPosition(true);
            mDestoryFlag = false;
            mAllowRotate = false;
            SetSpriteAnimation(0, 0, 1, 1, 10);
            FishSize = kInitFishSize;
            mCurrentEnemyType = EnemyType.BlowFish;
        }
```

5. Now we can implement the update function. In the function, perform the common
    operations such as updating position and velocity as well as the facing direction of the
    enemy if the enemy is not stunned. Additionally, utilize a switch case to call update
    functions for when the enemy is patrolling and chasing the hero.

```
public bool UpdatePatrol(Hero hero, out Vector2 caughtPos)
{
    bool caught = false;
    caughtPos = Vector2.Zero;

    mStateTimer--;

    // perform operation common to all states ...
    if (mCurrentState != PatrolState.StuntState)
    {
        base.Update();
        Vector2 toHero = hero.Position - Position;
        toHero.Normalize();
        Vector2 toTarget = mTargetPosition - Position;
        float distToTarget = toTarget.Length();
        toTarget /= distToTarget; // this is the same as normalization
        ComputeNewDirection(toTarget, toHero);

        switch (mCurrentState)
        {
            case PatrolState.PatrolState:
                UpdatePatrolState(hero, distToTarget);
                break;

            case PatrolState.ChaseHero:
                caught = UpdateChaseHeroState(hero, distToTarget, out caughtPos);
                break;
        }
    }
    else
    {
        UpdateStuntState(hero);
    }
    return caught;
}
```

a. Create the UpdatePatrolState() function, which updates the enemy's state
    depending upon its PatrolType. If the destination has been reached or the state timer
    expires, you can see that a different target generation function is called depending
    upon the PatrolType. Additionally, a check needs to occur to see if the enemy should
    chase the hero.

```
private void UpdatePatrolState(GameObject hero, float distToTarget)
{
    if ((mStateTimer < 0) || (distToTarget < kCloseEnough))
    {
        switch (mCurrentPatrolType)
        {
            case PatrolType.FreeRoam:
                RandomNextTarget();
                break;
            case PatrolType.LeftRight:
                GenerateLeftRightTarget();
                break;
            case PatrolType.UpDown:
                GenerateUpDownTarget();
                break;
        }
    }
    DetectHero(hero); // check if we should transit to ChaseHero
}
```

b. Now create the UpdateChaseHeroState() function, which handles the reaction of the
    enemy when colliding with the hero. You can see that depending upon the enemy
    type, different reactions occur. For BlowFish, the hero size is decreased and the
    BlowFish is destroyed; for JellyFish, the hero is stunned; and for FightingFish, a
    size comparison is done and either the hero feeds on the FightingFish or vice versa.
    Additionally, if the state timer has expired and the fish is not caught a new random
    target is selected.

```
private bool UpdateChaseHeroState(Hero hero, float distToHero, out Vector2 pos)
{
    bool caught = false;
    caught = PixelTouches(hero, out pos);
    mTargetPosition = hero.Position;

    if (caught)
    {
        switch (mCurrentEnemyType)
        {
            case EnemyType.BlowFish:
                hero.AdjustSize(-1);
                this.FishSize--;
                this.mDestoryFlag = true;
                break;
            case EnemyType.JellyFish:
                hero.StunHero();
```

```
                        break;
              case EnemyType.FightingFish:
                  if (hero.HeroSize > this.FishSize)
                  {
                      this.FishSize--;
                      this.mDestoryFlag = true;
                      hero.Feed();
                  }
                  else if (hero.HeroSize <= this.FishSize)
                  {
                      this.FishSize--;
                      this.mDestoryFlag = true;
                      hero.AdjustSize(-1);
                  }
                  break;
              default:
                  break;
          }
      }
      else if (mStateTimer < 0)
          RandomNextTarget();

      return caught;
  }
```

c. In the UpdateStuntState() function, simply wait for the state timer to expire and then transition to the chasing state.

```
private void UpdateStuntState(Hero hero)
{
    if (mStateTimer < 0)
        SetToChaseState(hero);
}
```

6. Next, add functions for changing between states that simply modify the enemy's current tint color, play, and audio cue and set the current state.

```
public void SetToStuntState()
{
    mTintColor = kStuntTint;
    mStateTimer = kStunCycle;
    mCurrentState = PatrolState.StuntState;
    AudioSupport.PlayACue("Stun");
}
```

7. Create a simple function for detecting whether the hero is within chasing distance. If so, change the enemy's state.

```
private void DetectHero(GameObject hero)
{
    Vector2 toHero = hero.Position - Position;
    if (toHero.Length() < kDistToBeginChase)
        SetToChaseState(hero);
}
```

8. The ComputeNewSpeedAndResetTimer() function remains unchanged from the previous version of patrol enemy.

```
private void ComputeNewSpeedAndResetTimer()
{
    Speed = kPatrolSpeed * (0.8f + (float)(0.4 * Game1.sRan.NextDouble()));
                                    // speed: ranges between 80% to 120
    mStateTimer = (int)(kStateTimer * (0.8f + (float)(0.6 * Game1.sRan.NextDouble())));
}
```

9. In the ComputeNewDirection() function, due to the side-scrolling nature of the game, if we allowed full rotation for enemies their faces would look odd. In order to avoid this, a new case is added which only allows the enemy to look left or right depending upon its facing direction. This is done by utilizing sprite sheet. For enemies without faces such as the JellyFish, the existing code still works.

```
private void ComputeNewDirection(Vector2 toTarget, Vector2 toHero)
{
    if (mAllowRotate)
    {
        // figure out if we should continue to adjust our direction ...
        double cosTheta = Vector2.Dot(toTarget, FrontDirection);
        float theta = (float)Math.Acos(cosTheta);
        if (theta > float.Epsilon)
        {
            Vector3 frontDir3 = new Vector3(FrontDirection, 0f);
            Vector3 toTarget3 = new Vector3(toTarget, 0f);
            Vector3 zDir = Vector3.Cross(frontDir3, toTarget3);
            RotateAngleInRadian -= Math.Sign(zDir.Z) * 0.03f * theta;
                                    // rotate 5% at a time towards final direction
            VelocityDirection = FrontDirection;
        }
    }
    else
    {
        VelocityDirection = toTarget;
        if (VelocityDirection.X > 0)
            SpriteCurrentRow = 1;
        else if (VelocityDirection.X < 0)
            SpriteCurrentRow = 0;
    }
}
```

10. The next set of functions is all related to generating a new random target. In the previous version of PatrolEnemy, you implemented RandomNextTarget(), which remains largely unchanged except for the addition of changing the enemy's tint color. However, two new variations of this concept are added. One generates targets vertically and the second generates targets horizontally. In these functions, if you examine the following code, you will notice that the camera is referenced in order to keep the patrol targets on screen except when patrolling to the left and right.

```
private void RandomNextTarget()
{
    mStateTimer = kStateTimer;
    mCurrentState = PatrolState.PatrolState;
    mTintColor = kPatrolTint;
    // Generate a random begin state
    double initState = Game1.sRan.NextDouble();
    ...
    ComputeNewSpeedAndResetTimer();
}

private void GenerateUpDownTarget()
{
    mStateTimer = kStateTimer;
    mCurrentState = PatrolState.PatrolState;
    mTintColor = kPatrolTint;
    float posY;
    float distToTopOfScreen = Camera.CameraWindowUpperLeftPosition.Y - PositionY;
    float distToBottomOfScreen = PositionY - Camera.CameraWindowLowerLeftPosition.Y;
    if (distToTopOfScreen >= distToBottomOfScreen)
    {
        posY = (float)Game1.sRan.NextDouble() *
                distToTopOfScreen / 2 * 0.80f + PositionY + distToTopOfScreen / 2;
    }
    else
    {
        posY = (float)Game1.sRan.NextDouble() *
                -distToBottomOfScreen / 2 * 0.80f + PositionY - distToBottomOfScreen / 2;
    }

    mTargetPosition = new Vector2(PositionX, posY);
    ComputeNewSpeedAndResetTimer();
}

private void GenerateLeftRightTarget()
{
    mStateTimer = kStateTimer;
    mCurrentState = PatrolState.PatrolState;
    mTintColor = kPatrolTint;
    float posX;
    if (Velocity.X <= 0)
    {
        posX = (float)Game1.sRan.NextDouble() * Camera.Width /2 + PositionX;
    }
```

```
        else
        {
            posX = (float)Game1.sRan.NextDouble() * -Camera.Width /2 + PositionX;
        }
        mTargetPosition = new Vector2(posX, PositionY);
        ComputeNewSpeedAndResetTimer();
    }
```

11. The ComputePoint() function ensures that enemies can generate targets offscreen. You'll notice that the Y value is always within the camera bounds but the X value varies depending upon the enemy's position.

```
private const float sBorderRange = 0.55f;
private Vector2 ComputePoint(double xOffset, double yOffset)
{
    Vector2 min = new Vector2(PositionX - Camera.Width/2,
                         Camera.CameraWindowLowerLeftPosition.Y);
    Vector2 max = new Vector2(PositionX + Camera.Width / 2,
                         Camera.CameraWindowUpperLeftPosition.Y);
    Vector2 size = max - min;
    float x = min.X + size.X * (float)(xOffset + (sBorderRange * Game1.sRan.
NextDouble()));
    float y = min.Y + size.Y * (float)(yOffset + (sBorderRange * Game1.sRan.
NextDouble()));
    return new Vector2(x, y);
}
```

12. The random position functions all received few or no changes. You can see this shown in the following code.

```
const float kMinOffset = -0.05f;
private Vector2 RandomBottomRightPosition()
{
    return ComputePoint(0.5, kMinOffset);
}
...
```

13. The last function you need to implement is used to generate a random position off-camera for spawning enemies. This is easily achieved by getting a random position within camera view and then shifting the position to the right.

```
public Vector2 RandomPosition(bool offCamera)
{
    Vector2 position;
    float posX = (float)Game1.sRan.NextDouble() * Camera.Width * 0.80f
                         + Camera.Width * 0.10f;
    float posY = (float)Game1.sRan.NextDouble() * Camera.Height * 0.80f
                         + Camera.Height * 0.10f;
```

```
        if(offCamera)
            posX += Camera.CameraWindowUpperRightPosition.X;

        position = new Vector2(posX, posY);
        return position;
    }
```

Now that the PatrolEnemy class has been modified to support multiple behaviors, it can serve as the base class for the game's enemy types. In the game design outline, defined earlier, there were three enemy types, each with their own behavior. These three enemy types can now easily be represented by changing the value of mCurrentEnemyType variable defined in PatrolEnemy class.

Creating the *JellyFish*, *BlowFish* and *FightingFish* classes

1. Begin by creating a new class called JellyFish that inherits from PatrolEnemy. Initialize the following variables in order to give the JellyFish the desired behavior. Remember to utilize the correct sprite sheet image and corresponding settings by calling the base constructor. The sprite sheet consists of two sprites; therefore, the row count is set to two and the column count is set to one.

```
public class JellyFish : PatrolEnemy
{
    public JellyFish() :
        base("ENEMY_3", Vector2.Zero,
            new Vector2(kInitFishSize * kEnemyWidth + kEnemyWidth,
            kInitFishSize * kEnemyWidth + kEnemyWidth), 2, 1, 0)
    {
        mAllowRotate = true;
        mInitFrontDir = Vector2.UnitY;
        mCurrentPatrolType = PatrolType.FreeRoam;
        FishSize = kInitFishSize;
        mCurrentEnemyType = EnemyType.JellyFish;
    }
}
```

2. Now create a new class called BlowFish that inherits from PatrolEnemy. Initialize its behavior variables to the following values. Remember to utilize the BlowFish sprite sheet. Notice that in the base constructor, the column count is now set to two. This is because the BlowFish sprite sheet consists of four sprites.

```
public class BlowFish : PatrolEnemy
{
    public BlowFish() :
        base("ENEMY_1", Vector2.Zero,
            new Vector2(kInitFishSize * kEnemyWidth + kEnemyWidth,
            kInitFishSize * kEnemyWidth + kEnemyWidth), 2, 2, 0)
    {
        mAllowRotate = false;
        mInitFrontDir = Vector2.UnitX;
        mCurrentPatrolType = PatrolType.UpDown;
```

```
                    FishSize = kInitFishSize;
                    mCurrentEnemyType = EnemyType.BlowFish;
                }
            }
```

3. Lastly, create a new class called FightingFish that inherits from PatrolEnemy. Initialize its behaviors to the following values and pass in the correct sprite sheet to the base constructor.

```
public class FightingFish : PatrolEnemy
{
    public FightingFish() :
        base("ENEMY_2", Vector2.Zero,
            new Vector2(kInitFishSize * kEnemyWidth + kEnemyWidth,
            kInitFishSize * kEnemyWidth + kEnemyWidth), 2, 2, 0)
    {
        mAllowRotate = false;
        mInitFrontDir = Vector2.UnitX;
        mCurrentPatrolType = PatrolType.LeftRight;
        FishSize = kInitFishSize;
        mCurrentEnemyType = EnemyType.FightingFish;
    }
}
```

Now that all of the enemy types have been created, the class to organize the enemies by controlling their creation and destruction can be implemented. This is achieved by creating a class to contain the enemies in a set in the same way that you have done in previous projects. This concept of combining objects to form a more complex object is known as composition in object-oriented programming.

Creating the *PatrolEnemySet* class

1. Create a new class called PatrolEnemySet. Similarly to the Hero, add static variables and functions for supporting particles. Next, add a constant for the number of enemies to spawn initially. Lastly, add a list to hold all the enemies and a distance interval at which a new enemy will be added.

```
public enum EnemyType
{
    BlowFish = 0,
    JellyFish = 1,
    FightingFish = 2
}

public class PatrolEnemySet
{
    #region Particles
    private const float kCollideParticleSize = 3f;
    private const int kCollideParticleLife = 80;
    private static ParticleSystem sCollisionEffect = new ParticleSystem();
    // to support particle system
    static private ParticlePrimitive CreateRedParticle(Vector2 pos)
```

```
    {
        return new ParticlePrimitive(pos, kCollideParticleSize, kCollideParticleLife);
    }
    static private ParticlePrimitive CreateDarkParticle(Vector2 pos)
    {
        return new DarkParticlePrimitive(pos,
                kCollideParticleSize, kCollideParticleLife);
    }
    #endregion

    private List<PatrolEnemy> mTheSet = new List<PatrolEnemy>();
    private float mAddEnemyDistance = 100f;

    //Constants
    private const int kNumEnemies = 5;


    ...

}
```

■ **Note**   An enum has been added above the `PatrolEnemySet` called `EnemyType`; this is to provide namespace wide access to the type. Also notice that each of the types has a distinct integer associated with it.

---

2.   Next, in the constructor, simply create the enemies by calling SpawnRandomPatrolEnemy() and add them to the set.

```
public PatrolEnemySet()
{
    // Create many ...
    for (int i = 0; i < kNumEnemies; i++)
    {
        PatrolEnemy e = SpawnRandomPatrolEnemy();
        mTheSet.Add(e);
    }
}
```

3.   Now create the SpawnRandomPatrolEnemy() function. You can easily do this by getting a random number and instantiating the corresponding enemy type depending upon its value.

```
public PatrolEnemy SpawnRandomPatrolEnemy()
{
    int randNum = (int)(Game1.sRan.NextDouble() * 3);
    PatrolEnemy enemy = null;
    switch (randNum)
    {
        case (int)EnemyType.BlowFish:
            enemy = new BlowFish();
            break;
```

```
            case (int)EnemyType.JellyFish:
                enemy = new JellyFish();
                break;
            case (int)EnemyType.FightingFish:
                enemy = new FightingFish();
                break;
            default:
                break;


    }
    return enemy;
}
```

4. Now create the update function. In it, first calculate whether an additional enemy should be added and then remove destroyed enemies, respawn new enemies, update existing enemies, and check for collision with the bubbles shot by the hero. Lastly, remember to update the particles and respawn off-camera enemies.

```
public int UpdateSet(Hero hero)
{
    int count = 0;
    Vector2 touchPos;

    //Add an enemy at 100m and every 50 after
    //Should an additional enemy be added?
    if (hero.PositionX / 20 > mAddEnemyDistance)
    {
        PatrolEnemy e = SpawnRandomPatrolEnemy();
        mTheSet.Add(e);
        mAddEnemyDistance += 50;
    }

    // destroy and respawn, update and collide with bubbles
    for (int i = mTheSet.Count - 1; i >= 0; i--)
    {
        if (mTheSet[i].DestoryFlag)
        {
            mTheSet.Remove(mTheSet[i]);
            mTheSet.Add(SpawnRandomPatrolEnemy());
            continue;
        }

        if (mTheSet[i].UpdatePatrol(hero, out touchPos))
        {
            sCollisionEffect.AddEmitterAt(CreateRedParticle, touchPos);
            count++;
        }

        List<BubbleShot> allBubbleShots = hero.AllBubbleShots();
        int numBubbleShots = allBubbleShots.Count;
        for (int j = numBubbleShots - 1; j >= 0; j--)
```

```
        {
            if (allBubbleShots[j].PixelTouches(mTheSet[i], out touchPos))
            {
                mTheSet[i].SetToStuntState();
                allBubbleShots.RemoveAt(j);
                sCollisionEffect.AddEmitterAt(CreateRedParticle, touchPos);
            }
        }
    }

    sCollisionEffect.UpdateParticles();
    RespawnEnemies();
    return count;
}
```

5. Create a function to respawn the enemies that are off to the left side of the camera. This
    is easily done by checking the X position of the enemy versus the left side position of
    the camera.

```
// Respawn enemies that are off to the left side of the camera
public void RespawnEnemies()
{
    for (int i = mTheSet.Count - 1; i >= 0; i--)
    {
        if (mTheSet[i].PositionX < (Camera.CameraWindowLowerLeftPosition.X - mTheSet[i].
Width))
        {
            mTheSet.Remove(mTheSet[i]);
            mTheSet.Add(SpawnRandomPatrolEnemy());
        }
    }
}
```

6. Lastly, create the draw function to draw each of the enemies and the particles.

```
public void DrawSet()
{
    foreach (var e in mTheSet)
        e.Draw();

    sCollisionEffect.DrawParticleSystem();
}
```

With the three enemy types now created, the last interactive object needed is the food. The design states that the food can be eaten by the hero fish and will periodically fall from the top of the screen. This behavior is similar to the Simple Physics project from Chapter 5, where you are simply applying a downward vertical velocity to the object.

Creating the *FishFood* class

1. Start by creating a new class called FishFood that inherits from SpritePrimitive. Add a constant for the food's size and a bool flag to keep track of the food's move state.

```
public class FishFood : SpritePrimitive
{
    private const float kFoodSize = 8;
    private bool mCanMove;


    ...
}
```

2. Now add a constructor to initialize the necessary variables to the following values. Utilize the worm sprite sheet provided. Remember to set the sprite animation's starting frame and tick timer.

```
public FishFood() :
    base("WORM_1", Vector2.Zero, new Vector2(kFoodSize, kFoodSize), 2, 1, 0)
{
    Position = RandomPosition(true);
    SetSpriteAnimation(0, 0, 1, 1, 10);
    mCanMove = true;
    Speed = 0.2f;
}
```

3. Next, create its update function. During each update, first check if the food has entered the camera's view from the right side of the screen. If so, apply movement in a downward direction. Then, check if the food has exited the left side of the screen. If so, move it to a new position off-camera. The last portion of the update function is to check its collisions. If it collides with the hero, feed the hero and respawn the food off-camera. If it collides with the seabed or seaweed, simply stop its movement.

```
public void Update(Hero hero, List<Platform> floor, List<Platform> seaweed)
{
    if (Camera.CameraWindowUpperRightPosition.X > PositionX && mCanMove)
    {
        VelocityDirection = new Vector2(0, -1);
        Speed = 0.2f;
        base.Update();
    }

    if (Camera.CameraWindowUpperLeftPosition.X > PositionX)
    {
        Position = RandomPosition(true);
        mCanMove = true;
    }
```

```
        Vector2 vec;
        if (hero.PixelTouches(this, out vec))
        {
            Stop();
            hero.Feed();
            Position = RandomPosition(true);
            mCanMove = true;
        }
        for (int i = 0; i < floor.Count; i++)
        {
            if (floor[i].PixelTouches(this, out vec))
            {
                Stop();
            }
        }
        for (int i = 0; i < seaweed.Count; i++)
        {
            if (seaweed[i].PixelTouches(this, out vec))
            {
                Stop();
            }
        }
    }
```

4. Add a function for calculating the random position to spawn the food off-camera. This function is similar to the random position function you created in the patrol enemy class, except that since you want the food to fall from the top of the screen, the Y position is always set to the camera's max Y value.

```
private Vector2 RandomPosition(bool offCamera)
{
    Vector2 position;
    float posX = (float)Game1.sRan.NextDouble() * Camera.Width * 0.80f + Camera.Width *
0.10f;
    float posY = Camera.CameraWindowUpperRightPosition.Y;

    if (offCamera)
        posX += Camera.CameraWindowUpperRightPosition.X + Camera.Width*2;

    position = new Vector2(posX, posY);
    return position;
}
```

5. The last function needed is the Stop() function; this simply prohibits the food from moving until it is enabled elsewhere.

```
private void Stop()
{
    mCanMove = false;
    Velocity = Vector2.Zero;
    Speed = 0;
}
```

With all the objects for the game created, you now need a method of building an environment and filling it with enemies. In the game outline, it states that the environment will go on endlessly. The concept of endlessly might seem daunting at first glance; however in a simple game such as this, it can be quite easy accomplished.

By now, we have implemented hero's self-protection mechanism (BubbleShot), the Hero, enemy behaviors (PatrolEnemy), the enemies (JellyFish, BlowFish, and FightingFish), the collection set for the enemies (PatrolEnemySet), and the hero's food (FishFood), all we need to do is to define the background (EnvironmentGenerator) and the game logic (GameState) to tie all of these classes together.

Creating the *EnvironmentGenerator* class

1. Start by creating a class called EnvironmentGenerator. Add a list of Platform objects for the floor and the small and tall seaweed. Additionally, add variables for the sign, the enemies, and the food. Lastly, create the constants shown in the following code.

```
public class EnvironmentGenerator
{
    private List<Platform> mTheFloorSet;
    private List<Platform> mTheSeaweedTallSet;
    private List<Platform> mTheSeaweedSmallSet;
    private Platform mTheSign;
    private PatrolEnemySet mEnemies;
    private FishFood mFishFood;

    private int mOffsetCounter;
    private const int kSectionSize = 800;
    private const int kFloorAndRoofSize = 40;
    private const int kSignSize = 30;
    private const int kInitialSignPosX = 100;
    private const int kSignUnitScaler = 20;


    ...
}
```

2. Now create a constructor which is responsible for setting the environment to its initial state. You can accomplish this by creating the floor, seaweed, enemies, sign, and food. Notice that the floor is laid out across the bottom of the screen, and five tall and small seaweeds are dispersed randomly across it.

```
public void InitializeEnvironment()
{
    Camera.SetCameraWindow(Vector2.Zero, 300);
    mOffsetCounter = -20;
    mTheFloorSet = new List<Platform>();
    mTheSeaweedTallSet = new List<Platform>();
    mTheSeaweedSmallSet = new List<Platform>();

    mEnemies = new PatrolEnemySet();
```

```
        for (int i = 0; i < kSectionSize / kFloorAndRoofSize; i++)
        {
            mOffsetCounter += kFloorAndRoofSize;
            mTheFloorSet.Add(new
            Platform("GROUND_1",
                    new Vector2(mOffsetCounter, 20),
                    new Vector2(kFloorAndRoofSize, kFloorAndRoofSize)));
        }

        mTheSign = new Platform("SIGN_1",
                    new Vector2(kInitialSignPosX, kFloorAndRoofSize / 2 + kSignSize / 2),
                    new Vector2(kSignSize, kSignSize));

        float randNum;
        for (int i = 0; i < 5; i++)
        {
            randNum = (float)Game1.sRan.NextDouble() *
                            mTheFloorSet[mTheFloorSet.Count - 1].PositionX + kInitialSignPosX * 2;
            mTheSeaweedTallSet.Add(new Platform("SEAWEEDTALL_1",
                            new Vector2(randNum, kFloorAndRoofSize),
                            new Vector2(kFloorAndRoofSize / 1.5f, kFloorAndRoofSize * 1.5f)));
        }

        for (int i = 0; i < 5; i++)
        {
            randNum = (float)Game1.sRan.NextDouble() *
                            mTheFloorSet[mTheFloorSet.Count - 1].PositionX;
            mTheSeaweedSmallSet.Add(new Platform("SEAWEEDSMALL_1",
                            new Vector2(randNum, kFloorAndRoofSize / 2 - 5),
                            new Vector2(kFloorAndRoofSize / 2, kFloorAndRoofSize / 2)));
        }

        mFishFood = new FishFood();
    }
```

3. You can now create an update function to support the endless regeneration of the terrain.
    There are several ways to achieve this, but one of the most straightforward is to simply
    replace objects that are moved off the left side of the camera to a new off-camera position
    to the right side of the screen. The length of the floor is longer than the camera's width, and
    when the last floor tile is reached by the right side of the camera, the entire floor array is
    moved forward. This can be done without any noticeable artifacts because all of the floor
    tiles are the same. Lastly, the sign is reposted at various intervals along the seabed.

```
public void Update(Hero theHero)
{
    mFishFood.Update(theHero, mTheFloorSet, mTheSeaweedTallSet);
    mEnemies.UpdateSet(theHero);

    if (Camera.CameraWindowLowerRightPosition.X >
                mTheFloorSet[mTheFloorSet.Count - 1].Position.X)
```

```
    {
        for (int i = 0; i < mTheFloorSet.Count; i++)
        {
            mTheFloorSet[i].PositionX += kFloorAndRoofSize * 10;
        }

        float randNum;
        for (int i = 0; i < mTheSeaweedTallSet.Count; i++)
        {
            if (mTheSeaweedTallSet[i].PositionX <
                        Camera.CameraWindowLowerLeftPosition.X - mTheSeaweedTallSet[i].Width)
            {
                randNum = (float)Game1.sRan.NextDouble() * kSectionSize / 2
                            + Camera.CameraWindowLowerRightPosition.X;
                mTheSeaweedTallSet[i].PositionX = randNum;
            }
        }

        for (int i = 0; i < mTheSeaweedSmallSet.Count; i++)
        {
            if (mTheSeaweedSmallSet[i].PositionX <
                        Camera.CameraWindowLowerLeftPosition.X - mTheSeaweedTallSet[i].Width)
            {
                randNum = (float)Game1.sRan.NextDouble() * kSectionSize / 2
                            + Camera.CameraWindowLowerRightPosition.X;
                mTheSeaweedSmallSet[i].PositionX = randNum;
            }
        }
    }

    if ((Camera.CameraWindowLowerLeftPosition.X - mTheSign.Width) > mTheSign.PositionX)
    {
        if (mTheSign.PositionX == kInitialSignPosX)
            mTheSign.PositionX = 0;
        mTheSign.PositionX += 500;
    }
}
```

4. Now you can create the draw function. This is simply a matter of calling each of this environment object's Draw() methods including the enemies' and the food's. In addition, notice that the sign's position is printed via its label.

```
public void Draw()
{
    for (int i = 0; i < mTheFloorSet.Count; i++)
        mTheFloorSet[i].Draw();

    mTheSign.Draw();
    String msg = (mTheSign.Position.X / 20).ToString() + "m";

    FontSupport.PrintStatusAt(mTheSign.Position, msg, Color.Black);
```

```
        for (int i = 0; i < mTheSeaweedTallSet.Count; i++)
            mTheSeaweedTallSet[i].Draw();

        for (int i = 0; i < mTheSeaweedSmallSet.Count; i++)
            mTheSeaweedSmallSet[i].Draw();

        mEnemies.DrawSet();
        mFishFood.Draw();
    }
```

With all the necessary objects for the game now created, it is time to modify the GameState in order to utilize them. The game state will handle the logic for the controls, the panning camera, and the swap between game screens.

Modifying the *GameState* class

1. Start by adding in enum for the three different states of the GameState object. Then, add instance variables for the splash screens, the environment generator, the hero, and the distance traveled.

```
public class GameState
{
    public enum GameStates
    {
        StartScreen,
        Playing,
        Dead
    }

    private int mDistantTraveled = 0;
    private GameStates mCurrentGameState;
    private TexturedPrimitive mSplashScreen;
    private TexturedPrimitive mGameOverScreen;
    private EnvironmentGenerator mEnvironment;
    private Hero mHero;

    ...

}
```

2. Next, in the constructor, set the current game state to StartScreen, start the background music, and initialize the start menu. In the start menu's initialization, set the splash screen to the camera's view and notify the user of how they can start the game.

```
public GameState()
{
    mCurrentGameState = GameStates.StartScreen;
    AudioSupport.PlayBackgroundAudio("Mind_Meld", 0.5f);
    InitializeStartMenu();
}
```

```
public void InitializeStartMenu()
{
    float centerX = Camera.CameraWindowUpperRightPosition.X - Camera.Width/2;
    float centerY = Camera.CameraWindowUpperRightPosition.Y- Camera.Height/2;

    mSplashScreen = new TexturedPrimitive("SPLASHSCREEN_1",
                new Vector2(centerX, centerY), new Vector2(Camera.Width, Camera.Height));
    String msg = "Press the 'K' key to start.";
    mSplashScreen.Label = msg;
    mSplashScreen.LabelColor = Color.Black;
}
```

3. Next, create functions for initializing the gameplay and the game over screen. When gameplay is initialized, simply instantiate the hero and the environment. When the game over screen is initialized, instantiate the game over splash screen and notify the player how far they have managed to travel.

```
public void InitializeGamePlay()
{
    mHero = new Hero(new Vector2(20f, 30f));
    mEnvironment = new EnvironmentGenerator();
}

public void InitializeGameOverScreen()
{
    float centerX = Camera.CameraWindowUpperRightPosition.X - Camera.Width/2;
    float centerY = Camera.CameraWindowUpperRightPosition.Y- Camera.Height/2;

    mGameOverScreen = new TexturedPrimitive("GAMEOVERSCREEN_1",
                        new Vector2(centerX, centerY),
                        new Vector2(Camera.Width, Camera.Height));
    String msg = mDistantTraveled +  "m traveled. Press the 'K' key to try agian.";
    mGameOverScreen.Label = msg;
    mGameOverScreen.LabelColor = Color.Black;
}
```

4. Now create an update function that updates the game depending upon the game's current state.

```
public void UpdateGame(GameTime gameTime)
{
    switch(mCurrentGameState)
    {
        case GameStates.StartScreen:
            UpdateStartScreen();
            break;
        case GameStates.Playing:
            UpdateGamePlay(gameTime);
            break;
```

```
        case GameStates.Dead:
            UpdateGameOverScreen();
            break;
    }
}
```

a. For the UpdateStartScreen() function, poll whether the A button has been pressed. If so, change the current game state and initialize the gameplay.

```
public void UpdateStartScreen()
{
    if (InputWrapper.Buttons.A == ButtonState.Pressed)
    {
        mSplashScreen = null;
        mCurrentGameState = GameStates.Playing;
        InitializeGamePlay();
    }
}
```

b. The behavior of the UpdateGameOverScreen() function essentially mirrors that of the UpdateStartScreen() function. In fact, another function could easily be extracted out of them to reduce redundancy.

```
public void UpdateGameOverScreen()
{
    if (InputWrapper.Buttons.A == ButtonState.Pressed)
    {
        mGameOverScreen = null;
        mCurrentGameState = GameStates.Playing;
        InitializeGamePlay();
    }
}
```

c. For the UpdateGamePlay() function:

- record the distance traveled

- check whether the hero has lost

- check whether the player has shot a bubble

- update the hero and environment

- allow the hero to pan the camera to the right

```
public void UpdateGamePlay(GameTime gameTime)
{
    mDistantTraveled = (int)mHero.PositionX / 20;
    if (mHero.HasLost())
    {
        mCurrentGameState = GameStates.Dead;
        AudioSupport.PlayACue("Break");
```

```
            InitializeGameOverScreen();
            return;
        }

        bool shootBubbleShot = (InputWrapper.Buttons.A == ButtonState.Pressed);
        mHero.Update(gameTime, InputWrapper.ThumbSticks.Left, shootBubbleShot);
        mEnvironment.Update(mHero);

        #region hero moving the camera window
        float kBuffer = mHero.Width * 5f;
        float kHalfCameraSize = Camera.Width * 0.5f;
        Vector2 delta = Vector2.Zero;
        Vector2 cameraLL = Camera.CameraWindowLowerLeftPosition;
        Vector2 cameraUR = Camera.CameraWindowUpperRightPosition;
        const float kChaseRate = 0.05f;

        if (mHero.PositionX > (cameraUR.X - kHalfCameraSize))
        {
            delta.X = (mHero.PositionX + kHalfCameraSize - cameraUR.X) * kChaseRate;
        }

        Camera.MoveCameraBy(delta);
        #endregion
    }
```

5. Finally, implement the draw function to draw the game depending upon its current state.
    During the gameplay state, remember to print out the distance traveled and size of
    the hero.

```
public void DrawGame()
{
    switch (mCurrentGameState)
    {
        case GameStates.StartScreen:
            if(mSplashScreen != null)
                mSplashScreen.Draw();
            break;
        case GameStates.Playing:
            mEnvironment.Draw();
            mHero.Draw();
            FontSupport.PrintStatus("Distance: " + mDistantTraveled
                                    + "  Size: " + mHero.HeroSize, null);
            break;
        case GameStates.Dead:
            if (mGameOverScreen != null)
                mGameOverScreen.Draw();
            break;
    }
}
```

Congratulations! You have completed the entire Fish Food game! As described earlier in this chapter, this game is non-trivial, but it was not too complicated either. Figure 9-2 shows an example of what you should see when you play the Fish Food game.

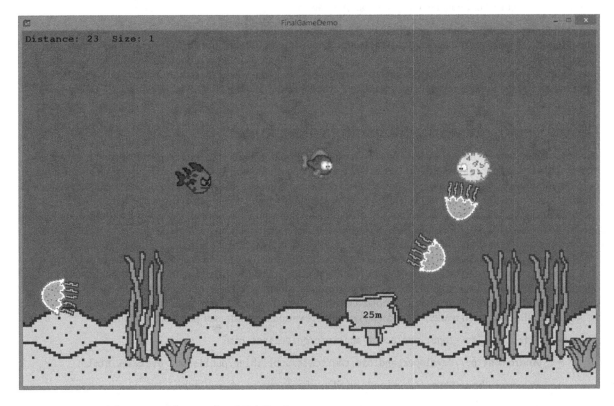

Figure 9-2. *Example screen of the completed Fish Food game*

Game criticisms and expansion

Now that the entire game has been implemented, build and run the code in order to try it out. Try and see how far you can travel and then see if you can beat that distance. What kind of impression did the game give? Was it too simplistic? How was the difficulty? How about the fun factor? Your answers to these questions are all relevant to the creation of your game. Overall, we hope you saw that the game is far from perfect. In fact, there are many areas of the game that could be improved. This includes areas such as gameplay, interface, controls, effects, theme, art, sound, and even the code itself.

If you have an idea that can improve the game in any of the areas, go ahead and implement it! If you're struggling with thinking of an area to improve, give one of the following suggestions a try.

- Content! Games can always use more content, such as enemy types, food types, hero character types, or even environment types.

- Gameplay and functionality! This can include things like camera zoom, hero or enemy abilities, or food bonuses.

- Effects! Often the best games have great effects such as satisfying sound or particle behaviors.

- Controls! Do the controls feel intuitive? Is there a more natural way to play the game? Awkward controls often dampen the game's fun factor.

- Code quality and understandability! Code can always be improved! Can something be re-factored or polished to provide a simpler approach?

Remember that some changes may have effects on other portions of the game. For example, if you are to implement the camera zooming feature, upon zooming out you may find that the environment no longer behaves as you expect. However, we encourage you to expand and implement your ideas, if not in this game perhaps in your own. There may be something in this game that is applicable to a game you have been thinking about. That's great! Cannibalize that section and or take what you have learned and start creating fun and challenging 2D games!

Device deployment and publishing your games

The MonoGame framework that we have worked with throughout this book is designed specifically to be a cross-platform library. With the philosophy of "Write Once, Play Everywhere," the framework currently supports most of the popular operating systems including devices that run on Linux, Windows, iOS, and Android. This means that once you have developed a game, you will be able to build and run the same game on all of these devices.

Ultimately, games are built for gamers and everyone out there who may appreciate our efforts. Publishing a game used to be reserved for absolute professionals. Fortunately, the recent opening up of marketplaces by all of the major vendors means that anyone can participate and self-publish their own games!

Together with MonoGame's cross-platform support, this means that you will eventually be able to publish your games on all of the platforms supported by MonoGame. As at the time of writing this book, though perfectly operational, the MonoGame cross-platform deployment mechanism is still undergoing significant changes. We encourage interested readers to refer to MonoGame website for up-to-date information at `http://www.monogame.net`.

Additionally, interested readers should also consult the various vendors' self-publication guides:

- iOS: `http://developer.apple.com/appstore/guidelines.html`

- Android: `http://developer.android.com/tools/publishing/publishing_overview.html`

- Windows Phone: `http://developer.windowsphone.com/en-us/publish`

Each vendor typically has separate and different license agreements that they would require you to sign, user interface design guidelines that they want your game to adhere to (e.g., font type, size), levels of testing that they expect you to perform on your game, documentations of machine capabilities and device sensors that your game requires, and for games on mobile devices, documentation of the kinds of player privacy information (e.g., location information, etc) that your game would access and how that information would be used. Please consult the preceding web sites for detailed requirements from each vendor.

Lastly, we should mention once again that this book focused only on the technical aspects of building games. As discussed in Chapter 1, technical know-how is a vital prerequisite for building fun games, but it is not the only factor. It is our opinion that, in general, it is a good idea to become knowledgeable with game design topics (please refer to Chapter 1 for some recommended references) before attempting to build games for self-publication, as the ideas and concepts presented are valuable tools that will help you make the most of your ideas. In fact, the reason you probably picked up this book is because you have many game ideas floating around in your head. The game design process is meant to assist you in documenting these ideas and making the jump from idea to the content and mechanics of a real game.

Finally, remember to enjoy the process! Building games is not a trivial task but if you enjoy the process of seeing your ideas come to life, it is well worth the time and effort. We hope that using the knowledge you have gained from this book, you can now begin the journey of creating your own 2D games. Good luck and have fun building and playing your first game!

Index

Get the eBook for only $10!

Now you can take the weightless companion with you anywhere, anytime. Your purchase of this book entitles you to 3 electronic versions for only $10.

This Apress title will prove so indispensible that you'll want to carry it with you everywhere, which is why we are offering the eBook in 3 formats for only $10 if you have already purchased the print book.

Convenient and fully searchable, the PDF version enables you to easily find and copy code—or perform examples by quickly toggling between instructions and applications. The MOBI format is ideal for your Kindle, while the ePUB can be utilized on a variety of mobile devices.

Go to www.apress.com/promo/tendollars to purchase your companion eBook.